THE LIBRARY MEDIA SPECIALIST IN CURRICULUM DEVELOPMENT

edited by
Nevada Wallis Thomason

The Scarecrow Press, Inc.
Metuchen, N.J., & London
1981

Library of Congress Cataloging in Publication Data
Main entry under title:

The Library media specialist in curriculum
    development.

    Bibliography: p.
    Includes index.
    1. Media programs (Education) 2. Curriculum
planning. 3. Instructional materials centers.
I. Thomason, Nevada Wallis, 1938-
LB1028.4.L5   371.3'07'8   81-50
ISBN 0-8108-1406-4

DEDICATED

In loving memory of my parents,
Mr. and Mrs. A. J. Wallis,
whose attitude and outlook on life
always inspired and guided me,

and

to my daughter,
Paula Ann Thomason,
who endured and grew up amidst
my own stages of professional growth.

ACKNOWLEDGMENTS

I wish to extend special acknowledgment:

To the authors and publishers cited throughout for granting
permission to reprint their materials.

To Dr. Albert W. Vogel at the University of New Mexico for
his constant encouragement to forget minor projects
and work on the book.

To the many students from all over the world who have taken
my courses, especially Nahla Al-Humood and Moham-
mad Al-Shuaibi of Kuwait at the University of Colorado
and Sahlu Alemayehu of Ethiopia at the University of
New Mexico, for their continued interest in the subject and belief in my professional abilities.

To the following colleagues for their encouragement, confidence, and helpful suggestions: Dr. Otis McBride,
Mr. Charles Timberlake, Miss Betty Ann Robinson,
and Dr. Janet Noll Naumer.

iv

CONTENTS

FOREWORD

The role of the library media specialist in the curriculum process has changed substantially over the years. There has also been a change in our concept of the school library. In the past the school library has not been in the "mainstream" of the educational program. Traditionally the school library has been relegated to the role of study hall or reference center, serving mainly as a place to house books. As Ruth Ann Davies points out in The School Library Media Center, a force for educational excellence (2nd ed. New York: R. R. Bowker, 1974), involvement of the library in the teaching and learning process in the past has been the exception, not the rule. So long as the educational program concentrated on textbook memorization, the library was not required to function in any other manner. However, as the educational program evolves from "traditional mediocrity to innovative excellence" the concept of the school library has to change from study hall or reference center to learning laboratory with direct participation in all aspects of the educational program.

According to Davies, direct involvement of the school librarian in the teaching learning program has changed the status of the school library from passive spectator to active participant in the educational program. As study hall monitor and book curator, the school librarian of the traditional curriculum days had little responsibility of an educational nature. Today's school library media specialist serves in the triple capacity of team teacher, media programming engineer, and curriculum consultant. The school library media specialist's responsibility extends beyond organizing and maintaining a materials collection. His/her responsibilities include planning cooperatively with other teachers as well as with the school administrator in working toward the goal of educational excellence.

The changing role of the library media specialist has

also brought on a change in title for the facilities--from school library to school library media center. No longer just a storehouse for books or the printed page today's library media center is not just a storehouse for all forms of print and nonprint material but rather a learning center where students gain knowledge by utilizing all their senses in the learning process. Educational technology is a basic part of education for today's learner.

Davies says that the contemporary definition of the term "curriculum" clearly requires the involvement of the librarian as a contributing member of every curriculum study group. Quoting from Putnam and Chismore, she wrote:

"... the curriculum is considered to encompass all the instructional activities planned and provided for pupils by the school or school system. The curriculum, therefore, is the planned interaction of pupils with instructional content, instructional resources, and instructional processes for the attainment of educational objectives. "

She further stated, "resources are the library media specialist's stock-in-trade; designing and implementing instructional processes are two of his specialized competencies; therefore, the library media specialist is a key figure and has a major responsibility in curriculum development. "

The administrator who values the library media center as an integral part of the educational program will expect the library media specialist to be an agent for change and to take an active part in all phases of curriculum development.

Joyce Elaine Saavedra
Albuquerque Public Schools
Albuquerque, New Mexico

PREFACE

During the past decade there has been a gradual evolution of the role of the public school library media specialist in curriculum development from just mere acceptance to an increasing awareness that this professionally trained educator has a tremendous contribution to make to the total educational process.

With the gradual change came the realization that not much has been written in the curriculum literature about this new role of the library media specialist. Difficulty in locating excellent information on the subject led to the idea of compiling an anthology of readings for students, researchers, and professors of library media education as well as for those employed as library media specialists. Teaching this topic in an administration class furnished additional proof that current information was not readily available. A file of resources was started, indexes were searched, and an ERIC computer search was conducted. No attempt was made to include books or pamphlet materials, only articles printed in current journals were included. All articles, with the exception of illustrations, are reprinted in the form in which they were published originally.

It is regrettable that several articles of exceptional value were located but could not be included in this volume. All authors contacted granted permission for their work to be included in the anthology, but some publishers would not release their articles for this publication. The compiler extends sincere appreciation to all authors contacted for their support, encouragement, and enthusiasm for a book to be published on this topic.

Nevada Wallis Thomason
Albuquerque, New Mexico
June 1980

Part I:

BACKGROUND HISTORY

THE SCHOOL MEDIA PROGRAM:
EMERGING MULTI-MEDIA SERVICES*

Carolyn I. Whitenack

An organized program of school media services exists
to serve the students, the teachers, and the educational goals
of the school.   Any description of emerging multi-media services and their evolutionary development is directly related
to the trends and problems of education in general.   These
media services have evolved over a period of many years
beginning with the development of schools and learning materials in the thirteen original states.   Many agencies, including schools, libraries, boards of education, state departments
of education, the professional associations (the American Library Association and the National Education Association and
its constituent departments), as well as private foundations
and interested citizens have been involved in the development
of these services.

Historically the first public support for learning resources was given for public school libraries by New York
and Massachusetts and dated in the early 1800s.   These school
district libraries were little used; their meager collections
were more suitable for adults than school students, and staff
and funds were small or nonexistent.   For the most part early school libraries were closely associated with public library
service to schools as well as with the development of a literature separate from that of textbooks.

The first comprehensive study of library service in the
United States deplored the fact that young people below the age
of fourteen were not served. [1]   In the years that followed pub-

*Reprinted by permission of the author and publisher from
Library Trends, vol. 19, no. 4, pp. 410-18, April 1971.
© 1971 by The Board of Trustees of the University of Illinois.

lic libraries developed children's rooms and services. [2]   In reports of the early history of the American Library Association and the National Education Association many studies were made of cooperation for library services to youth, although resources for teaching and learning planned especially for students were scarce.   Recommended lists of books, the debate over classroom collections versus central collections, and traveling collections from public or county libraries were the major efforts of the late 1800s. [3]

About 4,000 secondary school libraries were established by the turn of the century.   The Certain reports, as well as the publications of the Secondary and Elementary School Principals,   were important beginnings of standards for accreditation of schools in the early 1900s.   These reports gave a rationale for teacher-librarians and materials for school libraries and were the forerunners of standards developed by the five regional school-accrediting associations.   Typical of these concerns was the 1915 publication issued jointly by the National Education Association Committee on Library Organization and Equipment and the North Central Association of Colleges and Secondary Schools, which detailed the services and equipment which should be available in junior and senior high schools.

The American Council on Education has also been influential in the development of standards.   Its division, the National Study of Secondary School Evaluation, an organization in which all five regional accrediting associations are represented, has issued an Evaluative Criteria every ten years since 1940.   Instruments for qualitative evaluation of the instructional program including media services are provided in definitive schedules of criteria.   Originally the services were separated--one for library and one for audiovisual.   However, the 1960 edition, section F, was "Instructional Materials Services--Library and Audio-Visual, " and the 1969 edition, section 6, was "Educational Media Services--Library and Audio-Visual "[4]

Several private educational foundations,   including the Carnegie Corporation,   the General Education Board, the Rosenwald Fund and the Rockefeller Fund contributed to school library development and media services in the 1920s and 1930s. By 1927 forty-five of the forty-eight states had laws governing the establishment of school libraries.

In 1945 the American Library Association issued its

first national standards for school libraries--School Libraries for Today and Tomorrow. [5] This landmark served as a guide for objectives and as a program for the next fifteen years. Early in the 1950s, library and audiovisual specialists began to develop and establish a "unity of materials" philosophy and often this service came from the instructional materials center. New standards were issued again in 1960 by the American Library Association through its newly established division, the American Association of School Librarians. This publication--Standards for School Library Programs--provided goals for staff, users, materials, budget, facilities, and equipment. [6]

Early audiovisual units in schools began with museum services. Noteworthy were the school services from Philadelphia, St. Louis, and Cleveland museums. Large cities were also the leaders in establishing and organizing audiovisual education--St. Louis, Chicago, Newark, Detroit, New York, Los Angeles, Pittsburgh, and Philadelphia. The successful uses of training aids by the armed services in World Wars I and II gave added impetus to the movement. Audiovisual instruction in the 1950s and early 1960s was organized around 16 mm. films, filmstrips, tapes and recordings. The newer media for individualization of instruction--programmed materials, dial access, 8 mm. and super 8 mm., instructional television as well as miniaturization of equipment have been recent additions.

The professional association, Department of Audiovisual Instruction (DAVI) of the National Education Association (now the Association for Educational Communications and Technology), for the past fifty years has carried the leadership role in the continued growth and utilization of audiovisual communications.

A benchmark study--the National Education Association's Technological Development Project directed by James Finn--was unique in its thoughtful assessment of growth in audiovisual education since 1930. [7] The yearly surveys by Thomas Hope for the Society of Motion Picture and Television Engineers report production and sales of 16 mm. projectors and non-theatrical films in the Journal of the society. Eleanor Godfrey in her study, The State of Audiovisual Technology: 1961-1966, found that the teacher was the key to selection and utilization of audiovisual media. [8] Sherman and Faris[9] developed guidelines for a basic school program--personnel, materials, and equipment--which became the accepted Standards adopted by DAVI and the Association of Chief State School Audiovisual Officers in 1965.

Demonstration projects have been very successful in improving media services as well as serving as models for other schools. One of the most successful national demonstration projects in media utilization was the Knapp School Libraries Project funded by the Knapp Foundation and directed by the American Association of School Librarians. [10] The purpose of the project was to bring the library program in the eight project schools up to the 1960 Standards in services, staff utilization, resources, and facilities. A unique part of the project was the visitation program which allowed teams of leaders from school communities to observe the exemplary programs and return to improve their own media services.

A second promising new venture funded by the Knapp Foundation is the School Library Manpower Project. The first phase completed a task analysis of the jobs performed in media centers. [11] The second phase is the identification of competencies for the professionals who serve in school media centers and the restructuring of professional media education for these professional tasks. In addition to library science and audiovisual communications, the new discipline-- media sciences--will draw on psychology, sociology, administration, curriculum, business management, communications theory, computer science, educational research, and other fields.

Federal legislation has had a significant impact upon evolving media services. The units of the National Defense Education Act of 1958 made provision for strengthening instruction including much audiovisual equipment in "critical" subjects such as science and mathematics. Eventually it was enlarged to cover most areas of the curriculum. Under Title I of the Elementary and Secondary Education Act (ESEA) of 1965, staff and remodeling of facilities have improved services to educationally deprived children. Title II of the ESEA has certainly improved the quality and quantity of media collections. [12] Many states established elementary school library media programs. Title III made grants for supplementary centers and services and many projects had strong media components.

School libraries and audiovisual departments in schools greatly increased after World War II, although more than one-half of the elementary schools were without centralized services in the early 1960s. [13]

Until the twentieth century the body of information and

literature available was small, and the quality of resources for teaching and learning was poor. Research and scientific endeavors began to play a central role in improving the learning resources available to schools. Changes in instruction and the importance of the development of "library and audiovisual materials," rather than only text materials, were transitional stages in developing multi-media services. Many professional journals and books on curriculum change reflect the dawning of the "child centered" school with the development of each individual as a whole human being striving to become all that he can become. [14]

Many new curriculum studies planned by leaders in the academic disciplines emphasize the growing importance of independent study and the individualization of instruction. [15] Some of the more visionary curriculum leaders have urged team teaching, [16] the nongraded school, [17] the middle school, [18] and flexible scheduling [19] as new ways of organizing the school day.

Any history of the emerging school media program in the United States will identify the decade of the 1970s as a time of action. It is no longer a matter of conjecture that most quality schools have learning centers of all media for the instructional, inspirational and intellectual pursuits of students and teachers in today's modern educational program. One of the most significant developments in education at the turn of the decade was the preparation and issuance of new national standards for media resources, Standards for School Media Programs, [20] by the two professional associations directly associated with media--the American Association of School Librarians and the then Department of Audiovisual Instruction--in cooperation with an advisory board consisting of representatives from twenty-eight professional and civic associations.

This program of action has meant the adoption of new terminology and revised patterns of service that illustrate the vital, enthusiastic quality program required in teaching and learning for today's students and teachers. Since media and media programs exist to serve the constituents and goals of the school, terminology and patterns of administration may differ among schools. There are school libraries, instructional materials centers, learning resources centers, instructional media centers, library media centers, and audiovisual centers. Again the terms as defined in the Standards are cited for clarity:

Media--Printed and audiovisual forms of communication
and their accompanying technology.

Media program--All the instructional and other services furnished to students and teachers by a media
center and its staff.

Media center--A learning center in a school where a
full range of print and audiovisual media, necessary
equipment, and services from media specialists are
accessible to students and teachers.

Media staff--The personnel who carry on the activities
of a media center and its program.

Media specialist--An individual who has broad professional preparation in educational media. If he is
responsible for instructional decisions, he meets
requirements for teaching. Within this field there
may be several types of specialization, such as (a)
level instruction, (b) areas of curriculum, (c) type
media, and (d) type of service. In addition, other
media specialists, who are not responsible for instructional decisions, are members of the professional media staff and need not have teacher certification, e.g., certain types of personnel in television and other media preparation areas.

Media technician--A media staff member who has training below the media specialist level, but who has
special competencies in one or more of the following fields: graphics production and display, information and materials processing, photographic production, and equipment operation and simple maintenance.

Media aide--A media staff member with clerical or
secretarial competencies.

System media center--A center at the school system
level to provide supporting and supplemented services to school media centers in individual schools
of the system.

Unified media program--A program in which instructional and other services related to both print and
audiovisual media are administered in a single unified program under one director.

Teaching station--Any part of the school (usually but
not always a classroom) where formal instruction
takes place. Media centers are not included within this definition, although it is recognized that instruction is part of the media program. [21]

The school media program is a program of services

throughout the school to students and teachers from a specialized staff when and wherever the need for learning resources occurs. These services emanate in a center and range from assistance in independent study to serving as a member of team teaching; from direct teaching for a group of students in a subject discipline to dial access and computer-assisted instruction in very sophisticated learning areas such as in Oak Park-River Forest22 or Nova High School.

The key to such a program is adequate professional media staff (some generalists and some specialists) with support from technicians, aides and clerks. Personnel specialization should include reference, research, subject disciplines, and guidance in utilization, graphics preparation, message design or instructional technology, television, audiovisual communications, as well as learning theory and management.

Therefore, a good media service program serves the objectives of the total educational program of the school by:

1. Providing media professionals with sufficient supportive staff to consult, organize, and manage media resources, services, and facilities in media centers, in subcenters, in classrooms or wherever learning takes place.
2. Locating, gathering, organizing, coordinating, promoting, and distributing a rich variety of quality learning resources for use by teachers and students as individuals and in groups to improve learning, and by including involvement of teachers and students in the selection process.
3. Making available facilities, services, and equipment necessary for the selection, organization, management, and use of printed and audiovisual resources, including availability at all hours of the school day, before and after school, and extended hours.
4. Offering leadership and by counseling and guiding teachers and students in motivation, utilization, and experimentation in terms of the best media or combination of media for the particular learning situation.
5. Supplying a quality media environment with efficient work spaces for students, faculty, and media staff for reading, listening, and viewing activities.
6. Providing reference resources and specialized reference staff in reference areas to meet the informational needs of the faculty and staff.
7. Furnishing facilities for and assistance in the production of self-created instructional materials, displays, and demonstrations to meet the special needs of students and teachers.

8. Exploring the uses of modern technology, including exploratory use of computers, in attacking the control and synthesis of knowledge to encourage more learning in less time.

9. Encouraging supervisory and other supplemental services from districts or larger units, including investigating the desirability and cost of central services required in processing the varied learning media for all the schools of a cooperating area.

10. Offering information on new educational and curricular developments and participating in networks of knowledge for the benefit of students and teachers.

Such a program must have staff; collections of materials, equipment, and devices; facilities and funds. Each part is dependent upon the other. Basic to the program is the support of school board members, school administrators, curriculum specialists, classroom teachers, and community leaders. The concern for quality education must be shared by all citizens. [23]

The course of the school media program from a few books which a teacher owned to the computer-based multi-staffed, multi-media center represents the efforts of many dedicated professionals. That this goal will be accomplished remains with school administrators who have vision; dedicated library, audiovisual and media specialists; creative teachers and active learners supported by boards of education and community, state and national leaders.

References

1. U. S. Bureau of Education. Public Libraries in the United States of America; Their History, Condition, and Management. Washington, D. C., U. S. G. P. O., 1876, p. 412.

2. Broderick, Dorothy M. "Plus ça Change: Classic Patterns in Public/School Relations," School Library Journal, 14:31-33, May 1967.

3. Knight, Douglas M., and Norse, E. Shepley, eds. Libraries at Large; Tradition, Innovation and the National Interest. New York, R. R. Bowker, 1969, p. 90.

4. National Study of Secondary School Evaluation. Evaluative Criteria for the Evaluation of Secondary Schools. 4th ed. Washington, D. C., 1969, pp. 273-88.

5. American Library Association. Committee on

Post-War Planning. School Libraries for Today and Tomorrow, Functions and Standards (Planning for Libraries, No. 5). Chicago, ALA, 1945.

6. American Association of School Librarians. School Library Standards Committee. Standards for School Library Programs. Chicago, ALA, 1960.

7. Finn, James D., et al. Studies in the Growth of Instructional Technology, I: Audio-Visual Instrumentation for Instruction in the Public Schools, 1930-1960; A Basis for Take-Off (National Education Association of the United States. Technological Development Project. Occasional Paper, No. 6). Washington, D. C., 1962.

8. Godfrey, Eleanor P. The State of Audiovisual Technology: 1961-1966 (National Education Association of the United States. Dept. of Audiovisual Instruction. Monograph No. 3). Washington, D. C., 1967.

9. Sherman, Mendel, and Faris, Gene. Quantitative Standards for Audiovisual Personnel, Equipment, and Materials in Elementary, Secondary, and Higher Education. Washington, D. C., Dept. of Audiovisual Instruction, National Education Association of the United States, 1966.

10. American Association of School Librarians. Knapp Schools Libraries Project. Realization; The Final Report of the Knapp Schools Libraries Project. Peggy Sullivan, ed. Chicago, ALA, 1968.

11. National Education Association of the United States. Research Division. School Library Personnel Task Analysis Survey. Chicago, American Association of School Librarians, 1969. (Available from Robert Case, Director, School Library Manpower Project, American Library Association, 50 East Huron Street, Chicago, Illinois 60611.)

12. U. S. Office of Education. Descriptive Case Studies of Nine Elementary School Media Centers in Three Inner Cities. Title II (OE-10060). Washington, D. C., U. S. G. P. O., 1969; and _____. Emphasis on Excellence in School Media Programs, Descriptive Case Studies, Special-Purpose Grant Programs. Title II (OE-20123). Washington, D. C., U. S. G. P. O., 1969.

13. _____. Public School Library Statistics, 1962-63. (OE-15020-63). Washington, D. C., U. S. G. P. O., 1964.

14. Snygg, Donald, and Combs, Arthur W. Individual Behavior; A New Frame of Reference for Psychology. New York, Harper, 1949; and Rogers, Carl Ransom. On Becoming a Person; A Therapist's View of Psychotherapy. Boston, Houghton Mifflin Company, 1961.

15. Association for Supervision and Curriculum Development. Commission on Current Curriculum Developments.

New Curriculum Developments; A Report. Glenys G. Unruh, ed. Washington, D. C. , Association for Supervision and Curriculum Development, 1965.

16. The "Trump Plan, " proposed by J. Lloyd Trump as director of the commission describes the organization of the school's instructional day into 40 percent in large group instruction, 20 percent in small group instruction, and 40 percent in independent study. See: National Association of Secondary-School Principals. Commission on the Experimental Study of the Utilization of the Staff in the Secondary School. Focus on Change; Guide to Better Schools. Prepared by J. Lloyd Trump and Dorsey Baynham. Chicago, Rand McNally, 1961, p. 112.

17. Goodlad, John L. , and Anderson, Robert H. The Nongraded Elementary School. Rev. ed. New York, Harcourt, Brace, & World, 1963.

18. Alexander, William M. , et al. The Emergent Middle School. New York, Holt, Rinehart and Winston, 1968.

19. Bush, Robert N. , and Allen, Dwight W. A New Design for High School Education: Assuming a Flexible Schedule. New York, McGraw-Hill, 1964.

20. American Association of School Librarians. Standards for School Media Programs. Prepared by the American Association of School Librarians and the Dept. of Audiovisual Instruction of the National Education Association. Chicago, ALA, 1969.

21. Ibid. , pp. xv-xvi.

22. Crawford, Lura E. "The Changing Nature of School Library Collections, " Library Trends, 17:383-400, April 1969.

23. Whitenack, Carolyn L. "School Libraries and Librarianship. " In Miles M. Jackson, Jr. , ed. Comparative and International Librarianship. Westwood, Conn. , Greenwood Publishing, 1970, pp. 68-69.

Part II:

PROFESSIONAL DEFINITIONS

MEDIA SPECIALIST: SPECIALIST IN MEDIA*

Ted C. Cobun

Abstract

We consider those who participate in the vocation
of educational communication to be professionals.
At least, they should be professionals. Professional
means, in addition to being employed for reasons including financial gains, a quality of practice and development of product.   The terms we have which
identify the functions of professionals in educational
communication are one index of how well we know
what we are doing.   Terms should be, for a profession, accurate and descriptive.   Terms should
not be obscure.   Terms should be definitive, and
should employ definitive functions.   It should be possible to know whether a professional term, describes
predictable function better when the holder has one
kind of training than when he has another kind of
training.

Esoterics ought not be the name of the game!   But, if esoterics is not the name, the name must be confused diffusion.
Of course, no one ever hears that name.   What one hears is
the alias, "media specialist." All of the professional journals, house organs, periodicals of various persuasions, and
even some college catalogs carry the term "media specialist."

Definitions

The term, the name, the title, or whatever it is, of

---

*Reprinted by permission of author and publisher from Inter-
national Journal of Instructional Media, vol. 3, pp. 223-27,
1975-76.   © 1976, Baywood Publishing Co.

media specialist is a classic in esoterics. It is truly a
term intended for or understood by only a small group. It
might also be extended that even the small group doesn't
really understand it--not that it matters greatly to them.

Media Specialist

Let's define "media specialist." To eliminate the
more or less obvious, let's define "specialist" and get it out
of the way. A specialist is rather like an "expert." Will
Rogers had a good definition for "expert." He said that an
expert was a little man, a long way from home.

A specialist might then be an expert who specializes.
The dictionary, in a more serious vein, says that a specialist is one who has devoted himself to a particular branch of
study or research.

If one accepts that a specialist has devoted himself to
a particular branch of study or research, then a media specialist must have devoted himself to the particular branch of
study called "media." Well, back to the old dictionary again.
By the way, the word "old" in relation to dictionary is used
in the sense of endearment. It is really quite new. It is
the American Heritage dictionary. It was last printed in
1971. I checked it against a Random House dictionary and a
Merriam-Webster dictionary, all with 1971 publication dates,
and they all say essentially the same thing. The purpose of
the check was to define the word, "media."

Media

"Media" is defined by all three dictionaries as being
the plural of the word, "medium." Excepting certain posi-
tional definitions, and a mathematical one, "medium" is defined as (1) An intervening substance through which something
is transmitted or carried on. (2) An agency by means of
which something is accomplished, conveyed, or transferred.
(3) A means of mass communication. (4) One thought to have
powers of communicating with the spirits of the dead. (5) An
environment in which something functions and thrives. (6) A
means of expression as determined by the materials and creative methods involved.

Who needs them?--Obviously, most educational institutions would have little use for a media specialist whose de-
votion to study and research emphasizes communication with

the spirits of the dead. And, there doesn't seem to be sufficient scope and depth for a real specialist whose focus of
effort is on making fillers for test-tubes and Petri dishes to
grow germs, flies, etc.

It seems, since a medium can be defined as a <u>means</u>
of mass communication, one who could obtain the means
would be a means specialist or procurement specialist. The
same might be true, in definition, for one who could provide
the means suitable for expressions to massed audiences.

A medium is also defined as an agency by means of
which something is accomplished, conveyed, or transferred,
or an intervening substance through which something is transmitted or carried on. Thus, a media specialist is one who
devotes himself to a study of relevant <u>agencies</u> and/or <u>sub-
stances</u> useful for transmitting or carrying something.

The point is, to define a media specialist as having
functions beyond these limitations is to demonstrate that one
has never defined the terms, or, doesn't care to define the
terms. It could also imply that the esoteric connotations of
the terms are intentional, and their consequences directed
subjectively to suit and satisfy anyone for whatever are his
purposes.

<u>Who are they?</u>--Any teacher, at any level, and in any
subject-matter could be called a media specialist. Such
teachers should have specialized in training, or during professional experience, in agencies and substances which trans-
mit or convey subject matter. In the same vein, school administrators qualify as media specialists. One of the prime
concerns, and surely emphases of training of administrators
is the agency by means of which something is accomplished,
conveyed, or transferred.

It follows that library services personnel are also
media specialists. Their concerns are similar to those of
the teacher, except that, perforce, the concerns must be
more general since the attention of service is on a number
of teachers and learners.

On another track, the school bus is an agency which
conveys or transfers learners from wherever they are to
wherever they must go. Thus, the school bus driver is a
media specialist. He must have devoted some study--what-
ever he has devoted--to driving the bus and its concommital
functions.

It takes very little thought and practically no effort to demonstrate that almost everyone is a media specialist, depending on how and who defines the term. The term, media specialist, being so universally applicable, really defines nothing and is, therefore, useful only in a completely subjective sense. For a profession, its use borders on the hilarious--or, the sad--depending on how you look at it. It is a term like "audio-visual education" which means any learning event that can be seen and heard. Since, for the largest part, that is the kind of experience which most learners in most schools get, the term is meaningless. The term applies to everything, thus defines nothing.

JIMS says they are... --The Association for Educational Communications and Technology published, in 1970, a report entitled Jobs in Instructional Media (JIMS). On page 4, a career lattice is demonstrated. The lattice consists of thirty-six career titles, arranged in a hierarchical pattern. Each of these careers can be analyzed to show aspects of nine major functions.

The report also gives fourteen alternatives for job analysis with implications for job structure and for a training curriculum design. Also, there are thirty pages of study and course description related to "media support personnel," showing detailed and specific programs of skill development over two-year periods of study. There are some similarities in these courses but, each is different from the others.

The report is a good report! It is professionally executed in amazing detail! It can be used to describe job roles, and to eclectically produce other job roles. Depending on who does the interpretation and the synthesis almost any kind of professional in the field of "media" can be described. Within the huge complex of details lurk descriptions of technicians, specialists, and generalists who could be employed by any institution whose purpose is to change behavior. Trained, as described by the report, such technicians, specialists, and generalists could be optimally productive and beneficial to employing institutions.

Who they might be--But, to clear the air, to eliminate the confusion, and to place professionals in educational institutions as they are needed, and where they ought to be, the ambiguous, vague, misdirecting, meaningless title of "media specialist" should be recognized for what it is--superficiality, froth without substance, camouflage and pablum. Educational administrators, in particular, need to recognize an employee, or a set of employees, who can perform functions in the service of faculties and learners which will directly benefit the products of education in specifically accountable ways.

What they ought to be-- The schools do not need "media specialists." No one can tell, with professional clarity, what they are. What schools need as operational staff members are message design specialists, media design specialists, media production specialists, and developmental testing and validation specialists. All of these specializations may need to be performed by a single pertinently trained professional, because of financial reasons. Because of time and load, more than one such specialist might divide the roles and the load between them.

Especially for individualized instruction, and in open schools, the message design specialist cooperates with teachers or learning managers to design learning events. Such learning events could then take into account most of what is now mere lip-service, namely, learner analysis data, rationales for learning, and motivation.

More often than not, the design of a learning event will disclose that there is no existing medium which conveys, appropriately, required messages. It will also disclose that most existing media do not involve learners in learning activities beyond looking and listening. The research shows that far too many of such learning experiences are never assimilated, or are too quickly forgotten. The research also shows that when a learner does something and says something relevant to what he is experiencing he retains what he learns, as long as he continues to apply it, in nearly total amounts.

Therefore, a media design specialist designs media which are pertinent to specific learning events. He builds into the media requirements and opportunities for relevant responses. At times which are rational, the media induces the learner to do something related to what he is learning and its application.

When rational media are designed, they need to be produced. The reason for this is because commercially produced and validated media are far and few between. Therefore, a media production specialist is a valuable and required member of faculties.

<u>What they ought to be</u>--Since media of any kind require developmental testing, appropriate revision, and subsequent validation, a specialist of this order is implied.   This is a task of considerable intensity and volume.   Failure to accomplish validation is a weak link in the chain of accountability.

These, then, are the needs of education in contemporary society.   These are needs which failure to meet accounts for many of the conditions which are criticized about education.   One condition we do not need is more ambiguousity and confusion.   Let's specify the "media specialist"!

Direct reprint requests to:

Ted C. Cobun, Ed. D.
Director, Division of Instructional Communication
East Tennessee State University
Johnson City, Tennessee   37601

INTEGRATED SCHOOL RESOURCE PROGRAMS: A CONCEPTUAL FRAMEWORK AND DESCRIPTION*

Morris Freedman

School resource programs generally evolve from the perceptions of instructional technologists and/or librarians, with the possible additional inputs of supervisors and other interested personnel. There is usually a set of given conditions including the school plant, assigned facilities, personnel attitudes, skills, and budgets which too often serve to shape resource programs. The more seminal factors, such as the school's operating philosophy, curriculum planning, and holistic nature of schooling and instruction, learning problems, and characteristics of learners may not be the basic ingredients in designing school resource programs. A conceptual framework which may guide program development and help to describe its effective characteristics is needed by most schools.

Need for an Integrated School Resource Program

The following general assumptions point to the need for a descriptive and philosophical guide:

1. Schools do not have integrated resource programs based on a cooperatively developed school philosophy.
2. Students do not have available the variety of resource materials for learning which are possible through a planned integrated program.
3. School resource personnel have limited perceptions and

*Reprinted from Audiovisual Instruction, vol. 20, pp. 5-9, Sept. 1975, by permission of the author and publisher, the Association for Educational Communications & Technology.

skills to completely fulfill their roles and functions in an instructional resource program.

4. Existing resource programs are not concerned with the total school program.
5. Teachers do not have the skills needed for using resources effectively.
6. Resources are generally conceived as frills, rather than as essential components of the instructional process.
7. Staff and students are not involved in planning resource programs.

Definition of Terms

Phrases and words are used interchangeably in the field, resulting in ambiguity and lack of clarity in meaning. A few terms used in these pages are defined below:

1. Instructional resources are by virtue of their intended use not to be compartmentalized into print, nonprint, broadcast, or textbook media; rather, they are together the tools of the teaching-learning process and have value only insofar as they affect learner behaviors by serving as motivators, interest sustainers, clarifiers, explainers, image enhancers, informers, expanders, and attitude changers.
2. Instructional resources include materials, equipment, techniques, settings, messages, people.
3. Instructional resources users are those involved in the process of schooling.
4. Instructional resource specialists are those who can effectively assist users to maximize the values of media as they are applied to learning and teaching. Resource specialists are involved in total school development since their concern involves all grades, curriculum areas, and personnel.
5. Instructional resource facilities are all learning and resource spaces in which media are managed, used, presented, created, maintained, and disseminated.
6. The school instructional resource program is an instruction, service, and management system which is shaped by the school's philosophy, its learning objectives, teacher skills, the characteristics of learners, learning spaces, the curriculum, and the organization of students for learning.

A Conceptual Framework

The school instructional resource program is a system which evolves from the following: What is known about how children learn and what they learn, how teachers teach, the instructional process, the learner's uniqueness, teacher skills, the performance objectives which guide instruction, the methods and techniques of instruction, how teachers and students communicate in verbal and non-verbal forms, how instructional presentations are designed and created, which media are most effective for specific communications requirements, how learning spaces are designed, and how children are organized for learning.

The development of the school instructional resource program should be based on a descriptive analysis of the total school. Describing the characteristics of an optimum program provides a sound foundation and direction for action. Although the analytical approach may be the same from school to school, the unique conditions in each school will result in varying descriptions and lead to a wide range of program designs. Such descriptions are applied to all elements of the system, and include the needs, roles, requirements, and contributions of students, teachers, supervisors, parents, community, and community school district. The description serves as a guide to setting priorities, emphases, and a rationale for program organization.

The school instructional resource program as an integrated system is comprised of interrelated parts including people, learning objectives, spaces, facilities, budgets, evaluative instruments, and a broad range of tools within the school and the broader community. The interrelatedness of this system makes each element interdependent. Budgets, for example, affect staff, which affect training programs, which affect teaching skills, which affect use of resources, which affect learning. Similarly, program planning within this system must involve consideration of all components in a process of instructional developments.

Those persons who interact in the process of instructional development may include teachers, students, resource specialists, supervisors, parents, and other personnel. Space and facilities may include learning and resource areas, libraries, auditoriums, classrooms, production laboratories, darkrooms, projection booths, language laboratories, television studios and control rooms, master antenna and CATV devices, public address systems, backstage lighting and sound consoles, computerized instructional systems, intra and inter-school communications, and telecommunications.

The major objectives of the resource program relate to the philosophy and goals of the school. The implementation of the school's goals is the primary responsibility of the program. The more specific objectives of the instructional process and the needs of students and teachers should serve as a guide to the development of resource services and instruction. Since resources are a component of the instructional development process, its services and instruction should result from cooperative planning. Teacher-developed performance objectives provide an essential key to the resource program.

The range of resources for teaching and learning is broad and reflects the integrated nature of the service. Included are print and nonprint materials, real objects and the resources of the universe, the more vicarious learning opportunities in the form of 16mm and 8mm films, books, television or videotape, sound and silent filmstrips, photographic slides and large transparencies, audiotapes, disc recordings, photographs, microfilms, study prints, reference books, trade and textbooks, magazines, duplicated materials, models, mockups, and yet-to-be media of tomorrow. Multi-media data storage and transmission devices are also part of the service system. These include computers; electronic laboratories; information storage and retrieval devices; broadcast, cable, MATV and CATV, facsimile, satellite and microwave transmissions; information reduction systems such as microfilms; voice processing systems used for accelerated or compressed speech; programed projection devices; duplication and reproduction systems; audio, video and photographic systems; and those products of technology which will become components of teaching and learning.

Selection of media for school use must be based upon the careful review of primary users, teachers and students. Parents and supervisors should have direct roles in selection, especially where materials are highly sensitive or controversial. The specific roles of personnel in the selection process should be defined by local school boards, who should share with the superintendent his responsibility for the approval of resources used in the schools.

The resource program and its personnel have a responsibility to total school development in formulating its philosophy and goals and in implementing its objectives; in shaping instructional program, teaching skills, methods, and techniques; and in affecting the behaviors of learners by helping them to discover, use, and apply their learnings; and to have impact on their attitudes toward themselves and the world around them.

Description

With a conceptual construct established, it is then possible to describe program characteristics. Sample descriptions follow.

In an optimum school instructional resource program we would observe students:

1. Using a variety of resources for independent study, exploration, research, and self-instruction.
2. Using resources which relate to their interests, levels of ability, language skills, and other personal characteristics.
3. Using resources which are highly accessible, safe, simple to use, and in good operating condition.
4. Using resources which are current and relate to their learning activities.
5. Using resources which are motivating in format, presentation, and content.
6. Receiving assistance in using equipment and interpreting resource materials.
7. Having opportunities for experience with materials which relate to their strengths, and through which they may find success and positive feelings.
8. Receiving instruction in the uses of resources through which they may find alternative means for effective communication.
9. Receiving instruction in the creation of resources not only as a means of personal expression, but for the purpose of producing and being involved in the process of creating visual art forms.
10. Using concrete materials to support their understanding of verbal and visual abstractions.
11. Learning the skills for independently finding resources, and for selecting and using materials appropriate to their learning objectives.
12. Having a learning atmosphere that allows independent activities and peer interaction.

13. Having a variety of resources through which to communicate.
14. Using a variety of resources to generate and present information.

In an optimum school instructional resource program we would observe teachers:

1. Using a staff-developed philosophy to guide their teaching.
2. Directing students to a wide variety of resources for independent learning activities.
3. Using resources suitable to various patterns of pupil organization.
4. Using resources to assist in lesson development.
5. Using resources to resolve problems of classroom communications.
6. Using resource spaces in which materials may be constructed or produced.
7. Using resource collections of materials for study, reference, preparation of lessons, and self-development.
8. Using the expertise of resource specialists who can help select, create, produce, and guide the utilization of materials.
9. Using resources which are highly accessible, simple, and safe to use and are in good operating condition.
10. Using well-organized resource collections which simplify location and scheduling materials.
11. Participating in the selection of resources they will use.
12. Participating in planning the resources program.
13. Receiving the assistance of trained students and/or paraprofessionals in arranging and using resources.
14. Using resources which are current and relate to ongoing activities and objectives.
15. Receiving continuous updating and training in new resources and methods.
16. Using learning spaces which are efficiently organized for resource accessibility and utilization.
17. Receiving the support of supervisors and parents in media use and experimentation.

In an optimum school instructional resource program, we would observe the instructional resource specialist in the following categories:

Planning, Development and Management

1. Participating in planning school philosophy and goals.

2. Planning the resource program with staff.
3. Analyzing staff and student needs as basis for program design.
4. Planning resource space organization with staff.
5. Organizing resources which are accessible.
6. Scheduling services.
7. Integrating the resource program into total school program.
8. Managing the resource program to provide efficient services.
9. Organizing staff for appraisal and selection of new resources.
10. Maintaining resource spaces for effective use of resources.
11. Managing the resource program to integrate materials with instruction.
12. Organizing programs for efficient logistical support such as distribution and storage of resources.
13. Organizing and training students to provide services to learning spaces.
14. Arranging for and requisitioning resources from community and private sources.
15. Maintaining resource collections.
16. Maintaining catalogs and inventories.
17. Coordinating the utilization of all school resources, including those of broadcast, textbook, library, and audiovisual.
18. Providing resources for students and teachers to take home for study purposes.
19. Managing budgets.
20. Preparing proposals for funding.

Instruction

1. Providing instruction to students in selecting, locating, and preparing resources.
2. Providing instruction to students, enabling them to create and express themselves through verbal and non-verbal forms such as film, videotape, and photography.
3. Providing instruction in mass communications.
4. Providing instruction in the use of resources for self-expression.
5. Providing instruction in film study.
6. Providing extra curricular activities for enrichment in such areas as photography, filmmaking, radio, and television production.

Staff Development

1. Developing methods and techniques with teachers for effective resource utilization.
2. Training staff in new methods and techniques of utilization.
3. Training staff in equipment operation.
4. Training staff in constructing and preparing resources.
5. Training staff in organizing learning spaces for effective use of resources.
6. Providing new resource information to staff.
7. Providing orientation training to new teachers.
8. Preparing newsletters, bulletins, catalogs, lists to inform staff.
9. Demonstrating new resources, methods and techniques.
10. Organizing resources to assist staff with small and large group instruction or independent learning activities.
11. Identifying resources to support staff planning.
12. Helping staff prepare lessons.
13. Providing staff with unit resource kits.
14. Organizing community resources and field trips for staff.
15. Providing opportunities for preview of resources.
16. Experimenting with new resources, techniques, methods.
17. Evaluating resources with staff.
18. Evaluating resource utilization as an aspect of staff development.
19. Evaluating total program with staff.

Preparation of Resources

1. Organizing a resource facility to enable staff to construct or prepare instructional materials.
2. Developing staff awareness and confidence in preparing resources.
3. Providing training and assistance to staff and students to enable them to create instructional resources.
4. Training staff and students in use of production equipment.
5. Producing materials for staff.
6. Preparing originally designed materials.
7. Providing a broad range of services including copying, duplication, photographic, audio, video, projection, exhibit, graphics, display, construction with simple materials.
8. Providing materials for public relations and community-related programs.
9. Providing materials to support school supervision.

10. Providing programs enabling students to create materials for self-expression, demonstration, project activity.

Technical Service

1. Providing equipment set-ups for learning spaces.
2. Maintaining equipment in safe and efficient operating condition.
3. Evaluating new equipment.
4. Providing for microphone, lighting, and sound system set-ups.
5. Providing public address system operation.
6. Providing safe storage for resources.
7. Providing film and tape splicing and editing.
8. Planning facilities design and utilization.
9. Providing television studios, language laboratory, and other electronic facilities operations.
10. Inspecting new resources purchased by schools.
11. Maintaining repair facility.
12. Providing liaison with equipment dealers and repair services.
13. Maintaining equipment in learning and resource spaces.
14. Providing technical instruction to staff and to student and paraprofessional assistants.

In an optimum school instructional resource program, we would observe parents and people from the community who:

1. Understand and support the philosophy which guides the school program.
2. Understand and support the resources program.
3. Provide voluntary assistance to teachers and students.
4. Serve as resource personnel where special skills apply.
5. Have input into program planning.
6. Participate in the selection of resources as may be appropriate.

In an optimum school instructional resource program, we would observe personnel from the community school district:

1. Providing an educational philosophy and instructional goals.
2. Providing support and leadership encouraging school instructional resource program.
3. Providing budgetary support.
4. Providing resource services not available in the schools.

5. Organizing a district-wide committee to plan and organize district programs of support to schools.
6. Providing guidelines and standards to schools for staffing and organizing a program.
7. Providing training programs, in-service courses, and workshops for staff development.
8. Providing a long-range plan for resource acquisition and program development.
9. Keeping district staff informed of new media and techniques.
10. Providing a resource center for training and production.
11. Planning cooperative programs to better use staff skills and available funding.
12. Providing cooperative planning for funded projects.
13. Providing for program evaluation.

In an optimum school instructional resource program, we would observe <u>supervisors</u>:

1. Leading the school program with a cooperatively evolved philosophy.
2. Guiding the resource program with established goals and objectives.
3. Providing support and leadership to the resource program.
4. Providing programs for staff development.
5. Arranging for intergrade or interdepartment planning for integrating the resource program into the school curriculum.
6. Providing facilities and space for the program.
7. Providing budgetary support.
8. Helping plan the use of community resources.
9. Serving as liaisons with parents and community to involve their participation and support.
10. Providing orientation to new teachers.
11. Assisting in the dissemination of information to staff and community.
12. Providing security arrangements for resources.
13. Providing staff organization for the selection of new resources.
14. Providing for the organization of resources to make them easily accessible.
15. Providing for paraprofessional assistance to the resources program.
16. Arranging for student training as resource assistants.
17. Providing supervision and evaluation of programs as guides to improvement.
18. Organizing long-range planning to guide program development and resource requisitioning.

19. Providing leadership in seeking funding to strengthen resource program.

Conclusion

Most schools do not have integrated resource programs. The cooperative development of a broad-based school philosophy, from which a conceptual framework might be developed, would serve as the basis for building the integrated program. Descriptions of optimum conditions are useful as guides to setting goals and objectives. Teachers and students should be involved in this systematic process, and should have the continuous support of the school administration. This type of program development and implementation also reduces many of the interpersonal rivalries, interdepartmental squabbles, and inefficiences of separatism enabling professionals to get on with the primary tasks of schooling.

THE MEDIA SPECIALIST: EN ROUTE AND TERMINAL COMPETENCIES*

William E. Hug

With a unique degree of cooperation between professionals at all levels, Alabama has produced an innovative approach to the identification of competencies required of the media specialist. The competencies identified reflect the new relationships between librarianship, technology, and management theory which characterize the new role of the media specialist.

The competencies are reprinted from The Big M in Education--Media Specialist: A Role Defined[1] produced by the Alabama Committee for the Preparation of Educational Media Personnel. Participants included staff members from the Alabama State Department of Education, deans and faculty members from seventeen Alabama colleges and universities, and leaders of educational organizations in the state.

The final test or Terminal Competency expected of a media specialist is his demonstrated ability to make value judgments about media programs by applying internal[2] and external[3] criteria. This evaluation process is vital to any goal oriented program since evaluation enables the media specialist to (1) assess goal attainment, (2) make appropriate decisions, (3) project long-range needs, and (4) formulate requests for program support. The complex process of evaluation is based on the ability of the media specialist to apply what he understands and to analyze and synthesize[4] data in such a way that the entire program can be quantified for the purpose of evaluation and hence decision making.

*Reprinted from Improving College and University Teaching, vol. 24, pp. 59-60, Winter 1976, by permission of the author and publisher, Heldref Publications.

Terminal Competencies require the application, analysis, and synthesis of Enroute Competencies. Enroute Competencies are activities in which media specialists will be routinely engaged. Terminal Competencies are employed in the policy making process. For example, the media specialist must be competent in the evaluation of his management system (Terminal Competency). Contributing Enroute Competencies involve his ability to analyze (1) the arrangement of furniture, space, and materials, (2) the effectiveness of schedules, (3) the assignments of work load to para-professionals, (4) the appropriateness of operating policies, etc.

Detailed expertise needed for specific operations varies. Therefore, competencies are not meant to stand as equals. Some will be emphasized over others to meet the needs of specific programs. Enroute Competencies are in a constant state of change, evolving in order for Terminal Competencies to be more fully realized.

Task Analyses are the step by step procedure for performing specific operations. For example, an Enroute Competency is to specify the steps necessary in processing a book. The minute details in processing comprise the task analysis and are omitted from this report.

The remainder of this section consists of specifying six Terminal Competencies with Enroute Competencies immediately following. Terminal Competencies are the evaluation of (1) the instruction, (2) the management, (3) the organization and circulation, (4) the design and preparation, (5) the selection and acquisition systems of the media program in relation to the needs of the total school as well as the evaluation of (6) the pacesetting and innovative instruction systems in relation to their potential use and application in the total school program.

The committee is cognizant of the fact that certain Enroute Competencies are repeated under different Terminal Competencies. This apparent repetition tends to disappear when each Enroute Competency is considered in relation to the Terminal Competency under which it exists. Although Terminal Competencies are written on the evaluation level and in relation to the total school program, both Terminal and Enroute Competencies outlines are appropriate for media specialists working on all levels: school, district, county, state, or industry.

Instructional Competencies

Terminal Competency

Evaluates the instruction system of the media program in relation to the needs of the total school.

Enroute Competencies

- Assists staff in determining appropriate resources for meeting instructional objectives.
- Instructs staff in the preparation and repackaging of resources to better meet curricular and user requirements.
- Informs staff of trends in instructional systems, innovating schools and innovative practices, technological developments, and techniques for adapting and using media.
- Promotes the use of the effective techniques of information dissemination.
- Prepares workshops, formal presentations, informal discussions, newsletters, displays, demonstrations, etc., for the purpose of disseminating information and arriving at operational procedures.
- Guides students in information searches.
- Teaches students to use reference tools.

Management Competencies

Terminal Competency

Evaluates the management system for the media programs in relation to the needs of the total school.

Enroute Competencies

- Applies appropriate management technique.
- Participates in professional meetings, serves on committees, and maintains active membership in related professional organizations.
- Collects data in order to prepare for anticipated changes in the media program.
- Projects long-term needs.
- Directs the development of policies and operational procedures for the media program.
- Interprets policies and operational procedures.

- Prepares reports based on statistical data, direct observation, and expert opinion.
- Formulates task descriptions for media personnel.
- Prepares an analysis of functions and supporting operational components of the media program for the purpose of decision making.
- Establishes and manages system for the selection, acquisition, production, classification, circulation, and maintenance of media.
- Organizes and advises media clubs.
- Maintains the media budget.
- Determines priorities.
- Informs faculty and administration of media-related legislation.
- Initiates projects and proposals related to media for research and program development.
- Coordinates the media program of the school system with national, regional, and state organizations.
- Interviews and makes recommendations for staff appointments.

Organizational Competencies

Terminal Competency

Evaluates the organization and circulation system of the media program in relation to the needs of the total school.

Enroute Competencies

- Formulates policies and procedures for processing, classifying, cataloging, displaying, storing, maintaining, circulating, inventorying, and collecting media.
- Organizes collection to support the curriculum.
- Compiles catalogs, bibliographies and other listings of media.
- Insures easy access of collection to the user population.

Designing and Preparation Competencies

Terminal Competency

Evaluates the design and production system of the media program in relation to the needs of the total school.

Enroute Competencies

- Establishes policies and procedures for the preparation of media.
- Plans and provides means (space, facilities, personnel, supplies, guidance) for the design and preparation of media.
- Collects information and makes cost analyses between possible production techniques.
- Works with staff in the preparation of instructional sequences utilizing appropriate media.
- Applies principles of product development to the preparation of media.
- Redesigns mediated instructional systems in response to performance data.

Selecting and Acquisitioning Competencies

Terminal Competency

Evaluates the selection and acquisition system of the media program in relation to the needs of the total school.

Enroute Competencies

- Formulates policies and procedures for the selection and acquisition of materials.
- Locates and maintains sources of appropriate media.
- Arranges for media preview and selection activities.
- Obtains selected materials.
- Develops a system for the evaluation of media.
- Maintains media evaluation reports.
- Determines adequacy of collection.

Pacesetting and Innovative Competencies

Terminal Competency

Evaluates pacesetting and innovative instruction systems in relation to their potential use and application in the total school program.

Enroute Competencies

- Participates in curriculum planning.

- Assists in the preparation of learner objectives, instructional sequences, and the evaluation of entry, enroute, and terminal behaviors.
- Cooperates with staff in the designing of new instructional systems.
- Adapts promising new systems of instruction into proposals for implementation.
- Gathers and disseminates information about innovating schools and innovative practices.
- Promotes continuous progress, individualized instruction, team teaching, and differentiated staffing.
- Uses multi-media to fulfill instructional objectives.
- Advises curriculum workers of the appropriate use of filmstrips, programmed instruction, single concept films, realia kits, 16mm films, study prints, audio and video recordings, etc.
- Analyzes the function of the media staff in relation to new programs.

Footnotes

1. Copies available from Mrs. Nina Martin, Library Consultant, State Department of Education, State Office Building, Montgomery, Alabama, 36104.

2. Internal criteria are those cooperatively formulated by the operating unit usually involving the superintendent, building principal, lead teachers, and media specialist.

3. External criteria are those standards formulated by state, regional, and national agencies.

4. Usage of evaluation, understanding (knowledge and comprehension), application, analysis, and synthesis based on Bloom's Taxonomy of Educational Objectives, Handbook I: Cognitive Domain.

Part III:

EDUCATIONAL CHANGE AGENTS

THE MEDIA SPECIALIST AS AN AGENT FOR CHANGE*

Betty Fast

No one ever accused the traditional school library of revolutionary tendencies; its serene and studious atmosphere epitomized a passive role in the educational scene. Its function was to support the curriculum of the school in a subservient handmaiden fashion. The leadership that a few outstanding librarians managed to demonstrate in their schools came despite and not because of their positions.

When the librarian was building a book collection and offering reading guidance to students at one end of the school, the audiovisual specialist was tending ailing machines and offering teachers how-to-do-it instructions at the other. Occasionally, an audiovisual educator like Carlton W. H. Erickson envisioned the AV director as a change-agent in the school; in actuality only a few people were even able to change their after-teaching media duties into a full-time job.

Moaning Librarians and AV Tinkerers

While librarians bemoaned the advent of newer forms of media and spent their time scanning the horizon for readers, and AV tinkerers scouted the terrain and announced an imminent takeover by librarians as the major hazard to avoid, true media specialists began to put the strengths of their two fields together and found they had the capacity to become "shakers and movers." The new breed of media specialist, functioning on the school level, quietly assumed the position of curriculum coordinator in the school.

*Reprinted by permission from the May 1975 issue of the Wilson Library Bulletin, vol. 49, pp. 636-37+. Copyright by The H. W. Wilson Company.

Who would suspect that a merger of the fields might result in a combination whose sum is far greater than its two parts? Although Frances Henne led a small band of prescient educators toward the unified media concept, even today most people do not realize the potential of the fusion. It is a force whose time is yet to come.

One reason for the time lag in recognizing the potential of the media specialist has been the do-it-yourself aspect of the situation. Since library and education schools have moved with less than deliberate speed in the direction of integrated programs to educate media specialists, the major impetus has come from perceptive professionals in the field who grasped the unified philosophy and found their own means to acquire the necessary skills and knowledge.

In individual schools some talented media specialists have interwoven curriculum and media to encourage learning. Occasionally these new media-curriculum specialists are classroom teachers, especially English teachers, who understand that media is the language of today's youth and have become effective media teachers. Fortunately, there is a growing number of educators who believe that curriculum and media cannot be considered as entities.

Changing Learning Patterns

Media programs are vital in education because of the great changes in the learning patterns of youngsters, caused largely by their exposure to television and other mass media. If schools are to move from a classroom and teacher-dominated routine--already declared outmoded by the students--to a learner-oriented environment, the media program must emerge as a key component, an integral part of the learning process. Media must play an active, not a passive, role in the school experience, since the success of the educational program depends in large part on the way learners use resources to find, evaluate, and apply information.

The media specialist--with the ability to make connections between the people, ideas, and media that are the essence of learning--has become a key member of the educational team. In fact the logical conclusion of this learning interplay is an educational program in which media and curriculum, media and learning, and media specialists and teachers have become identical. There is no such thing as a separate media program or a physical entity called the media center apart from the rest of the school. Since the media program's goal is the improvement of instruction, it is possible that the media program might self-destruct when it becomes totally integrated into the learning process.

Although such integration is in the future, for the present the innovative media specialist is in a unique position to have an impact on the entire school. Example is still a successful way to cause change, and the example of the media center is easily observed. Unlike a teacher, whose classroom door is closed and who works with only a small segment of the student population, the media specialist can touch every student's life. The media center should present a model for media use with a variety of learning opportunities (including media production) replacing the class instructional or study hall mode. In a good media center program, the time saved by utilization of self-instructional materials could be used to help students develop an appreciation of media and to encourage its improved use in the classroom.

Innovative changes can originate in the media program and cause fundamental alterations in the life of the school. The media specialist, working with one part of the curriculum or one group of teachers at a time, can bring about changes in the style of teaching in the classroom. Often it will be necessary to set up some of the new learning methods in the media center with classroom-related subject matter. Then teachers can send their students there to use materials individually or in groups until the teacher feels confident and enthusiastic enough to incorporate them into the classroom situation. In some schools taped teaching, individualized reading programs, use of simulation games, and learning center techniques have been initiated by the media specialist and then have moved into the classroom.

How to Export Innovation

Instead of building larger and larger centers to accommodate most of the media use in the school, media specialists should consider farming out the activities, the equipment, and even the carrels into the classrooms. There is no reason why the individual use of media cannot become part of the regular classroom life. The ultimate goal of a media program, including student production, should be to integrate it into the school's learning program. As each activity moves out of the media specialist's domain, the specialist is freed for another innovation which will also be exported when it proves its worth in the curriculum.

At the same time that the media specialist is working as a master teacher using resources in innovative ways in the media center, s/he must also wage a campaign for active involvement in curriculum planning. Although it is vital to have media specialists function as part of the team that designs curriculum guides at the district and/or school level, it is equally important to have this input on the firing line where the student meets the curriculum. By its use in co-operative lesson planning, the media specialist's expertise can help teachers clarify objectives and select the mix of media and method which can be used most effectively. As the media specialist becomes indispensable to the improvement of learning through demonstrations of innovative practice and curriculum planning, it will become easier to justify additions to the staff and to the collection.

How can this concept of the media specialist as a change-agent become a reality rather than a rarity? The vision must precede the realization: Media specialists must have this self-image before it can become a reality. The new national guidelines for media programs, Media Programs: District and School, describe this person functioning at the center of the learning program. The combined roles of curriculum consultant and innovator should attract educators with leadership qualities to the field. What is needed are flexible people with a receptivity to change and the courage to overcome institutional inertia: media specialists who are eager to work with people as well as with media. Educational training programs must assume an influential position as well as offer the background necessary to help media specialists to meet their destiny. This presupposes an understanding and commitment that many programs have been slow to recognize.

The New Improved Media Specialist

The name of the game is important, for a label helps to create the mental set. Changing names to media center, media specialist, and media program is crucial if the new program is to dramatize how it differs from the traditional library. Although imposing a name change does not create an instant media orientation without an attitude change in the media center staff, the school library that clings to the traditional label and attempts to operate a change-oriented media program must cope with a residue of stereotyped associations that impede its progress. The quickest way to change the image is to change the label; by calling the program something different, we make people aware of a change to a new improved entity.

Written philosophies of education to the contrary notwithstanding, the idea of a truly learner-centered school program is revolutionary in the real world of the public schools. Why can't the media specialist and the media program lead the way toward this fundamental change in education?

THE CASE OF THE MEDIA SPECIALIST: THE OVERLOOKED EDUCATIONAL CHANGE AGENT?*

David M. Moore

Abstract

The media specialist (e. g. , the Director of Learning Resources, Director of Media Services, A-V Director) has had many responsibilities in the past. His duties have been many and varied. Sometimes he likes to think of himself as an educational change agent. It is the author's contention that no case can be made for the media specialist to be a true educational change agent unless he becomes a trusted consultant to the faculty who knows and skillfully uses the ideas and concepts of instructional design. He, of course, will have to still be responsible for hardware and software management, but his impact and ultimate accountability will be to the faculty in the direct improvement of instruction.

There is no denying that the age of technology is upon us and that it permeates nearly every phase of our lives. In the past few years, there has been an expansion in the acquisition and uses of all types of educational media such as television, film collections, audio tapes, videotapes, computer-assisted-instruction, and others.

Most teachers and administrators are aware of the teaching advantages offered by many uses of media, but that awareness may not be enough. What is needed is a commitment on the part of teachers and administrators to begin

---

*Reprinted by permission of the author and publisher from International Journal of Instructional Media, vol. 3, pp. 109-15, 1975-76. © 1976, Baywood Publishing Co.

to redefine that role of the teacher in light of the new opportunities offered by technological developments. It is apparent that the mere availability of educational media has not
and in fact should not be the cause of change. The technology only provides a means by which certain desired ends can
be achieved.

As a result of the new technology, the teacher has the
opportunity to become less a giver of information and more
coordinator of information and even a co-learner with the
student. Education must become more of a cooperative endeavor. A great deal of learning occurs outside the classroom. The quantity of information from sources such as
television, newspapers, magazines, and films provides important inputs into the educational process. Children are
coming into the classroom with more experience, though
many times vicarious, than ever before. Teachers must
learn to orchestrate the great variety of printed and electronic media both in and out of class. Students know and teachers must learn, that there are many sources of information.
To behave as if the teacher is the only source of information is counter productive to the educational process and is
a very narrow sighted view. [1]

But the teacher should not be allowed to bear the
burden of making the transition alone--the one of becoming
a coordinator of information. He or she must have help,
strong administrative leadership, and a source of professional
advice and support in the design and the development of instruction. Hopefully at this point the media specialist[2] enters the scene.

The use of media has offered some promising opportunities to help the teacher improve instruction but there are
some reasons why this has not necessarily happened. Some
of these are:

1. The necessary equipment and particularly materials have
   not been immediately available.
2. The large bulk of teachers have had little impact at the
   developmental and selection stages of commercial
   media production.
3. Teachers have been unduly influenced by the fads and
   promises of the "new" media.
4. Teacher training and in-service programs have done little to prepare teachers to deal effectively with technology.

5. Lack of use of comprehensive instructional design in course and lesson development by most teachers.
6. The media specialist has done nothing more than change projection lamps and pushed carts.

Assume for a time that the following premise is fairly true, that technology probably will cause some type of change in the role of the teacher and that the use of media in education still is not as effective as it should be.   Also, assume that instruction is the focal point of a school's activities.   Then what is the role of the media specialist and how is his or her accountability in the media management process connected with the changing role of the teacher and the improvement of instruction?

The media specialist historically has been charged with many responsibilities, among these are supervising

1. the production of instructional materials,
2. the maintenance of materials,
3. the development of in-service program in the media area, and
4. the purchase of equipment and materials.

He or she has been responsible for scheduling and keeping equipment and materials in good repair and has spent some time in consultation with the faculty.   Should the media specialist be asked to do more, or only be held accountable for what he already does?   Because his or her training and experiences with the media technology should give the media specialist unique skills in the educational process, he should be called upon to do more than manage equipment and materials.   He should, of course, be held accountable for these management functions.   These duties will be discussed briefly.   However, the ever increasing, complex and most important role is of educational consultant, and this resulting accountability to the instructor will be discussed in greater detail.   For it is the author's contention that the consultant role will be the most vital responsibility of the media specialist and all of the other functions will play only a supporting role in this process.

Personnel Management

The media specialist must determine the functions of his organization, thus his personnel needs.   The personnel needs of a media center will be based around efforts to improve instruction generally at two levels: (1) Providing professional design, development support to the teacher's planning and (2) Providing the necessary clerical and technician support to effectively implement the above design and development work. Effective communication of media center activities is vital both within the internal organization of the center as well as with the clientele and administration. Personnel management should be designed to support the ongoing activities of the media center to support and improve instruction.

Hardware Management

Most media specialists are given the responsibility of managing the hardware needed for instruction. This equipment, of course, would include that which is necessary for self-instruction, large and small group instruction and for in class or out of class activities. The primary goal, however, should be teacher availability of equipment. It has been shown over and over again the more available the equipment the more use it will enjoy. It is also desirable that this usage be encouraged to be high in quality as well as quantity.

Software Distribution

Where it once may have been considered unusual to see combined collections of media hardware and library materials under the same roof and managed by a person with training in both media and library science, today it is becoming fairly common place. Many librarians and media specialists are realizing that they are both in the same game: instruction. Since there is no one best educational media or method for all types of instruction, it is an advantage to combine resources and use the best for a particular purpose. What software to purchase or to produce will become very important in the improvement of instruction. The role of the media specialist working with the teacher to select and develop materials becomes the first step in performing the most important task, that of becoming an active consultant with the teacher to improve instruction. This consultive role if done in depth has taken the name of instructional design.

Instructional Design (Consultant)

Many teachers, administrators and media specialists are not familiar with or have not had contact with the ideas and concepts of instructional design, e. g. , the systematic development of instruction using all resources available including educational media. The idea is to redesign the entire lesson around objectives and to use media as an integral part of the lesson, and not necessarily as an adjunct or supplement to teaching.

The following is a quote from the Illinois Audiovisual Association's 1972 Leadership Conference's final report on the role of the media specialist as a consultant to an individual teacher.

> ... Because accountability most certainly will be concerned with the outcome of student learning, the director of media services and staff must be responsible for working in depth with the teacher to develop materials and packages for both in and out of class. This would involve a great deal of time and some of the activities would be:
>   1. Working with teachers to develop objectives
>   2. In class observations
>   3. Out of class consultation
>   4. Studying prospective audiences
>   5. Development and production of materials for both in and out of class use
>   6. Developing testing tools
>   7. Evaluation of efforts
>   8. Redevelopment of materials where necessary
> As it might be indicated, this effort implies the cooperative redesign of entire courses or at least units of study not just a lesson or segment of a lesson. ... [3]

Almost all media specialists spend some time with teachers, but how many spend the time and do the activities stated above? I would guess very few, and this is where they can make the greatest impact in education. If the teacher has an opportunity to work closely with a person, e. g. , the media specialist, who has extensive knowledge in the use and selection of media and in systematic development of instruction in a team approach the end product should, of course, be more effective instruction with or without the use of educational media. It should be remembered, however, that the use of media is not always the answer to improve instruction, but instructional design may be. Teachers are also being held accountable, wise decisions and hopefully wise usage will result from coordinated efforts. And it is here where the role of the teacher will begin to change to a coordinator of instruction and where the media specialist becomes a true educational leader.

Few teachers have had the opportunity to make inputs on commercially produced media. It may be a fact that most teachers will have to accept the role as a consumer rather than a developer of commercial materials. The media specialist in the role of consultant can work with the teacher as a reviewer, critic and a suggester of ideas. While teachers generally cannot affect the development of commercially produced materials they can in cooperation with the media specialist develop locally produced materials which in most cases will fit the exact need of a teacher's particular subject, lesson, or unit. Media specialists should have the opportunity to act as a buffer, because of their knowledge of media, between the teacher and the zealous media salesman who may or may not have a useful product. Many of the past "fads" in educational media might have been dampened somewhat if there had been a closer cooperation between the media specialist and the teacher and the administration.

Some colleges and universities have not equipped teachers and administrators to deal with the problems of the technology. In many cases the university academic climate is oriented to the past, rather than the future. Even though many teacher education institutions may provide a required course in the selection and use of educational media, many of these courses are not able to do more than allow teachers opportunities to learn how to operate equipment. The enlightened media specialist in his management role of consultant should provide more in-depth, interesting in-service programs either individually or in small sessions for teachers to improve their skills in designing and developing instruction.

Summary

There is no doubt that the media specialist must be held accountable for all of the management functions, hardware management, software management, personnel management for these support the more important, the prime role of improving instruction. In addition, the media specialist may be the only person to whom a teacher can turn for professional advice in the selection or design of materials for instruction. The media specialist because of his access to support materials e. g., media, and hopefully his skill in instructional design may also become the logical team member with the teacher to design and develop instruction. The ultimate accountability of the media management processes will be whether or not a positive role was played in the improvement of instruction. As teachers must change to deal with new technologies, the media specialist must also develop consultant skills trusted by the teachers. If this is not done there is no case for the media specialist as an Educational Leader or change agent.

References

1. David M. Moore and Robert M. Bruker, Technology and Teachers: Combatants or Collaborators?, Illinois Schools Journal, 52(3):81-82, Fall-Winter, 1972.
2. Media specialist will be used in this paper to mean Director of Media Services, A-V Director, Director of Learning Resources, etc.
3. Illinois Audiovisual Association, IAVA 1972 Leadership Conference Final Report, p. 41, Illinois Audiovisual Association.

Bibliography

Brown, J. W., Norburg, K., Administering Educational Media, McGraw-Hill Book Co., New York, 1965.

Erickson, C. H., Administering Media Programs, Macmillan Publishing Co., New York, 1968.

Illinois Audiovisual Association, IAVA 1972 Leadership Conference Final Report, Illinois Audiovisual Association, 1972.

Kemp, J. E., Instructional Design: A Plan for Unit and Course Development, Fearon Publishers, Belmont, California, 1971.

Moore, D. M. and Bruker, R. M., Technology and Teachers: Combatants or Collaborators?, Illinois Schools Journal, 52:80-84, 1972.

Part IV:

TOTAL CURRICULUM INVOLVEMENT

THE ROLE OF THE SCHOOL MEDIA
PROGRAM IN THE CURRICULUM*

Shirley L. Aaron

Every time an educator enters the classroom he or
she is faced with the overwhelming problem of how to provide the variety of instructional experiences necessary to
meet the individual needs of students. Many teachers cannot cope with this problem so they gear their instruction to
the nonexistent "average" child. An educator who follows
this procedure can often be heard to say "I teach on a third
grade level since my students are in the third grade." Other teachers provide some learning alternatives to meet individual learning needs when possible, but they are constantly frustrated by their inability to offer many of the instructional activities indicated. These teachers frequently lament
the fact that not enough time, materials, space, etc. are
available for them really to do the kind of job that would
produce an optimum learning environment for every student.

Certainly these factors have a great influence on the
teacher's ability to individualize instruction in any part of
the curriculum, but before factors such as amount of materials needed or space required can be placed in the proper
perspective, another question must be considered. One must
ask whether a teacher working alone, no matter how talented,
can provide the variety and types of complex learning experiences needed by today's students.

In order to determine an answer to this question some
of the essential ingredients for successful implementation of
an individualized instruction program need to be examined in
an objective fashion. Basically an effective individualized

*Reprinted from Southeastern Librarian, vol. 27, pp. 221-
26, Winter 1977, by permission of the author and publisher.

instruction program requires the sound utilization of many different types of appropriate materials and experiences. When a teacher attempts to provide for the differing needs of students, he or she accepts the necessity for making available a variety of effective learning alternatives of multiple levels to help students achieve each instructional objective. Since a number of learning activities are occurring simultaneously in this kind of educational environment, the teacher is required to alter his or her perception of the traditional teaching role and perform instead as a manager of instruction whose chief responsibilities are to provide and prescribe suitable alternatives at the appropriate time. The focus of the instructional experience then shifts from the utilization of a limited number of materials with emphasis on teacher centered activities to the use of a wide range of resources that include members of the community and locally produced materials developed by students.

For the wide range of learning alternatives to be made available for classroom and individual student needs, the following tasks should be performed: identification, selection and evaluation of materials and other resources according to student needs and concepts being taught; production of needed materials that are not available commercially; organization of resources so that they can be obtained by students in the forms required when and where they are needed; and aid to students in the production of their own materials to enhance and broaden their learning experiences through direct involvement. When each of these essential ingredients is analyzed in terms of expertise, time, and inclination toward media use required, and when the other duties and responsibilities assigned to the teacher are also considered, the enormity of the job moves beyond the capabilities of the classroom teacher.

Many teachers simply lack the time, expertise, and inclination to offer the variety of media oriented experiences necessary to individualize or personalize instruction in an educational program. In many cases a large part of a teacher's pre-service training is focused on learning the content of the area in which he or she intends to teach rather than on mastering the processes of communicating the content. Consequently the teacher becomes a content specialist but many times has little experience in utilizing techniques such as selecting and using films effectively, helping students to produce photographs to improve visual literacy, and other activities of this nature. Further, time constraints severely limit the teacher's ability to carefully select, produce and evaluate much of the media which have potential value as bases for learning alternatives in the classroom.

Recognition of the magnitude of these problems by many educators has led to the exploration of alternatives aimed at combining the content expertise of the classroom teacher with the communication process expertise of other specialists in the school to form a strong teaching team. Within this context the unique skills of the library media specialist are being acknowledged increasingly as essential ingredients in an instructional program focused on meeting the individual learning needs of the student.

To determine specifically the unique contribution of the library media staff to the teaching team and to students in the school, one must examine the functions generally associated with the media program. These functions are divided into instructional support or indirect services to the educational program, such as selecting materials for the media collection, and instructional or direct services such as helping the teacher to design materials needed in the classroom or teaching media skills to students. Each of the functions performed in the media program is aimed ultimately at effective utilization of appropriate materials and media activities at the time they are needed.

Support Functions

Four important instructional support functions provided by the library media center form the foundation for the direct involvement of the media staff in the planning, implementation and evaluation of a specific curricular unit.

Selection

Initially, relevant commercially produced materials must be selected for the media collection, and they should then be made available in the media center when they are needed for instructional units or activities. In order to accomplish these tasks, the media staff attempts to involve teachers and students in the selection of high quality materials which can be used most effectively in the classroom. During this selection process the media specialist brings new and pertinent materials to the attention of the teachers and suggests other materials which might replace materials initially selected by instructors from publishers' catalogs and similar sources. Through the continuing interaction of the media staff with teachers and students, and through investigation of curricular objectives and the text materials which provide basic information about the curriculum, gaps and weaknesses in the school's media collection become evident. The media specialist then selects additional materials to fill the gaps and to eliminate the weaknesses.

Acquisition

Once the decision has been made about the selections, the media staff then orders the materials required in the most efficient, cost effective manner so that the materials will be available as soon as the teachers need them. The acquisitions functions are carried out within the constraints of budgets and the school's own purchasing policies and procedures. The need for planning and cooperation between media staff and teachers is obvious if the teachers and students are to get the materials when they are wanted.

Organization

After the materials arrive in the school, they must be organized and accounted for in a way which will make them accessible to teachers, students and others desiring to use the materials for the purposes of instruction, information and personal fulfillment or interest. The media specialist applies his or her organizational skills to this task and assigns appropriate subject headings, classification numbers, and other aids which place each item where it will be most useful in the media collection. The card or other type of catalog systematically provides the user who wants particular materials with a description of every piece of material contained in the media center's inventory and an indication of where specific materials are located. Without the knowledgeable application of this type of organizational system materials in a media center or in other parts of the school are inaccessible to all but those who are in direct possession of the materials. Consequently, if the eighth grade language arts teacher decides to put the material she orders in a classroom collection without processing these materials through a central organizational system, the ninth grade language arts teacher or the social studies teacher who might need to use the same materials may not be aware that these materials are already in the school. This often results in unnecessary duplication and inefficient utilization of existing resources.

Circulation

After materials are organized in a logical way to serve
best the instructional organization of the school and the needs
of the users of the media collection, a circulation system is
developed by the media staff. The circulation system keeps
track of where the materials (and often the equipment) are at
any given time when on loan from the media center, and it
is intended to insure the widest use of the media resources.
If the circulation system is not adequate, or if it is too cum-
bersome, teachers and students may find that the materials
they need are unavailable even though the materials can be
identified as part of the school's media collection. The materials (and equipment) may be housed in the media center
as part of its permanent (but nonetheless circulating) collection, or placed on temporary or permanent loan to a classroom or a subsidiary learning resource center. The important consideration should be a system by which the materials and equipment are made accessible when and where
they are needed or wanted. It is the responsibility of the
media staff to devise a system that is workable and to assure that it works.

Direct Instructional Role

Each of the instructional support functions described
above is essential to the educational program of the school,
but the library media staff can also play a more direct instructional role in any classroom where the teacher is attempting to individualize instruction. This complementary
curricular role of the library media staff can be illustrated
by looking at the direct media services provided to a language arts teacher, as an example, who may be working on
an American folklore unit or module.

Planning

The library media specialist meets frequently with the
language arts teacher during the planning stages of the unit
to insure that communication or basic skills objectives dealing with reading, listening and viewing are included and that
materials and other resources which are needed for the unit
are available when they are needed. In these meetings and
at other times the media specialist suggests activities which
will help students achieve unit objectives through such activities as viewing sound filmstrips on "Our Heritage of Ameri-

can Folk Music, " reading magazine articles on different aspects of American folklore, videotaping a reinactment of a folk tale by members of the class, or listening to a tape of "The Legend of Sleepy Hollow. " The teacher's attention is called to new materials of folklore and additional resources which may be tapped. These resources can be identified at least partially through a central community resources file often developed, organized and frequently updated by the media specialist. In numerous instances the media specialist also acts as the contact person to obtain materials and information services for the school from other community, state and federal agencies.

Materials already in the media center are evaluated by the library media specialist and the teacher in terms of their quality and ability to help students attain unit objectives. The library media specialist, by virtue of professional training as a materials specialist, can help the teacher choose the finest materials technically to include in the unit. In an increasing number of situations where the media specialist works effectively and continually in a curricular role with the teachers, the media staff also screen the available materials for an instructional unit so that the teacher will not have such an overwhelming number of materials to examine. Over fifty percent of the materials on folklore obtained from various sources may obviously not be suited for this teacher's language arts class. They may be poorly produced, on too difficult a reading level, or contain a large portion of irrelevant material; consequently, the media specialist who is aware of unit goals and objectives can sometime eliminate those from consideration before the teacher examines materials for the unit. A close working relationship between teacher and library media specialist during the planning stages of the unit also enables the media staff to suggest materials and activities for specific objectives, a service which tends to do away with much of the frustration experienced by teachers who are overwhelmed by the great numbers of materials they must investigate before deciding which materials and media activities will finally be included in the unit.

After the possible activities and materials related to each unit objectives are identified, a variety of questions such as the following must be answered by the teacher before a final selection of activities can be made:

1. What skills are needed to present the learning activities to students? Are these skills presently available?

If not, can these skills be obtained in a practical way?

2. What materials, other resources, and equipment must be scheduled in what place at what time?
3. What students will participate in which activities at what time?
4. What resources must be locally produced for the unit? How can this be accomplished?
5. What means of prescription and evaluation will be used in the unit?
6. What limitations are presented by the time frame of the unit?

The media staff can be of much assistance in supplying possible answers to many of these questions by offering unique services in the area of instructional design, media production, basic skills development, administration of materials and equipment systems, staff development and consultation and information.

Production

If the language arts teacher decides to include the range and types of materials and activities necessary to accommodate the learning orientations of the students completing the unit, a number of preliminary decisions relating to the design of materials must be made. First, the teacher will need to make a final selection of the materials to be used from the media collection. Then with the consultation and technical assistance of the media specialist, the teacher can decide which additional materials need to be designed, created and/or adapted. Once this decision has been made methods of creating the materials are explored. In many schools production facilities such as a dark room and TV studio are part of the media center facilities. When more complicated techniques must be employed to prepare materials, the services of the district media center are utilized by the media specialist or the teacher. In schools where there are sufficient media staff with specialized technical skills, such as graphic artists, for example, locally produced materials are prepared by media personnel for the teachers when certain production services are required. In other situations where lack of adequate staff does not permit such service on a broad scale, media specialists provide in-service training programs for teachers in the design, production and utilization of instructional materials. In this way teachers can become more proficient in creating different types of materials and utilizing media effectively with their students.

Another aspect of media production which can be pertinent to the teacher in planning and implementing a unit is student involvement in the production of materials. The media specialist who has skills in cinematography, photography, TV production, graphics and other media production techniques can work directly with students to help them utilize media techniques effectively to convey concept, information, and attitudes related to the unit. In this way a teacher who lacks these skills or feels hesitant in this area can still make these learning experiences available to students.

Developing Student Skills

Skills taught to students through the media program encompass a much broader area, though, than media production. As the library media staff and the language arts teacher work closely together, they develop a sequence of planned activities which help students to acquire skills in locating, selecting, using and evaluating all forms of media on folklore and in other areas of language arts as they work on group and independent projects. Students are given the competencies they need to use the library catalog and other tools to find materials on subjects such as Paul Bunyan or Pecos Bill, to evaluate these materials in terms of their appropriateness and quality, and then to utilize them effectively. Emphasis is always placed on providing instruction in media skills at the time the skills are needed by students. Any approach to the teaching of media skills which does not integrate these skills in a meaningful way into the curricular program is generally ineffective. Students need to receive reinforcement at the time of instruction; otherwise they will not retain what they have been taught.

Each of the areas of expertise attributed to the library media staff in a school should receive consideration as a teacher decides the most advantageous way to present unit activities. However, factors such as the time which the staff can give to working with students to produce materials, the facilities and resources available, the teacher's areas of expertise in media utilization techniques, the teacher's perception of the library media program's role, the administration's perception of the media program's role, and the media staff's perception of its curricular role all will have a major influence on the manner in which the media staff will participate in a curricular unit. Once the level and type of media program participation has been decided by the teacher and the library media specialist, the media staff carries out its curricular responsibilities as the unit is implemented and evaluated.

Guidelines for a Curricular Role

For those librarians who are just beginning to become involved in a curricular role for the library media program, the following guidelines may be helpful:

1. Educate your principal and teachers about the role that you can perform on the teaching team and let them know what resources are required to allow you to act in this role. Do not assume that they are already aware of the benefits to be derived from allowing the library media staff to function in this role.

2. If your staff and other resources are limited and you want to demonstrate effectively the meaningful contribution you can make in the curricular area, select a teacher to work with who has exhibited a positive attitude toward media services, and work intensively with that teacher. It is extremely important to experience success in this first instance since this effort will provide the impetus for other teachers to request the same kind of service.

3. Become a member of the curriculum committee and participate in a variety of ways, such as offering suggestions about materials to be considered, information on new curricular approaches and developments in an area, and similar activities.

4. Do not try to provide the full range of media services to everyone if you have limited resources. Instead, use your resources most effectively to achieve your top priorities and then focus your attention on those activities. If your efforts become too diffused in an attempt to provide all media services at some level, your program will suffer and people will regard your area as incidental to the educational program.

5. When asking for additional resources to perform in a curricular role, always relate your request directly to the benefits which will be experienced by students in the classroom.

6. Be very careful about criticizing the teachers with whom you are working in a curricular capacity. Some teach-

ers will feel very insecure in this cooperative role; they will need continuing positive reinforcement.

7. Do allow yourself a realistic time line when working with teachers. It is not uncommon to need four to six weeks lead time to have materials locally produced as needed as well as to offer the inservice training desired, coordinate the logistical arrangements for materials and equipment, locate, acquire and evaluate materials which may be appropriate for the unit, and perform other similar tasks. It is better to give teachers a reasonable estimate of time required to complete responsibilities rather than to disappoint them with inadequate products or no products at all.

8. Be flexible about meetings with teachers. If possible meet when and where they can. Their planning schedule may not conform to or be limited to their planning periods during the school day.

9. Use your communications skills constantly to inform people in the school of the potential of your program for them and of the resources required to reach that potential.

10. Study texts and other curricular guides used in the classroom to obtain basic information about curricular directions in specific courses.

These guidelines when followed should move the media specialist closer to the exciting implementation of a unique role which will have far reaching positive effects on the way in which educators are able to meet the learning needs of the child. It is the responsibility of all media professionals who are committed to this concept to provide the leadership necessary to convince educators and others that these changes will result in much improved learning environments for individual learners.

ROLE OF THE LIBRARY MEDIA SPECIALIST
IN CURRICULUM DEVELOPMENT*

D. Joleen Bock

Curriculum development, a time-honored activity, has run the gamut from the "I think we need a course in--" approach, to extensive industry surveys in order to determine job markets in a specific field. In all practicality, we probably still need both approaches as points of departure for considering curricula, but within the framework of a logical progression to final decisionmaking. Some curricular decisions are pre-determined by state education agencies, but even those require local decisions to make them operational. Where does the library/media specialist fit into this process?

Curriculum Committees

The library/media specialist role in curriculum development has evolved from the passive role of receiving minutes of the curriculum committee (if lucky) to that of being actively involved in the decisionmaking process. It is important that this individual be a member of the curriculum committee. Regulations regarding committee structures often make this difficult to attain. If this is not feasible, then the specialist should attend as an observer, actively participate from the floor when it is appropriate, and ask to receive agendas and minutes. Whether an observer or a committee member, the specialist can become an integral part of the process by providing research for the committee.

*Reprinted from Ohio Media Spectrum, vol. 29, pp. 57-59, Oct. 1977, by permission of the author and publisher, the Ohio Educational Library Media Association.

Individual Instructors

For the instructor presenting a course, the library/ media specialist can provide catalogs from other institutions for comparison purposes and can, in conjunction with the instructor, determine:

(a) What materials currently in the collection will be useful to this course.
(b) What materials are available commercially, and their cost.
(c) The cost to locally produce materials, and the feasibility of time lines to assure their availability when needed.
(d) Whether audio-visual and library equipment on hand is sufficient to support the activities suggested.
(e) Whether available facilities are of the type needed: e.g. Do large groups of students need to be accommodated in the Learning Resource Center at one time? In small groups? At special times of the day?

In addition, the library/media specialist can give assistance in writing course or program objectives, usually required on submittal forms to curriculum committees.

This process not only is helpful to the instructor, but assists the committee in making decisions by providing accurate cost data. It also introduces the instructor to the materials and equipment available and opens the door for instructor input into materials selection, a process which is a constant problem to library/media specialists.

Institutional Involvement

To participate in all the activities suggested above can be very time consuming if there are many curricular changes occurring in one year, but the importance of them to the operation of the Learning Resource Center cannot be over-emphasized. Full participation at this point reaps later benefits in increased student and instructor utilization of materials and equipment.

In reality, probably few library/media specialists are involved to the extent mentioned above. If the involvement is casual, one of answering questions from faculty or administrators if asked, what should be done to change that approach?

A common concern in schools and community colleges today is not only whether a new course be of benefit to the student, but whether or not the institution can afford to add it to the curriculum. Some institutions have an unwritten agreement that if a new course is added an old one will be withdrawn, unless it involves an entirely new program. With or without this regulation, administrators need to know specifically what each recommended course will cost in personnel, facilities, equipment and materials. You, the library/media specialist, are in a good position to be of assistance in several of these areas. If the institution does not require library/media information on the curriculum request form, a section similar to the following could be recommended:

INSTRUCTIONAL RESOURCES:
(To be completed with the assistance of
the library/media specialist)

		Currently Adequate	Additional Cost
a.	Materials		
	Books	_____	_____
	Periodicals (paper & micro)	_____	_____
	Maps, Charts, etc.	_____	_____
	AV Materials	_____	_____

b. Equipment
If current equipment will not adequately serve this proposed course, list items needed:

Item	Cost
_____	_____
_____	_____

If the curriculum change form is one which requires signatures, a signature line should be added for the library/media specialist so that administrators are assured participation in the process.

Curriculum Consultant

If this treatise sounds like the library/media specialist

should become curriculum consultant, you're right. This is a major responsibility of such a specialist and one which has taken on more significance each year as libraries have developed into learning resource centres. As instructors and administrators realize that the library/media specialist is knowledgeable in this field and that it is an integral part of the entire instructional process, they begin to use this expertise.

Many of us received little or no instruction in college in such things as writing objectives, psychology of learning, and curriculum development. What can we do to insure that we have adequate background for the curriculum consultant role which is now thrust upon us, in varying degrees? School systems have curriculum consultants, but at the building level, the library/media specialist may be IT, and in community colleges this is usually the case also.

If it is not possible to attend summer or evening classes to get further background, there are innumerable materials available for individual study.

In addition, educational periodicals are filled with articles about instructional processes. Professional conferences provide much information on current trends and techniques. If you are an individual entering a doctoral program, here is another excellent opportunity to take courses in psychology of learning, instructional development, etc. The most important thing whether you take courses, read, listen to speeches, or whatever, is to have a positive attitude toward the process of curriculum development and your role as a library media specialist in it. With this you can go far, and the curricular process at your institution will benefit.

THE LIBRARY MEDIA SPECIALIST AND
TOTAL CURRICULUM INVOLVEMENT*

Mary Margrabe

If a feeling of indifference or lack of concern and ex-
pectation from your faculty and students toward the Library
Media Center (LMC) gnaws at you, you may want to take
steps to alter the situation. You may establish several objectives that could result in greater interplay between the
LMC and the total school.

Six goals for involving the LMC in the curriculum
will be discussed in this article. First, to attract the size-
able body of students who never voluntarily enter the LMC;
secondly, to provide techniques and a framework for teaching library skills, combining individualization with pleasure;
third, to identify and stimulate gifted and talented students
not otherwise recognized outside the LMC, or to enrich those
already identified; Fourth, to turn on the "turned-off" by
exposing them to success-assured activities; Fifth, to become so enmeshed with the school's curriculum that scarcely
a unit is begun without input from the librarian; Sixth, to
provide the youngest children with a library/librarian-based
orientation to school.

Attracting Students to the LMC

If students never find their way to the Library Media
Center under their own initiative, then it's up to the Library
Media Specialist to make it so inviting and accessible that
the students won't stay away for fear of missing something.
Accessibility depends directly on the attitude of the LMS,

*Reprinted from Catholic Library World, vol. 49, pp. 283-
87, Feb. 1978, by permission of the Catholic Library Association.

who can open or close, invite or repel students. The use of posters, displays, contests and interest centers attracts attention; perhaps some of the following suggestions may help you achieve the first goal:

1) Morning programs for the school prepared under the leadership of the LMS with only library aides sharing a role.

2) Conduct weekly contests with questions whose answers are found in the LMC. These will attract pupils who can't resist the possibility of winning that ice cream prize. Frequent contests can invite entries in the form of mobiles, models, dioramas, posters, etc., a different form each week. Entries may be group-produced or individually made, in class or out. Door decorating contests with changing themes can be sponsored.

3) All-school voting in the LMC reveals school favorites, such as records, books, teams, whatever.

4) Student-of-the-Week can be selected by vote; his biography can then be presented "over the air" (public address system). Contests similar to the TV show "It's Academic" can be held. The questions can be geared to the "high interest, low difficulty" group: recent sports records, outstanding athletes, athletic rules, and miscellaneous world records.

5) Large commercial posters showing drag racing, sporting activities, motorcycles, and other high-interest topics can decorate the media center along with pithy mottos, pennants and bumper stickers of favorite athletic teams.

6) Treasure hunts in the library, displays of summer souvenirs, graffiti boards, on-going board games, a comic book exchange, or a gentle touch on the shoulder may be the "open sesame" that fills your library. There's something for each of us to use.

The idea is to attract the students to the library long enough to learn that the media center is a joy to visit, and that its director is a human being who likes kids enough to make the LMC an attractive and colorful place where they are welcome.

Skills Teaching: Games and Stations

After the student body knows you really want them in the media center, offer them some fare they can handle. Skills stations, including games, offer pleasure and encourage individualization. Adapt a simple game the children already play, such as "Fish." Use those extra sets of catalog cards. Shuffle about ten sets, and deal. Take turns drawing from the person to your left. When a player has a complete set, he displays it in front of him. When all the cards are played the person with the most sets wins; or the first person to clear his hands of cards wins. Decide your rules in advance.

You may wish to create a board game. Decide on your objective: to learn LMC rules. List the (however many) rules you wish to emphasize. Lay out a board with squares to proceed through. Leave some squares empty, but on others write: "You have a book overdue, go back three steps"; "You shared your material generously, advance two"; "You forgot to return the book you were examining, so stay where you are"; "You left your book on the ground, start over." Decide on numerous such directions. Provide dice or spinner for determining the numbers of moves. Use buttons or other objects to represent each player. Presto! a game, at no cost, but with a generous dividend--in that the originator will give thought to the guidelines for efficient library usage, and the player will receive similar exposure to LMC usage.

Publicize the creators of the games, thus encouraging others to play them or to attempt to invent a new game. Here is an opportunity for enrichment and creativity for the gifted student, and fun-learning for those students who are not-so-gifted but who can profit from playing their friends' games.

Another activity that has spread from the classroom to the Library Media Center is the use of "learning stations." At its simplest, this device of recent years consists of a single attractive chart or poster which allows a child to self-teach a single concept or objective. In a more complex form, it may include audiovisual equipment and software, realia, even a human resource on occasion.

You decide what you want the student to learn, for example, where the index of a certain encyclopedia is located.

Your station might contain a drawing of an encyclopedia
opened to the back showing page entitled "Index." The station is located near the sets of encyclopedias in question.
Instructions are listed for the learner: 1) Look at the front
pages of any three volumes. Is there an index in the front
of the volume? 2) Look at the last pages of any three volumes. Is there an index at the back of these volumes?
3) Look over the entire encyclopedia. Is the first volume
an index? 4) Is the last volume an index? Where is the index located? 5) Is there one or two means of indexing in
the encyclopedia?

The same procedure could be required of all sets of
encyclopedias in your reference section. Even if the student
does not remember which encyclopedia has an index at the
end of each volume, which has a single-volume index, and
which has both, he at least has the experience of looking for
an index and may remember to do that when the occasion demands it.

As you decide which media skill to teach, think through
the steps for self-learning and create a station with simple
activities for learning that one skill. If you consider 30
skills important for the children in your school, you will
soon have a store of 30 stations to select from as a need
for each skill surfaces.

The material for stations and games can be costly,
when there is no money budgeted for it. However, there are
alternative methods to consider. If there is a paper mill
near you, you might ask for cardboard rejects to be donated
or sold to your LMC at a reduced price. Other imaginative
sources include cardboard boxes. One side of a large mat-
tress carton can be creased, folded in thirds, and painted.
This station stands on the floor in use. If only smaller sec-
tions of corrugated cardboard are available, they may be
hinged by book repair tape into a triptych which will hold up
to six stations. Or remove the top and bottom from a box,
separate at the seams, then paint the cardboard or cover it
with the colored roll paper used as background on bulletin
boards. This makes a foldable, four-panel station.

Work books which contain some exercises relative to
LMC usage may be disassembled, then each page covered
with clear plastic adhesive (like Con-Tact), then filed together in a small box. Thus, one book does the work of a
dozen, and no copyright laws are violated.

Also, cake boards may be obtained from a local bakery or bakery supplier. They are corrugated circles, white on each side. When you mark "cake slices" for each learning objective, and use pincher clothes pins inscribed with corresponding answers, another world of stations appears.

In addition manila folders, with independent study lessons inside, and with outside cover decorated, offer another source of stations. Discarded folders may be used. Similarly, folders with pockets, while more expensive, provide a place for storing exercise sheets and answers, and are more colorful.

There must be dozens of other sources of material for this purpose. Once the material need is determined, the LMS can imaginatively search for material that can be adapted to meet that need.

Displaying stations and games may at first appear to be a great challenge. They may be suspended from the ceiling and cover an entire wall. To hang stations and games: use twine over the metal ceiling strips or attach it to a molding; punch two holes in the bottom of one and top of another station; tie one under another until the row of stations hangs from wall to floor, if desired.

In addition, simple wooden frames can be created to hold two stations sandwich board style. They can be stacked in bulk in an upright storage box, with the titles of the stations protruding beyond the top of the box for quick selection and use, or the stations may be made freestanding.

The Talented and Gifted Student

While many teachers intuitively spot talented and gifted students in their care and teach to their abilities and needs, far too many such youth pass their years of formal learning without being identified.

The librarian can work alone, or she can become part of a team to develop units for these gifted students who are often "lost" amid more pressing demands, and are expected to succeed on their own.

With gifted students the LMS' role can be divergent. It can be limited to directing them to an ever-expanding appreciation of good literature through book talks, discussions, reports, and annotations; or, it can be as complicated as sponsoring youngsters in the operation of a book store for which the students preview, order, and sell books as well as maintain the business part of the enterprise.

The "Turned Off" Student

For the student that is less gifted or merely "turned off," the LMS has a role to play. He/she may find himself helping some of the "otherwise gifted" students create something with their hands relating to the library media center, such as book marks.

The LMC becomes a "turning on" place when interest centers invite pupils to view filmstrips, slides, records, tapes, and kits on their favorite subjects, such as sports, monsters, motorcycling, gymnastics, snakes or ESP.

Total Curriculum Involvement

Since the "library" has evolved from the storage place for books to a "media center" with the goal of Total Curriculum Involvement (TCI), the LMS is fast becoming enmeshed with the whole faculty and the needs of the school's programs. The role may have to include a "readiness" program which makes both students and teachers aware of the possibilities of the media centers, and then turns the possibilities into reality.

This process will require a public relations program within the school using not only printed bibliographies, public address system announcements, programs and contests, but also a one-to-one relationship of librarian to client. It is most important that the LMS "sell" the LMC at faculty meetings, join teaching teams as they plan, contact individual instructors, know the school's curriculum, and anticipate teacher needs.

Chance meetings and informal discussions with teachers in the lounge and at lunch may be utilized to spread the word. An in-service day in the LMC for the teachers to explore, view, listen, and produce media will provide a hands-on endeavor.

Involvement in the total curriculum is not limited to elementary and secondary schools. It's happening at college and graduate school level, where visual and sound programs have been created in-house for every level and every course, where students can master a subject on a "cafeteria" basis at their own pace and at their own rate of intensity.

Self-teaching with audiovisual materials at the higher level should dispel any idea that audiovisual materials are intended as a substitute for the ability to read. Rather, their use may provide the incentive for elementary and secondary students to want to read, and may start them reading. Multimedia is proving itself a springboard for reading, not a substitute.

What does this mean in specific terms to the school librarian? It means that upon learning of the teacher's sustained reading program, the LMS will help by making reading material available through circulating a cart of books, magazines, and newspapers; by ordering duplicates of the popular magazines; by offering an interest inventory to ascertain the students' needs; and by providing a vehicle for swapping materials.

After a successful, appreciated experience or two in the direction of TCI, it will be difficult for the LMS to meet with a teacher or a team without feeling himself a part of the planning mechanism responsible for "hooking" the children on learning.

Orienting the Very Young

The very youngest children have a definite niche in the library's scheme of things. First, the kindergarten teacher prepares her classes for the special kind of behavior their school expects of them when they visit the media center. A positive attitude toward the care and use of media discussed and demonstrated, especially during the first several weeks of school. The children are taught how to share materials and how to behave, in anticipation of their first visit to the media center.

After this introduction, the very minimum to offer children in kindergarten is a weekly visit to the LMC for a book exchange, supported by the close personal relationship of the LMS.

First grade children deserve an orientation far beyond a weekly half-hour meeting in some secluded corner of the LMC with a story read to them and an exchange of books.

1. A general tour of the entire facility, including a visit to the inner sanctums, will provide an idea of the size and function of their LMC.

2. Careful practice in withdrawing and returning books, along with IMC codes of behavior and care of material, needs to be acted out, reviewed, and evaluated week after week.

3. At the least, the children's weekly visits can take them to different areas of the media center. Read a book to them from each section to provide an introduction to the different types of materials shelved at each location (Easy books, fairy stories, biographies, holiday books, verse, nursery rhymes, pre-cyclopedia reference books, and magazines.)

4. When fairy tales are presented, several forms of the same story as told in different countries can be read to introduce a new dimension to fairy tales. This activity has endless possibilities.

5. A distinction between realism and fantasy can be conveyed by first reading a fanciful story on a given subject, then a very realistic and possible story, followed by a discussion of the target idea.

6. Practice for all in using the individual and group filmstrip viewer and the sound filmstrip viewer will help develop motor skills and assist in independent use of media. Provide expendable practice films for this session.

7. Another orientation may have the youngsters "read" and record a story for books without words. This offers them an opportunity to exhibit creativity and imagination, and provides them with an opportunity to perform before the class.

8. Many and varied exercises in alphabetizing can include practice in shelving carded Easy books, and in "reading" and tidying Easy shelves. These activities will not only help to develop good attitudes, but help teach children to use the library efficiently. This leads directly into what "call numbers" are and how they are determined for Easy books.

9. Acquaint the children with the parts of a book. This can be successfully done at the first grade level. Provide an opportunity for them to react and participate in stories with actions, facial expressions, and verbal responses. Such intimate involvement provides another means with which to secure their attachment to the content of books.

10. Directed reading lessons may aim at familiarizing children with terms like setting, character and plot, with listening or reading for a specific purpose, and with noting sequence of events.

11. Help students learn to use the card catalog to locate special materials for special occasions or on such favorite subjects as Christmas, cats, or clowns.

After about six months of orientation to the library media center, the good readers and the independent workers among the first year students will be ready for an adventure into library stations that teach basic media skills. Other students will continue an exchange of books as needed.

Storytelling

Fortunate are the children whose LMS is not just a reader, but a storytelling artist. The LMS becomes an artist with the flannel board by using this time-honored technique to capture the children's fancy. For occasional use, individual or group flannel boards are welcomed by the children (but preparing figures in multiples requires time). The small boards may be made from two pieces of cardboard 11" x 14", creased at 5", and folded. Overlap the two 5" bases and staple them together. Tape the 11" edges together at the top and cover the front with flannel or corduroy. The children can place characters on the board as the storyteller places her characters during the narration.

The use of puppets, whether doll, hand-puppets, or stick-puppets, will enliven any story session. Other props are used as needed, such as, hats, flowers, toy figures, anything to visually enhance the story. Scrolls, overhead projectiles and slide-tapes can help spellbind the little listeners.

For the older students, dramatized book talks have proved to be powerful incentives to broaden pleasure reading.

The LMS who feels inadequate to the task can look around for a parent or patron who is active in community theatre to provide the professional touch.

Conclusion

The successful LMS must be a teacher, housekeeper-administrator, and technician.

An ambiguity frequently exists for the teacher-librarian in determining her primary role. The role of story-teller and book reviewer competes with the role of teacher. Today's goals for the LMS far exceed a union with students and teachers. The LMS has become a slave to two masters, one human, the other curricular. The need to know and help implement the school's curriculum may be covered by the umbrella term--"total curriculum involvement."

The LMS is further torn apart by two other-selves. The housekeeper-administrator who manages a staff, whether paid, volunteer or assigned, and must somehow accomplish the housekeeping chores, albeit haphazardly at times; and the librarian-technician, who must select, acquire, process, and circulate media.

The multi-faceted role of the LMS can be formidable. Indeed, the delicate balance among the many responsibilities requires hard decisions. In the final evaluation, my psyche tells me that orderly minds are more to be desired than orderly shelves, and turned-on students are to be cherished more than turned-in books.

THE MEDIA SPECIALIST AND THE
DISCIPLINED CURRICULUM*

Marjorie Sullivan

In a recent editorial pleading for improved communications skills, Norman Cousins declares that modern education is scatter-prone. He asserts that schools, in want of
a philosophy of education, are producing a generation of idea
hoppers. [1] Cousins posits that "it is not necessarily true
that the school is helpless to cope with the onrush of increasing specialization. Major emphasis can be given to the in-
terrelationships of knowledge and to the points of contact
and convergence. It may not be possible to keep the student
up to date in the accumulation of new knowledge--or even instruct him fully in the old. But what is possible is to define the significance of what is happening and to identify the
juncture at which different areas of knowledge come together. "[2]

The school media center, which provides resources
for teaching and learning, shares responsibility for the quality of the educational program. Standards for School Media
Programs, issued jointly by the Division of Audio-Visual Instruction and the American Association of School Librarians,
states the purpose of the media center: "The pupil will not
only need to learn skills of reading, but those of observation,
listening, and social interaction. He will need to develop a
spirit of inquiry, self-motivation, self-discipline, and self-
evaluation. He will need to master knowledge and develop
skills. Ultimately he must communicate his ideas with his
fellows. "[3] Further, it is important that "every media specialist participate actively in shaping the design of instruction, and that every media facility, piece of equipment, book

*Reprinted by permission of the author and publisher from
Journal of Education for Librarianship, vol. 10, pp. 286-95,
Spring 1970; a publication of the Association of American
Library Schools.

or material to be selected, produced, and used so that the students in our schools are challenged to a dynamic participation in a free, exciting, and enriched life. "[4] Educational excellence is directly related to the school media center and to the performance of the media specialist.

In formal education, the students' learning experiences, planned and supervised by the school, are organized into a pattern, a curriculum. Disciplined subjects, those drawn from the content of the sciences and the humanities, have as their purpose the liberation of mind and spirit. Non-disciplinary subjects, those providing vocational skills, driver training, homemaking skills, and physical education supply other urgent needs (Figure 1). This paper considers, in the main, the disciplined curriculum.

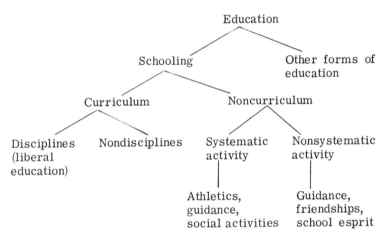

Figure 1. The Disciplines of Knowledge in Education. [5]

The media center program, however, implements the entire curriculum. Intimate involvement with students and teachers engaged in learning is indicated in the 1969 <u>Standards</u>:

A media program provides:

Consultant services to improve learning, instruction, and the use of media resources and facilities.

Instruction to improve learning by use of printed
and audio-visual resources.

Information on new educational developments.

New materials created and produced to suit special
needs of students and teachers.

Materials for class instruction and individual investigation and exploration.

Efficient working areas for students, faculty, and
media staff.

Equipment to convey materials to the student and
teacher. [6]

Basic to this program of services are the media, the
carriers of information. Narrowly defined, information refers to facts and data. Broadly conceived, information em-
braces all meaningful communication, be it intellectual or
aesthetic. So interpreted, McCracken's A Guide to Fortran
Programming, Gray's Anatomy, and Wallace Stevens' "The
Blue Guitar" are equally information. Although information
and knowledge are often used interchangeably, the latter refers more particularly to a body of facts gathered by study
and observation and implies an understanding of what is
known.

Classified in a variety of ways throughout history,
knowledge is now often categorized in reference to the know-
er or to that which is known. Fritz Machlup's ontological
classification designates five classes of knowledge:

1. Practical knowledge of the workaday world.
2. Intellectual knowledge concerning humanistic
   and scientific matters.
3. Small-talk and pastime knowledge.
4. Spiritual knowledge.
5. Unwanted knowledge. [7]

P. H. Phenix's epistemotological classification designates and characterizes nine generic categories (Figure 2).
These broad classes have three broad components of peda-
gogical significance: the disciplines, providing sources for
curricular content; characteristic methods and representative
ideas defining the structure of the disciplines; and, basic
patterns of meaning providing a rationale for determining the
scope of studies in general education and a means for ascer-
taining general structures that promote transfer of learning. [8]

Each discipline within these generic divisions has its

Figure 2

Extension	Intension	Designation	Disciplines
Singular	Fact	Synnoetics	Philosophy, psychology, literature, and religion, in their existential aspects
Singular	Form	Aesthetics	Music, visual arts, the arts of movement, literature
General	Form	Symbolics	Ordinary language, mathematics, non-discursive symbolic forms
General	Fact	Empirics	Physical sciences, life sciences, psychology, social sciences
Singular	Norm	Ethics	The various special
General	Norm	Ethics	areas of moral and ethical concern
Comprehensive	Fact	Synoptics	History
Comprehensive	Form	Synoptics	Philosophy
Comprehensive	Norm	Synoptics	Religion

Figure 2. The Generic Classes of Knowledge[9]

distinctive content, structure, and mode of inquiry. It is inquiry in the natural and social sciences and the humanities that generates new knowledge. From the accumulated knowledge of the disciplines, liberal education selects its subject matter. J. E. Bruner reminds us, however, that "education is not only the transmission of culture ... but it also gives shape to the power and sensibility of mind that each person may learn how to acquire for himself an interior culture of his own."[10]

Bruner sees knowledge as a model projected to give meaning and structure to regularities in experience. "The organizing ideas of any body of knowledge are inventions for rendering experience economical and connected. ... Experience is not had direct and neat, but filtered through the programmed readiness of our senses. The program is constructed of our expectations and these are derived from our models or ideas about what exists and what follows what. "[11]

To A. R. King and J. A. Brownell, the disciplines are a "community of discourse" providing a theoretical model for devising theories and subtheories of curriculum. The curriculum is a series of encounters between a neophyte and the communities of discourse. [12] The several autonomous disciplines display these isomorphic aspects:

> A discipline is a community of persons.
> A discipline is an expression of human imagination.
> A discipline is a domain.
> A discipline is a tradition.
> A discipline is a syntactical structure--a mode of inquiry.
> A discipline is a conceptual structure--a substance.
> A discipline is a specialized language or other system of symbols.
> A discipline is a heritage of literature and artifacts and a network of communications.
> A discipline is a valuative and affective stance.
> A discipline is an instructive community. [13]

Now a legitimate question would be: Why focus attention upon the content, structure, and methods of the scholarly disciplines instead of upon some other theoretical framework? King and Brownell list over 30 familiar curriculum theories --ranging from "college preparation" to "social competence" --and reject them all as loosely construed, vaguely philosophic, and by no means scientific. The disciplines, however, are rooted in man's symbolic capacity. They serve his need to arrive at free choices, to be expressed symbolically. They also offer a functioning organization of symbols in usable and learnable form, with built-in devices for correction and addition. [14]

Bruner's testimonial for the efficacy of learning disciplinary structures is impressive. He hypothesizes that learning structures of disciplines:

> Is learning how things are related.
> Makes a subject more comprehensible.

Slows forgetting.
Permits reconstruction of detail through patterns.
Is the main road to transfer of training.
Narrows the gap between advanced and elementary
knowledge.
Leads to intellectual excitement.
Supplies bases for and enhances intuitive thinking.
Is the bridge to simplicity.
Provides a path for progression of learning in each
discipline. [15]

Quite possibly disciplined learning assists students toward
clarity of thought and self-expression. Norman Cousins con-
cludes in his previously mentioned editorial that "institutions
can be built upon clarity" and that "clarity is one of the truly
distinguishing characteristics of the educated man. "[16] Scholarly consideration of teaching and learning during the past
decade has righted to a considerable extent the imbalance between liberal and practical elements of the curriculum. Educators now accept the creation of the educated man conver-
sant with ideas and modes of thought a worthy aim. Media
center learning resources implement this quest for individual
excellence.

Jerome Bruner's The Process of Education provides
a touchstone for the attainment of educational excellence.
Bruner develops four themes basic to disciplined teaching and
learning: structure, readiness, intuition, and desire. [17] Derived from these, the following corollaries indicate broad relationships between Bruner's themes and the school media
center serving the disciplined curriculum:

To facilitate the mastery of the structures of knowledge, the media specialist assembles and arranges for
access materials of excellence embodying these structures.
To support the spiral curriculum--early introduction
of fundamental principles in simple form for subse-
quent elaboration--the media specialist must collect
materials translating fundamental themes and structures into the students' varying ways of viewing things.
To foster intuitive thinking, those leaps which bypass analytic procedures, the media specialist provides
a collection rich in possibilities--from poetry to poli-
tics to Picasso to pixies--and a climate conducive to
mental meandering.
To spark and sustain the desire to learn, the media

specialist devises a program to pique curiosity and invite discovery, hoping that intrinsic rewards will lead to extended episodes of independent study.

Bruner asserts that the teacher himself is the principal agent of instruction. To aid the teacher and extend the student's experience, however, he would provide special devices:

1. Print and non-print materials for direct, vicarious experience.
2. Experiments, demonstrations, models and sequential programs to reveal basic ideas and structures.
3. Dramatizing devices to lead to identification with a phenomena or an idea.
4. Automatizing devices for individually paced learning. [18]

And finally, Bruner asserts that the teacher must be not only a communicator, but a model learner, competent, and enthusiastic. [19] The same observation applies to the media specialist. How can either infect students with a disease he has not caught?

The school media specialist, a learner exemplar, summons intuition and research to develop the educated man, the individual characterized by clarity of thought and expression. In consultation with other educators, scientists, scholars, and psychologists, the specialist contributes to curriculum improvement. His media center program facilitates mastery of the themes and structures of the disciplines, supports the spiral progression of ideas from the simple to the complex, nurtures intuition, and promotes discovery. He provides easy access to a range of resources to mediate instruction. [20]

The landmark Standards for School Media Programs designates the elements essential to maintain a program adequate to support "the needs and requirements of today's educational goals"[21] and unifies for optimum service print and audio-visual media. The crucial integrant in this supportive effort is the school media specialist. At this moment library educators are reshaping curricula to prepare students to assume this demanding and exciting role. If the media program is to facilitate a curriculum of depth and sophistication, the professional education of the media specialist must embrace intellectual substance. Logic dictates that he be grounded in the structures of the sciences and the humanities.

From the disciplines springs his essential expertise concerning curriculum content and methods of inquiry, to which learning and communication theory must be related--all on the several grade levels. Rooted in the disciplines also are his essential skills in the analysis, evaluation and selection of media, the carriers of knowledge, [22] and the design of materials and instructional systems--all components of the media program organized and administered to implement educational aims. To assist the learner in discovery, the school media specialist must carry in his professional kit a map of the terrain.

Schooling in the structures of the disciplines should sharpen the media specialist's professional competencies, [23] provide a foundation for sixth-year subject or technical specialization, and furnish a background for continuing education. [24] His familiarity with the structures of liberal knowledge could yield other educational benefits:

1. Provide an invaluable background for interdisciplinary study.
2. Encourage the integrated use of print and nonprint media as information sources.
3. Provide a common element in the education of master teachers and media specialists and a basis for their professional collaboration.
4. Provide a basis for the integration of the classroom and the media center.
5. Promote optimum use of media center resources.
6. Add rigor to teaching and learning.
7. Place clerical and technical activities in the school media center in proper perspective.
8. Supply purpose and direction to administrative activities.
9. Supply a framework for new knowledge and for new trends in the subject areas.
10. Establish a base for experimentation and research.
11. Provide stability in a time of rapid change.

Designing the proper course content and sequence for the media specialist's mastery of disciplined structures may require considerable trial and modification. Library educators may never agree upon a one best way. Figure 3 shows a conservative approach embodying Bruner's spiral pattern. The undergraduate enjoys a broad introduction to liberal

Level	Hours Credit	Course	Emphasis
Undergraduate 1-4	50-60	General education	Accumulation of knowledge and understanding
	30-40	Major area	
Masters 5	1 of 5 hours	Foundations of Librarianship	Knowledge: definitions, functions, classification, media, production, proliferation.
		Literature of the	The disciplines, their structures, modes of inquiry and literatures.
	3	Sciences	
	3	Social Sciences	
	3	Humanities	
	3	Elementary School Curriculum	Basic Principles and present trends.
		or	
	3	Secondary School Curriculum	
	3	Materials for the Elementary School Media Center I	Materials related to the grade school curriculum.
	2	Materials for the Elementary School Media Center II	
		or	
	3	Materials for the Secondary School Media Center I	Materials related to the secondary school curriculum.
	2	Materials for the Secondary School Media Center II	L Language Arts, Fine Arts, and Practical Arts. II Social Sciences, Physical Sciences, and Extra-class activities.

Figure 3. The School Media Specialist's Education for the Disciplined Curriculum

learning. As a novice entering library education he sharpens his conceptions of knowledge somewhat. Next he turns to specific disciplines to understand their themes and to become acquainted with significant literature incorporating them. Finally, he relates appropriate print and non-print media to the various school curricula, which are in part, derived from the disciplines.

Even the best curriculum guide is a dead thing incapable of endowing the media specialist-to-be with either the required know-how or the desired personal qualities. Needed are vitalizing learning experiences to enliven our purposes and plans--or better still, those of our students. As library educators advocating active learner involvement, do we do as we say? Are learners in our classrooms alive with excitement of purposeful, self-directed inquiry? Do these learners grapple with the substance, structures, and themes of knowledge? Do they draw information from a variety of media? Do individuals and groups probe critically to discover and test intellectual, aesthetic, and moral values?

After graduation the school media specialist going forth to spark fireworks between learners and learning may well reestablish in his domain the learning climate recently experienced in our library school classrooms and libraries. He may well incorporate into his professional practice the mode of learning acquired under our tutelage. In part, his success --or failure--in implementing the new Standards will be ours.

References and Notes

1. Cousins, Norman: Are You Making Yourself Clear? Saturday Review, Feb. 22, 1969, pp. 31-32.
2. Cousins, p. 32.
3. American Association of School Librarians, A. L. A. , and Department of Audio-Visual Instruction, N. E. A. Standards for School Media Programs. Chicago, American Library Association, 1969, p. 1.
4. A. A. S. L. and D. A. V. L , pp. 1-2.
5. King, A. R , and Brownell, J. A. : The Curriculum and the Disciplines of Knowledge. New York, Wiley, 1966, p. 119.
6. A. A. S. L. and D. A. V. L , p. 4.
7. Machlup, Fritz: The Production and Distribution of Knowledge in the United States. Princeton, New Jersey, Princeton University Press, 1962, pp. 21-22.

8. Phenix, P. H.: The Architectonics of Knowledge. In: Education and the Structure of Knowledge. Chicago, Rand McNally, 1964, p. 62.

9. Phenix, pp. 60-61.

10. Bruner, J. E.: After John Dewey, What? Saturday Review, June 17, 1961, p. 78.

11. Bruner, p. 76.

12. King and Brownell, pp. 67-94.

13. King and Brownell, p. 95.

14. King and Brownell, pp. 99-115.

15. Bruner, J. E.: The Process of Education. Cambridge, Massachusetts, Harvard University Press, 1960, pp. 56-57, et passim, cited by King and Brownell, pp. 90-91.

16. Cousins, p. 32.

17. Bruner, pp. 17-80.

18. Bruner, pp. 81-84.

19. Bruner, p. 90.

20. Considering the librarian's "more active educational role" in the Instructional Media Center geared to efficiency and academic achievement, Ernest Roe predicts that the librarian's relationship to the child will become "more intellectual, less emotional." Roe, Ernest: What Kind of Librarian? School Library Journal, April 15, 1969, p. 1718.

21. A. A. S. L. and D. A. V. I., p. x.

22. Roe states also "that the IMC must become increasingly an evaluation rather than a storage center." p. 1718.

23. A. A. S. L. and D. A. V. I., p. 12.

24. Grazier, Margaret H.: Effects of Change on Education for School Librarians. Library Trends, April 1969, p. 418.

CURRICULUM CHANGES AND THE LIBRARIAN*

Alexander Frazier

New respect for the young learner, new independence for the learner at every age, and new insistence on depth of learning--these are three of the major characteristics of curriculum development today. Inherent in each of them and in all three combined is a series of challenges to school librarians. Suddenly, from a variety of sources and forces, the capacity of the young learner has become a matter of new interest. He knows more than we have thought, and he can learn more. In consequence, his needs as well as his potentialities are being reexamined. Our interest takes many shapes.

At present, the best publicized of these is the earlier teaching of reading. Children younger than six or six-and-a-half can learn to read, at least some of them can, as we must always have known. After all, in some cultures five-year-olds have been taught to read for centuries. But for us, another development in early reading may be of more lasting importance. That is the use of a broader base of materials in reading instruction. The movement to individualize the teaching of reading, in part by encouraging children to select books on their own almost from the very beginning of the literate experience, has tremendous implications for both teacher and librarian.

With the new interest in earlier and broader reading has come an accompanying phenomenon--the publication of more books for the youngest readers. While still largely oriented toward the fun conception of "books for young chil-

*Reprinted by permission of the author and publisher from the January 1965 issue of the Wilson Library Bulletin, vol. 39, pp. 389-91. Copyright © 1965 by The H. W. Wilson Company.

dren, " the various early reading series in trade-book format
are indicative. We can expect that more books with content
worthy of study by the very young reader will continue to be
published. One new social studies program, for example,
has the study of exploration as a major theme in the first
grade. Because there are no suitable books for use by children of this age (after all, the topic belongs in the fifth
grade!), a special series of biographies of Magellan, Columbus, and John Glenn is being compiled for the project.

Similarly, in the effort to provide worthy materials of
study, attention is being given to the production of nonprint
resources for the young learner. Two new social studies
programs are notable here. One has issued a talking textbook for first graders, a picture book which is to be "read"
while listening to a recorded narrative commentary. The
other study project, which will emphasize lessons to be
learned from primitive cultures, maintains camera crews on
location in countries around the world to prepare films offering information, impressions, and ideas that the young learner is not yet ready to garner from print.

At the high school level, new respect for young learners has taken numerous directions. Perhaps the advanced
study program has been the best organized and most influential, but all the efforts to build a more stimulating program
promise to have impact on the school library and its functions.

The new concern we feel for providing the learner
with greater independence doubtless related to our awareness
for his capacity. But here most of the efforts are aimed at
altering the situation in which the learner is placed rather
than being centered on the redevelopment of content. Many
efforts are under way to find some better method of providing time for study opportunities within the school day. The
first of these was tied in with experiments in large-class instruction. More recently, attempts are being made at the
high school level to reduce the number of class meetings per
week, possibly by analogy with college practice, and to
schedule time for independent study or "research" under
school sponsorship.

Another major movement has been aimed at removing
the limitations inherent in the graded structure of American
schools. The intent has been to free the learner to move
ahead at his own pace or to accommodate the slower rate of

the student who needs more time. Individualization of instruction is usually the goal proposed for these ungraded or nongraded programs, which are still found mostly in the earlier years of school. Often there is an increased emphasis on independence and self-direction. Accompanying the interest in self-directed study has been the growth of materials that lend themselves to independent use. Programmed materials have been widely promoted from this point of view as have a variety of other kits or packages. Places set aside for private study, cubicles or stations, have been provided in a good many new school buildings.

In the long run, however, the emphasis on discovery by learning will make more of a difference than the majority of these efforts involving the alteration of the use of time or the reorganization of the way learners may be grouped. Most of the new science and mathematics programs seem to be as much concerned with method as with content. As the first subject fields to be restructured, they have been in the forefront, but inherent in the new social studies programs are proposals that young learners be given opportunities to examine raw data, generalize, and test out their findings. The same focus on independence in thinking things through may be expected to characterize other subject areas as they are reworked.

The new insistence on depth of learning takes many forms. Certainly the provision of more opportunity for independent study is basic to the phase of our current curriculum thinking as is the new respect for the learner. However, here we may look chiefly at the size of the task of learning as it is being redefined. One of the most pervasive themes in this period of curriculum change is helping the learner get at the essence of a discipline. However conceived, this essence is usually defined as the relationship of the key concepts and generalizations of a particular field. Increasingly the task of the teacher is interpreted as one of helping the learner establish and consolidate these relationships at increasing levels of maturation. In order to provide such help, immersion in the discipline is necessary.

Again, we are most familiar with what this may look like in the new science and mathematics programs. But of greater significance to the school library may be the analogous developments in two other fields. We have already noted the growth of a broader base for the reading program in the elementary school. There the attention is being extended to the development of the higher order reading skills, skills that must in fact be based on more materials than a single book or the books of a single series of readers. Critical reading and literary analysis depend upon selective emphasis within a range of books from which choices may be made. Attention to close reading of literary texts is well established now in the high school and is receiving more time in the new reading program at the earlier levels.

In the new social studies programs there is also concern for greater depth. One program involves the introduction of documentary materials at the junior high school level, which will enable students to work with the original sources from which historians and other social scientists have come to their conclusions. With this program will also come artifacts in replica to enable the young learner to handle the objects and utensils of other and earlier cultures. These developments tend toward depth in study compared to the more superficial opportunities provided in the past.

These three factors, then, are the major centers of current curriculum concern: the learner receives greater respect in terms of his capacity to learn; he is supported in his search by more opportunities for independent learning. And he is expected to achieve greater depth. What challenges will this involve for the school library?

Perhaps the first challenge is the recognition by most of the curriculum projects of the essential importance of materials and resources. With justification, the librarian may point out that curriculum makers have only now really caught up with the thinking of materials specialists. But something more is at stake here. How the materials are selected, organized, and supplied for use will determine in large part how effectively the new concern for materials is realized in practice. Some of the curriculum projects, out of naïveté, may attempt to meet all their own materials needs in a single package or may propose ways of assuring a supply of what they consider the basic study resources that would short-circuit the effectiveness of their use. They will probably need help in understanding the relationship of new materials to the broader collection and to its attendant facilities and services.

A second development that may seem to have been slow in coming is the awareness of the uniqueness of varied materials. Films and pamphlets and charts and models are

being supplied by the recent curriculum projects as something more than relief from the book.   Particularly, as we
have pointed out, in providing for the newly understood needs
of the very young learner, some of these media are now
recognized for their potential in supplying data earlier as
well as supplying different kinds of data.   In a good many
cases, a set of materials or a system, as it is sometimes
called, is being prepared to make use of the uniqueness of
differing resources.   The librarian has an obligation to help
the users of these materials assess their probable value and
test their adequacy as well as relating what is proposed for
use by a given project with whatever else is or could be made
available.

Another major thread in current curriculum thinking
is the value attached to a broader base of study materials.
This is more than valuing variety in kind.   Abundance is
seen as desirable in its own right.   The emphasis on self-
selection and independence, on discovery, and on depth is
accompanied in most cases by the assumption that the learner will have about him a wealth of materials from which to
learn.   In fact, learning to use many study materials or
"learning to learn, " as it is often phrased, is one of the prevailing principles of the new curriculum.

The Learner as Searcher

A fourth characteristic of the new developments is a
larger role for the user of materials.   Perhaps this may
seem to be a restatement of the emphasis on a broader base;
certainly it grows out of the belief that more materials for
study must be supplied.   But from his first days in school,
the learner is now seen as being of necessity a searcher.
The weight placed on the development of skills that go with
the continuous use of many materials, as compared with
those needed on occasion for reference or auxiliary use of
a collection, will undoubtedly cause many school librarians
to evaluate their present programs of teaching the use of
library resources.

Finally, the total curriculum context today provides
a much more integral place for the specialist in materials.
This involves more than knowing what is available and finding, organizing, and supplying the best.   Surely these functions remain of central importance.   But very essential is
the professional viewpoint of the librarian who values, to an

almost absolute degree, the need to keep the full range of resources for learning always in the middle of the picture. In truth, the prospect of the school library's coming into its own as a result of the new curriculum projects is very real. Helping to keep it there is the ultimate challenge to the librarian.

NEW CURRICULUM TRENDS AND
SCHOOL LIBRARIES*

Elenora C. Alexander

Basically, most of the educational goals underlying recent curriculum changes have been constant for some years. The newness is in the methods of instruction being employed to help each student develop to the maximum of his ability, to become self-reliant, to have a positive attitude toward himself, and to acquire skills that will provide for continuous learning. The newer instructional methods for achieving these educational goals place more emphasis on independent learning by means of investigation or by discovery than did former methods. Thus, students are being required to seek out sources of information, formulate problems, state hypotheses, check data, and come to conclusions on their own. It is this emphasis that has special significance for school libraries.

In preparing this paper, I decided to take a look at the effect the new directions for learning have had on our school library program in Houston, for I judge that what is happening in our one hundred and fifty-four elementary and forty-three secondary schools is typical of what has happened or will be happening in other systems. In fact, the very growth of the elementary school library program in Houston from its small beginning of nineteen WPA administered libraries in 109 schools to a library in every school, since 1950, reflects healthy curriculum trends. Again, the increase in the city-wide average number of books per pupil from almost zero to the present average of four, while still far below national standards, is indicative of the necessity of change. The same can be said of the increase in the number of elementary school librarians from a meager four in 1954 to seventy, ten years later.

*Reprinted by permission of the author and publisher from Illinois Libraries, vol. 47, pp. 291-99, April 1965.

Scheduling of Classes

To begin with, the increased emphasis on independent learning has brought about a re-examination of the scheduling of classes to the library. While most of our elementary school classes still have regular weekly library periods, the trend is to provide more unscheduled time blocks, where school enrollment permits, for classes as a whole or in part, or for individuals to come to the library as the need arises. In a number of team teaching situations, part of the class may come to the library to explore personal interests or to find information on subjects introduced in the classroom, while other members of the class remain with one or more of the team teachers.

What is even more apparent is that principals and teachers, who once thought that primary grade children could get along solely with changeable classroom collections borrowed from the school library, are now saying that library opportunities for these youngsters are even more essential than for those in the upper elementary grades. They want these younger students, as soon as they enter school, to begin acquiring skills in using books and libraries as well as to develop an appreciation for good books. As a result, even kindergarteners are now privileged to take books home, this despite the once vehemently voiced fear that the wear and tear on books would mount. Parents are generally sent a note at the beginning of the school year informing them that their primary grade children may bring home a book that he is unable to read on his own and suggesting that the parent read to him. When the size of the school library collection permits, no restrictions are placed on the number of books that may be borrowed.

There was a time when elementary school children were herded, so to speak, through the library to select and check out a library book just as quickly as possible. Now, more thought is given to planning rich, rewarding experiences that relate to classroom instruction, and which help to develop a desire to read on the part of students, and also allow for individual reading guidance.

At the secondary level, where students spend more time in research for class assignments, we have to create opportunities for him to enjoy the library for his own personal pursuit. Study halls have become practically extinct in our secondary schools as most students now take a full program of studies. If the student is to have access to the library during the school day, his subject teacher must arrange for him to have this privilege during her regular class period. Not all teachers have realized this obligation, so various scheduling programs are being tried out to provide students with the opportunity to engage in individual projects in the school library. A team teaching arrangement in one junior high school in Houston has been so patterned that individual pupils may have four library periods per week for independent study. One period per week for every major subject is spent in the library. In other words, four periods per week are spent in the regular classroom and a fifth in the library. These periods are staggered so that the student has no more than one library period per day. Each student may select from a teacher presented list, a topic for independent study in the library on his scheduled day, or he may choose a topic on his own which has been approved by his teacher. Several students may find topics of sufficient scope to justify group work.

In other secondary schools, the more capable students may elect to have a library period in place of a subject. Students granted this privilege are self-governed. No formal permits are required of them. They pursue their chosen interests, but they are also free to call upon their teachers and librarians for guidance if they desire. Study carrels are provided for their use. The library for these students has become a true university. They frame their own problems and then seek to find information on their own.

Some fears were voiced by librarians; first, that this plan for capable students to be regularly assigned to the library would result in the library becoming a glorified study hall; and second, that service to the student body as a whole may be sacrificed for a few, especially in those schools where the library quarters are small. So the administration is moving into the program cautiously, but we anticipate that much learning will take place and that in time, access to the library will not be limited to the academically able. Lack of opportunity for students to use the library during the school day has also resulted in extending library hours. By staggering staff time, the library is now open from thirty to sixty minutes before classes begin in the morning and sixty minutes after school. In selected senior high schools, the library is open several evenings during the week.

Summer Programs

Practically all of our secondary schools have summer programs varying from six to twelve weeks. The library, at such times, is open not only to those taking courses, but to any student who regularly attends the particular school.

The library program, within the last four years, has become a definite part of the forty-two elementary school summer centers. Each is open one or more mornings a week depending upon the number of programs offered and the number of students enrolled. A librarian is on duty in each center for ten weeks during the summer. Children are encouraged to use the libraries in summer centers within their neighborhood, even though they attend other schools during the regular school term. All of this endeavor is to make learning materials as available as possible, and to help students maintain and strengthen reading skills acquired during the long term.

Library Collections

The emphasis on independent learning has resulted in the need for larger library book collections with a broader representation of many aspects of many subjects written at various levels of reading difficulty. Elementary school library book collections, I have observed, have had to include more mature books, generally thought to be of high school reading level, and secondary school library collections have, in turn, included more books written at the college or adult reading level. At the same time, the needs of those students we are trying to keep in school, who so frequently have serious reading problems and require materials less mature in composition yet mature in thought, are not being neglected. The school library has had a vital part in what we term the Talent Preservation Program.

We have been mindful, too, of new topics being introduced into courses of study, of new approaches in the teaching of modern languages, arithmetic, and other subjects, and of new knowledge gained.

There was a time, not long ago, when a library's collection of mathematics books would fill less than a shelf. The increase in the number of library owned volumes has not been due to the number of mathematics books being published, but rather to the demands for them made by students and teachers. These books are being used. What was once considered an easy counting book for the primary grades has become a valuable teaching tool. The National Youth Physical Fitness Program has made us aware of our inadequate library holdings in this area, and we are hastily trying to meet its requirements in the way of materials.

Technological developments, such as the splitting of the atom, have necessitated the frequent weeding of obsolete materials from the collection. Francis H. Horn, president of Rhode Island University, in his article, "The Ends for Which We Teach," states: "Never before has what is taught one year so likely to be out-of-date only one year later."[1]

Not only are our science collections being reevaluated but also the modern languages. The practical approach to teaching language as a tool for communication has necessitated this. More careful selection of these books is being taken into consideration. For example, we would never choose a French book that has the English translation parallel to the French text. New emphases, new understanding, as well as new truths require more than ever before that we choose wisely any materials for inclusion in our school library collections. The collections must support the new approach to learning. It also means that librarians need to know many books thoroughly.

In the New Curricula, edited by R. W. Heath, we are advised that the provision of collateral reading matter for all subjects "becomes almost an inescapable obligation of the major curriculum revision, arising both out of its mode of operation and its purposes. The process of elimination which takes place in organizing the course implies that gaps will be left. For some students, these gaps may represent the very areas of the subject in which personal enthusiasms have been engendered, and it is only reasonable that the student be enabled to fill such gaps by his own efforts and his own time. Collateral reading prepared for the purpose, can help in this task."[2]

There is greater variety as to types of learning materials. In so far as physical facilities, funds, and size of staff permits, our school libraries are making available a variety of instructional resources from which students and teachers may choose those most appropriate for a given situation. There are rapidly growing collections of teacher-librarian prepared transparencies on every subject, including ones on teaching the use of the library.

For awhile, efforts were made to bring together into the library all instructional materials. Now the trend is to disseminate a number of them throughout the school buildings in a variety of ways, so that they are more accessible to classes. Some materials may remain indefinitely in classrooms, science laboratories, language laboratories, and the like, but records of these are kept in the library. They are also available to classes other than those in which they have been placed. Convenience, size, and arrangement of the library quarters affect the extent to which materials are placed elsewhere than in the school library. The placement of materials throughout the building has brought about a revision of the policy pertaining to the purchasing of duplicate copies. Once we set an arbitrary figure; now we have a flexible plan based upon the number of students enrolled in a particular grade or class. Size and breadth of the collection, however, are also deciding factors.

Teaching the Use of the Library

Teaching students how to use books and libraries effectively has high priority, when emphasis is placed on independent learning. No longer is it merely a matter of teaching a specific number of lessons at each grade level or limiting particular skills to certain grades. Instead, instruction is given frequently, as the need arises, either formally or informally, to an entire class, or to an individual student in terms of what the particular situation demands. Why wait until Mary is in the eighth grade to teach her how to use the Readers' Guide to Periodical Literature, if she has occasion to consult it in the fifth grade and is capable of mastering it?

Frequently instruction is given in the classroom, either by the teacher or librarian, in relation to course content with the follow-up or actual application of the skill in the library. Skills for using books and libraries have been written into practically all courses of study so that a functional approach is achieved. There are repeated opportunities to master these skills, as this is important in independent and individual learning. The functional approach undergirds the foundation for continuous learning.

Library Quarters

Current trends in instruction are affecting the plans for senior high school library quarters now on the drawing board. In these schools, the library is to be located adjacent to a large area termed a "mall" which will accommodate an overflow of students when all seats in the main reading room of the library are occupied. These libraries are located so that they are blended into the building complex as a unifying unit rather than a separate area. The extensive use of glass walls puts the library on display, making it a colorful, inviting place and producing a favorable climate for learning.

The School Library and Change

This discussion of curriculum trends would be incomplete if their significance for the school librarian were omitted. The most difficult problem, that we have had to face, has been our willingness or unwillingness to accept and adjust to change. Because of the greater demands student needs have on our time, we have had to discard some familiar and traditional ways of doing things. Fortunately, we had never used Cutter numbers in cataloging school library collections, so no decision regarding them had to be reached. The omission of accessioning was first viewed with alarm, but once this step in processing books was eliminated, practically all wondered why it had ever been necessary. The elimination of author letters on the spine of books, on book cards, and on catalog cards is now under study. The idea of underlining the author's surname on book spines, in place of using the author letters, is being considered as a means of making the student more aware of the author, in addition to being a time saver.

Our school librarians long ago accepted the philosophy of the school library as a materials center. Moreover, they are attempting to use the newer media. The overhead projector has been found to be most effective in teaching the use of books and libraries. Practically all presentations of formal library lessons lend themselves to this media. A program entitled "Book Look" is televised quarterly to further the reading of good books at the secondary school level. In-service telecasts are given at intervals to create a better understanding of the place of the school library in instruction.

At the administrative level, we are exploring the application of data processing to relieve the librarians of clerical tasks and thus to provide them with more time for reading guidance. Basic orders for new schools are now being machine processed. Once so recorded, we envision being able to keep the list up-to-date by monthly deletions and additions. Previously, revisions were made about once every five years. Annual periodical and supply orders will be prepared in a similar fashion this fall. Eventually, annual book orders will undergo the same modernization of procedure.

Along with our attempts to adjust to change we have been exerting some efforts to bring about change, not for the sake of change but for the direct or indirect improvement of instruction. When the movement toward individualized reading instruction gained momentum, there was concern that it would weaken the basic reading program. That guided independent reading would strengthen the reading program had to be demonstrated. A simple action research project was initiated in six elementary schools to ascertain the effects of regular, directed use of the school library on pupils reading below grade level in second and fifth grade classes. The results were most gratifying, not only for the underachievers on whom records were kept, but on all others in these classes. The outcome has been to provide more library books for the extension of the library reading program in all elementary schools. The study decidedly changed the attitude that some principals and teachers had toward primary grade students using the school library, which I referred to earlier.

A similar study was undertaken in a junior high school when a class of eighth graders were allowed to read widely, library books of their own choosing on topics covered in their science, social science, and English classes. Reading scores were recorded at the beginning and again after the study had been in progress for a year. Remarkable improvement on the part of the underachievers, the average student, and the above average student was noted. Here again, a project in one school brought about a different approach to teaching in many schools, and the library budget benefited, too.

Another pilot program was undertaken to improve the teaching of literature in the elementary grades. The purpose, in this instance, was to determine the advantages of a study of literature by able readers in place of a study of a second basic reader, and to identify some profitable methods of teaching literature. One book in a category such as biography, myth, legends, folk tales, historical fiction, history, fanciful tales, and the like, was read in common by a group. At the same time each student within the group read independently many other books in the same category. Freedom was allowed the teacher so that the literature study took off in different directions. For example, a group of fifteen who read Invincible Louisa by Cornelia Meigs (Little, Brown, 1933), became interested in the biographies of the illustrious friends of the Alcotts. The Alcotts' love of John Bunyan's Pilgrim's Progress led them to read that classic. George Washington's World by Genevieve Foster (Scribner, 1941), created a desire to learn more about many persons, times, and places. Because of the demonstrated values students derived from this study, the program is being extended to all sixth-grade classes.

A job analysis study of the secondary school librarians has made the principals and administrators aware of the need for clerical assistance. The amount of time spent on specified clerical and professional duties was recorded in fifteen minute intervals for a period of six weeks. The findings revealed that more clerical help was needed. Such studies as these have created a demand for more funds for library materials, and more staff.

In discovering that we have a responsibility to take the initiative and to help set the course that new curriculum changes dictate, we find that the resulting contributions to the improvement of instructions bring their own rewards to the school library itself.

CURRICULUM DELUSIONS*

Rosalind Miller

"The [library] collection meets the requirements
of the various curricular areas and provides for
the diverse learning skills of individuals representing all levels and types of ability. "1

Curriculum design and implementation in the schools
has been the focus of much criticism and change in recent
years. Each year brings new studies, new materials, new
designs. School librarians know they have many roles to
play other than curriculum resource persons. But our raison
d'etre as a library within the school is to support the curriculum and programs of the school, not as we wish they
were, but as they are in reality. A rational consideration
and study of curriculum and curriculum materials will help.

"Why don't the students use the materials?" For
many lean years I as a school librarian believed that if I
ever had a proper budget I could create a school library or
media center that would bring about wonders in the learning
process. Thanks to Federal monies and the upgrading of
regional accreditation standards, I found that eventually I
had the budget and the materials. Unfortunately, very few
teachers or students seemed to be using them, and there
seemed to be little difference in the library's role in the
educational process. I could only take comfort in listening
to other school librarians who would share with me the same
frustrations at conventions. We all felt certain we were
"meeting the requirements of the various curricular areas in
our media centers. " How we came to this certainty is un-
clear--few of us had studied curriculum, few of us served

*Reproduced, permission of the author and publisher from
School Library Journal, vol. 99, pp. 3028-29, Nov. 15, 1974,
R. R. Bowker Company/A Xerox Corporation.

on curriculum committees, and even fewer were ever consulted about textbook selection. We did, however, cherish
certain common delusions about curriculum practices while
ignoring realistic facts.

● Delusion one: In any adequate collection there should
be materials for the reader and the nonreader, for the motivated and the unmotivated. Compare materials about American
history, for instance, with materials dealing with other subjects and you might discover that the media center will not
only be meeting the requirements of the various curriculum
areas, but does include materials "for the diverse learning
skills of individuals, representing all levels and types of
ability." When these carefully selected and expensive materials gather dust it is not surprising that librarians have
often bitterly agreed with Carolyn Leopold's statement: "A
survey ... showed an average library use of one half book
per student per month. Except for the presence of warm
bodies flirting or doing homework ... our school libraries
are only expensive storehouses."[2]

● Delusion two: Textbooks come and go. They do
not concern the librarian and they do not belong in the media
center. Their adoption should have only a peripheral influence on materials selection.

● Delusion three: Teachers must bear a large part
of the blame for unused materials. Surely once they are
made aware of the availability of materials and vast resources of the media center they should be able to make use
of them in some way. If they do not they must be doing
something wrong.

● Delusion four: Librarians belong on curriculum
committees. Their role on such committees is to inform
teachers of what resources are available in the media center.
This can probably be done best by a bibliography. (The fact
that librarians do not serve on curriculum committees explains why resources are unused.)

A brief summary of curriculum practices will demonstrate why these assumptions have not, and probably will
not work.

Despite the shibboleth "the library is the heart of the
school" the textbook, a standby in the self-contained classroom, has in reality been the heart of the matter. Unfor-

tunately, this is still true in many schools. In such a situation it has been almost impossible for even the most energetic librarian to play a central role in complementing the educational process. This traditional textbook oriented model is now considered inadequate, in theory at least. Educators are moving to different curriculum designs and varied approaches.

While librarians are busy celebrating the downfall of the tyrannical textbook they may be appalled to learn that the substitution of a curriculum package or instructional kit makes little difference to the media center. "The bald fact is that most teaching in our schools is and must be from a textbook or curriculum package. We do not trust teachers to write their own materials, we do not give them the time or money, and we insist on standardization. So long as this is true the suppliers of teaching materials will have a potentially powerful effect on the curriculum."[3]

Few librarians are aware of the exigencies placed on teacher and student by textbook, kit, or whatever. Some of the time now spent carefully studying selection aids might profitably be diverted to examining the instructional materials used in the classrooms. Unless librarians carefully study ways to integrate media center materials with units emphasizing multimedia approaches and original documents, students may well bypass the center.

The Media Center as a Resource

Providing a collection of interesting and varied materials (and many media centers have such collections) vaguely related to the curriculum areas of the school has not proven effective in most situations. Librarians search for guilty parties and often blame teachers, students, and schedules. In reality, the problem is often the focus of textbooks and instructional kits. Many of these units make a point of providing all instructional materials deemed necessary to obtain the objectives of each unit. As a result the media center is often bypassed as a resource. A librarian faced with this must become over-familiar with these units in order to suggest specific alternatives to teachers who undoubtedly will find a time when all the components of the unit are simply not working with each student.

The majority of librarians seem to feel that if teach-

ers made meanginful assignments students would be flocking
to the center and using the materials purposefully.   Professional library literature abounds with such meaningful assignments and complete units involving the use of the library,
demonstrating at least that it can be done.   Teachers, however, are not teaching from such sample units nor, for the
most part, are they teaching from self-devised materials.
They are teaching from guides that clearly outline what to do
and how.   In fact, as instructional kits become more varied,
teachers' guides become more specific and detailed.   They
even include the correct way to answer a student's question.
Teachers are more discouraged than encouraged by the structure of the materials they use to seek out alternatives in the
media center.   Again, only a librarian extremely familiar
with the objectives of the classroom material can really help
the teacher.

Serving on Curriculum Committees

Could the presence of the librarian on the curriculum
committees improve use of the media center?   This is an
excellent learning experience for librarians and may be a
way of introducing some useful materials to teachers.   Librarians certainly should be included in curriculum planning.
However, practical realities usually prevent the librarian
from having as much influence as desired.

Many school districts have organized personnel committees for curricular development.   These groups, struc-
tured by subject matter areas, usually meet during the summer.   Occasionally the librarian may be assigned to a group,
usually social science or English.   There is little guarantee
that this will be a rewarding experience.   Often the librarian
is simply regarded as an outsider as such problems are de-
bated as "should we offer drama to freshmen" or "should
Hamlet be retained at the senior level."   Ideally the librarians would not serve on one committee, but as a resource
person for all.   In reality many school districts hesitate to
pay for such service--"Can't the teachers go in and look at
what is available?" or "Can't the librarians prepare a list?"
It is doubtful if curricular committees, concerned with goals,
needs, behavioral objectives and evaluation, will ever use
such a list or visit the media center or utilize the knowledge
of the librarian.

Often curriculum committees meet to select textbooks,

instructional materials, or commercial curriculum packages. Again the librarian will probably not be consulted. The math committee selecting a new math textbook would not consider asking physical education, history, or drama teachers for a critique of its usefulness. Why should they ask the librarian (who probably won't allow the book in the media center anyway)? Assigning librarians to curriculum committees will not effect the increased use of a media center unless the specific purpose of the curriculum committee is to find ways to increase this usage.

If librarians really want to more closely integrate materials in the media center with the materials used by the students in the classroom they should consider these questions:

1) Am I familiar with every officially adapted text, kit or instructional package used in the school? The significance of these, and their influence on use of materials in the media center, cannot be minimized.

2) Am I familiar with every current curriculum guide in the school? Curriculum guides may offer teachers anything from broad sets of recommendations to detailed lesson plans and their content will influence students' use of the center.

3) Do I know the perimeters of the choices teachers are offered: by departmental guidelines, by their instructional materials, etc. in developing learning opportunities with students? Only if I know what the teacher can or will consider a reasonable or suitable learning experience can I provide materials that will be used.

4) Am I familiar enough with course objectives to offer specific alternatives to meet these objectives?

5) Am I familiar with curriculum terminology? If a teacher, involved with a curriculum committee, asks for a list of materials relevant to heuristically oriented methods, could I help her?

6) Am I familiar with the objectives of the extracurricular activities and how these activities implement the curriculum? Does the media center support this program?

Unfortunately an adequate answer to even one of these

questions could involve hours of study on the part of the librarian--these hours are not easily found. As was suggested, some of the time devoted to selection of materials might be more usefully devoted to curriculum study, an advanced curriculum course may prove to be of more value to school librarians than an advanced reference course. Often, as an added bonus, such courses offer increased opportunities to interact with teachers than does serving on curriculum committees.

References

1. American Library Association (ALA) and National Education Association. Standards for School Media Programs. ALA, 1969, p. 20.
2. Leopold, Carolyn Clugston. School Libraries Worth Their Keep: a Philosophy Plus Tricks. Scarecrow, 1972, p. 21.
3. Kirst, Michael W. & Decker F. Walker. "An Analysis of Curriculum Policy Making." Review of Educational Research, December 3, 1971, p. 492.

Selected Bibliography

Sanders, Norris M. & Marlin L. Tanck. "A Critical Appraisal of Twenty-Six National Social Studies Projects," Social Education, April 1970.

Saylor, J. Galen & William M. Alexander. Planning Curriculum for Schools. Holt, 1974.

Part V:

CURRICULUM INVOLVEMENT THROUGH
PROFESSIONAL RELATIONSHIPS:
ADMINISTRATORS AND TEACHERS

THE PRINCIPAL AND THE
MEDIA CENTER*

Phyllis R. Kuehn

How can you, as a principal, be sure of having the best possible media center for your school? A media center is a school library which provides all types of learning materials--print and nonprint--and the equipment to use them.

You have heard reports of and read articles on current trends in education, including the swing toward accountability, individualization of learning experiences, and the motivational force of making learning more relevant to students' needs. You want to upgrade media services in your building to meet present and future needs. How can this be done?

Reasons for Wanting to Improve Media Center

First, you must believe that the media center is an essential and integral part of the school and its curriculum. Do you have any poor readers? Research has demonstrated that a multi-media approach to instruction motivates students to do more voluntary reading.[1] To reach students who are "turned off" to school, learning materials must be relevant and interesting. Many authorities have concluded that media are relevant to youth and heighten motivation for learning.[2] In fact the evidence in favor of providing quality media centers is so overwhelming that one can only wonder why this part of the instructional program has been ignored for so long in some school districts.

*Reprinted from NASSP Bulletin, pp. 51-60, Sept. 1975, by permission of the author and publisher, The National Association of Secondary School Principals.

Quality media programs are expensive, and a great deal of communication may be needed before taxpayers are convinced that they are essential and not "frills." Administrators sometimes take the same view as taxpayers. When there are budget cuts, what sort of things are likely to go first? Certainly not classroom teachers, which is understandable, but if your media center is what it ought to be-- if its program is integral to the educational goals and philosophy of the school, if it is vital in supporting the curriculum, if students are enthusiastic about visiting the media center-- you will not want to see cuts made in this area.

People Most Important

People are the foremost ingredient in any program. Not new buildings, spacious facilities, huge materials budgets, or the latest, most sophisticated hardware--but people. And the key people in providing quality media services at the building level are the principal and the media specialist, working cooperatively to implement philosophies they share. So get the right person to run your media center, one who is qualified both by education and personality. An enthusiastic, energetic person can work wonders even under circumstances that are far from ideal, but not without a supportive principal!

Some qualities to seek might include interest, enthusiasm, energy, non-punitive attitudes, and the idea that kids are more important than guarding materials. Look for a person who wants to see materials used. You can learn a lot by asking individuals how they envision the role of media specialist.

Educational qualifications are important, too. Principles of materials selection, reading guidance, use of reference materials, AV equipment and materials, technical processing, etc., are taught in library schools. And the person running your media center needs to know these things in order to function effectively whether he actually performs all the tasks involved or not. It's time we get rid of the idea that "anyone can run a library." This notion is a carryover of the old concept of a little old lady sitting at a desk and stamping cards.

Understanding the Specialist's Role

Research has demonstrated that provision of professional personnel is well worth the cost. A 1960 study analyzed the provision of eight kinds of professional specialists whose employment does not reduce class size in relation to a criterion of school system quality. He found the highest zero-order correlation between the quality criterion and the provision of specialists per thousand students to be with the provision of the school librarian, while guidance counselors ranked fourth and reading specialists sixth. [3] Minimum educational qualifications for your media specialist should include certification as a school librarian or media specialist by the state department of education. Better would be a masters degree in library or media from an American Library Association accredited university.

After you find the right person, it is the administrator's duty to have a clear understanding of the role of the media specialist, preferably through a written job description. Types of tasks involved are outlined in Standards for School Media Programs, [4] a handy little booklet that also can provide information concerning facilities, materials, and equipment. You will realize that the media specialist's role is partly administrative and that a good, cooperative working relationship with adequate lines of communication is necessary for both of you to achieve your common goal: the best possible media center under existing circumstances.

It is part of your responsibility to see that professional talents are not consumed with minutiae. Processing materials is one of the most time-consuming tasks faced by the media specialist. Work to convince the superintendent of your district that centralized processing might be advantageous. If you do not, or cannot, have centralized processing, urge your media specialist to take advantage of pre-processing by jobbers whenever possible. Provide clerical help. This is absolutely essential if you want your media specialist out there helping kids and teachers rather than sitting around typing. Realize too that some clerical work is unavoidable for the professional. See that your media specialist has a preparation hour to work on reports, lesson plans, bibliographies requested by teachers, preparing orders, etc.

Work toward improving the materials selection process. As an NASSP committee pointed out recently in Sharper Tools for Better Learning, [5] materials selection is important and extremely time-consuming. Our current selection procedures are woefully inadequate, and many more persons should be involved. The committee added that scientific evaluation of materials is needed, with products developed and revised on the basis of actual student performance. "Some 200,000 items of instructional materials--books, films, tapes, kits, etc.--are on the market today. This is 20 times more than two decades ago!"[6]

When one considers the 200,000 items, it becomes apparent that item-by-item evaluation in individual schools is a physical impossibility. A written selection policy containing guidelines and evaluative criteria is advisable at the building or school system level. This policy would include guidelines for dealing with objections to materials by citizens, using the form provided by the National Council of Teachers of English in their excellent pamphlet, "The Student's Right to Read." Selection should be coordinated by one person in each building, probably the media specialist, in order to avoid duplication, and materials should be centrally located in the media center to guarantee accessibility.

Standard Selection Aids

In order to wade through the 200,000 items, some shortcuts are necessary. And they are available in the form of standard selection aids and review periodicals. Naturally, producers' catalogs are advertisements designed to sell by those who have a vested interest in selling their products. Yet this is the sort of thing most often used by teachers who request purchase of an item.

Standard aids are objective, as are review periodicals, and more and more of them are including widened coverage of AV materials as well as print materials. The Booklist, published by American Library Association, includes reviews of books, films, filmstrips, records and tapes, and other materials. Previews, an offspring of Library Journal and School Library Journal, is devoted entirely to reviews of AV hardware and software. Standard lists are available for building book collections--such things as the Standard Catalog series by H. W. Wilson Co. Unfortunately, a similar evaluative, selective listing of AV materials has yet to appear! NICEM indexes are sometimes useful, but they are neither descriptive nor evaluative. They serve only as a starting point in locating what is available on a given topic.

Using these aids takes time, and lots of it! The media specialist usually maintains a Consideration File. Cards for this file contain complete ordering information as well as brief quotes from reviews to indicate why the item seems desirable. Name of the magazine, page number, and date are included so that the full review can be located if needed. Reading reviews and making cards are usually done at home, since there is no time in the busy day at school. When AV items appear to fit the school's curriculum, the media specialist shows the review to teachers of the subject involved. If it sounds good to the teachers, the item is ordered for preview and later purchased if teachers recommend this. Teachers also initiate suggestions, and every effort is made to purchase what they request.

It is certainly wise to involve as many people as possible in the selection process, and students as well as teachers and administrators have much to contribute. Student requests that cannot be met often point up a lack in the collection, and these requests are added to the Consideration File for purchase when funds are available. The more people involved the better! One of the main reasons for involving lots of people is that, if they suggest purchase of certain items, they will be more likely to use them. And that's what having materials is all about. If they are not used, funds have been wasted.

A Coordinator Is Needed

A coordinator of building purchasing is needed when a large number of persons turn in orders. For example, when Teacher A orders a sound filmstrip set and puts it in his closet, Teacher B may not be aware that it is in the building. A year or so later, Teacher B may receive an advertisement for the same thing and order it. In addition to the duplication problem is the waste that sometimes occurs when orders must be sent in quickly. Persons with no time to spend on selection hurriedly order expensive items that may not be needed, in order to "use up the allocation." We have all seen this happen. With small budgets and rising costs, such waste is really tragic, and it can be avoided by maintaining a Consideration File and putting one person in charge of coordinating materials requests.

Selection also involves some sort of interweaving consideration of the following factors:

1. Knowledge of the curriculum, student interests, and student abilities as demonstrated through standard test results and item analysis data.
2. Knowledge and evaluation of the existing collection--what is already available in the school--and identification of needs.
3. Knowledge of what is available on the market to fill these needs--through studying standard selection aids and review periodicals.
4. Keeping a record of student and teacher requests that cannot be filled.
5. Knowledge of the community and its expectations for children.
6. Understanding of the application of evaluative criteria, as documented in the school's written selection policy.
7. Knowledge of teaching methods employed and the philosophy of the school.

Media specialists receive training in the selection process through their college courses. They are taught to establish objective criteria and evaluate materials critically. Because of this, unless there are strong reasons for not doing so, it would seem logical to put the media specialist in charge of collecting suggestions for purchasing new materials, with the possible exception of textbooks which will be used only by classroom teachers.

The Principal Has Responsibilities

As an administrator, there are specific things you can do to upgrade selection. First, have one person coordinate it. Then, conduct interservice meetings with teachers to help them realize that advertisements from producers should not be used as a basis for requesting or ordering materials. Show them the selection aids that are available in the building, and urge that these be used. When they express interest in expensive AV materials, suggest that they preview the items first and evaluate whether they will be as good as they appeared in the producer's description. If a teacher walks in with an advertisement for a new textbook, show him El-Hi Textbooks in Print, 7 which lists every available textbook for grades K-12 together with price and grade level. Perhaps he would have as many as 50 items to choose from on the same subject!

As for pilot testing and scientific evaluation of materi-

als, principals and media specialists as a group should urge
that this be done nationally, with results published in journals
that are already being read by persons involved in selection.

Actually, selection, important as it is, is only a first
step. Next must come guaranteed accessibility of materials.
As materials proliferate, accessibility can be guaranteed only
by keeping materials in a centralized collection run by a person who wants to see things used. Accessibility is further
ensured by having all materials listed in a centralized catalog.

Organization according to a standardized subject-
oriented scheme, such as Dewey Decimal Classification, will
group materials by subject and make them easier to retrieve.
The card catalog may be used by the media specialist to prepare lists for teachers of what is available on a given subject. While the collection is still relatively small, it will
be possible to distribute lists of all audiovisual materials
in the building, so that every teacher has a copy.

Processing Must Be Done

Remember that materials are not available for use until they are processed: stamped, labeled, and complete with
a set of catalog cards. Processing takes time, even when
card kits or preprocessing are ordered. Sometimes a delay
of almost two school years can occur before materials are
available for use.

Suppose that, in September, a need is recognized.
For example, a teacher needs a filmstrip on city government. This need is noted in the Consideration File, but the
filmstrip cannot be ordered until spring when funds are available. It arrives during the summer and is placed in a storeroom with other new materials. Now if the media specialist
is working as he should be with people and does not have
assistance, it might take until the following June to get that
storeroom emptied. Or, in other words, there could be a
time lapse of two years before the filmstrip is processed
and available for use. One solution, of course, is to hire
media specialists to work during the summer, and many
school districts are doing this.

An important objective in having centralized collections in individual buildings is that students as well as teach-

ers will have access to AV materials and equipment. Materials in teachers' closets are generally used by the teacher, not students. Materials in regional or district-wide collections are available for loan to teachers, not to students. But in a building media center, students may use all materials and equipment available to pursue their studies or interests, and this is a very important consideration in the individualization of learning.

When a film is shown in class, a student may or may not be interested in the film's content. He may get something out of it, or he may turn off completely and daydream or go to sleep. When this student comes to the media center and by his choice watches a filmstrip entitled "Who Should Go to College?" he is getting something out of the experience. This activity has been chosen by him. It is something which interests him, information he wants, and he is going to pay attention and listen.

Accessibility is improved through the use of flexible scheduling in media centers. A media specialist who is tied to a rigid schedule, with a class arriving every half hour, has time for nothing else. Free your media specialist to be able to respond to individual needs of students and teachers at least part of the time. If possible, extend media center hours to beyond the normal school day if sufficient staff is available.

System-Wide Sharing Is Economical?

System-wide use of all instructional materials is another desirable goal. Expenses can be lowered if materials are shared between buildings. To do this, it is necessary to include a centralized cataloging system in the centralized processing department. Duplication of listings is not an overwhelming chore if it has been started from the beginning.

A model system of this type has been developed in Grand Haven, Mich. It includes a pickup and delivery system. Teachers in any school may request books or AV items owned by another school and have them delivered in a relatively short time.

In Grand Haven this system works beautifully, but a warning is in order. To institute between-building sharing in an established district where collections have been run independently for a number of years would require a large investment of both staff time and funds. It might be too expensive to consider, or it might be worth the effort. Each system should decide this in light of cost and obstacles to be overcome.

Administrators who believe in quality media centers will want to work to increase budgets to meet demonstrated needs. Program budgeting, as opposed to function-object or "line-item" budgeting is advocated by some authorities. [8] Program budgeting involves a great deal of planning; specific objectives of the program must be identified and justified by a rationale. A built-in evaluation system will judge program success and provide objective evidence that goals have been achieved. Feedback through the evaluation system will indicate changes that should be made to achieve program objectives. Administrators, media specialists, and persons in the testing and evaluation field may work together to set up such a "program budget."

This sounds like a good system. But whatever the system, one must be realistic about how costs have increased. Good media centers are expensive, but their expense can be justified as an essential component of quality education. Inflation has touched every aspect of our lives, and the cost of media--books and AV materials--is no exception. According to Statistical Abstract of the United States, 1972 edition, [9] the average cost of a clothbound fiction book today is $5.98 as compared with the 1960 average of $3.59! Prices have risen astronomically. In light of this, it is laughable to attempt to supplement a curriculum on a 20-year-old budget figure such as $1.00 per pupil for materials, yet this is happening in some districts. With federal aid evaporating, it is absolutely essential that local budgets be increased.

Supporting Innovations in Curriculum

As well as working to increase budgets, administrators can contribute to improving programs by supporting innovative ideas. Media centers today are getting into new areas, including production as well as provision of materials. Facilities for graphic work, production of transparencies, laminating, dry mounting, and photography are being incorporated in new and remodeled buildings.

Get a couple of movie cameras and let students produce films. They can show their movies in class while they narrate, or they can add sound on tape or use one of the new 8 mm sound movie cameras. Some of the better student efforts can be put in a super 8 cartridge for use by other students with a loop projector. Ask students to produce a slide series that is a tour of the school. Show it to new students, new teachers, and parent groups. Let kids get involved in videotape productions, in showing filmstrips to their classes as part of a report, in making their own transparencies to illustrate points. They will be improving communications skills while becoming more interested in school. And the ideal place for most of this production activity to originate is the media center.

Do you want to improve your media center? You, as principal, can accomplish a great deal. In summary, put the right person in charge. Understand the media specialist's role, and free him of excessive clerical work and rigid schedules. Do what you can to improve the selection process. Insist on accessibility of materials. Speak up for increased budgets whenever possible, and support good ideas. Your enthusiastic leadership will be contagious, and your students will benefit by having an active, busy, vital place to go to pursue their needs and interests--the media center.

Notes

1. Nicholas P. Georgiady, Louis G. Romano and Walter A. Wittich, "Increased Learning Through the Multimedia Approach, " Audiovisual Instruction, 12 (Mar. 1967), p. 251.

2. Edgar Dale, Audiovisual Methods in Teaching, 3d ed. (New York: Holt, Rinehart and Winston, 1969), p. 150. Jack Tanzman and Kenneth J. Dunn, Using Instructional Media Effectively (Englewood Cliffs, N. J. : Parker Pub. Co. , 1971), p. 24.

3. Merle E. Landerholm, "A Study of Selected Elementary, Secondary, and School District Professional Staff Development Patterns. " Ed. D. project, Teachers College, Columbia University, 1960.

4. American Association of School Librarians and Department of Audiovisual Instruction, Standards for School Media Programs (Chicago: American Library Association, 1969).

5. Sharper Tools for Better Learning (Reston, Va. : National Association of Secondary School Principals, 1973).

6. Sharper Tools for Better Learning, p. 3.

7. El-Hi Textbooks in Print 1973: Subject Index, Author Index, Title Index, Series Index (New York: R. R. Bowker Co., 1975, annual).

8. James W. Brown, Kenneth D. Norberg, and Sara K. Srygley. Administering Educational Media (New York: McGraw-Hill, 1972), p. 359-81.

9. U. S. Dept. of Commerce, Statistical Abstract of the United States, 1972 (Washington, D. C., 1972), p. 503.

LIBRARIAN, TEACHER, ADMINISTRATOR
RELATIONSHIPS*

Peggy Sullivan

The Need for Communication

The problems that exist among librarians, teachers, and school administrators are surely not unfamiliar to us as librarians. From having worked with school librarians and from my experiences in having taught in library sciences programs, I am convinced that one of the greatest initial shocks and a shock which continues throughout a school librarian's career is to realize that although one may have come to school librarianship from teaching assignments, one may no longer be considered by other teachers as a colleague on the same level. This, incidentally, was the main thrust of an item headed "Librarians Take Over School," which appeared in the April 1974 issue of the Wilson Library Bulletin, in which it was noted that at some mythical school, the announcement was that "... former teachers, athletic directors, and administrators will not be thrown out but will be given routine typing, cartage, and shelving assignments. Every attempt will be made to find jobs menial enough to fit aptitudes and training. Librarian status for former teachers and administrators will be considered every decade, if not later." While it was amusing, part of the impact lay in the fact that it struck a chord with most of us who have been concerned at some time to realize that librarians are not always recognized as the peers of teachers, far less as people whose teaching experience and academic background should provide them more points of similarity than dissimilarity. I have watched library school students react throughout the first term of classes though they were teachers coming to school to see how to make libraries run better. During their

*Reprinted by permission from Catholic Library World, vol. 46, pp. 282-85, Feb. 1975.

second terms they may realize that they are vulnerable as librarians and that their attitudes may be changing. In their first experiences as working librarians they are often appalled to realize that they are not always considered as real colleagues of teachers. I believe that much of this misunderstanding and many of the problems which exist stem from these problems of adjustment of attitude on the part of librarians as well as the attitude of teachers.

As communicators, we must be concerned with the whole problem of bridging that distance between librarians and teachers and, more than bridging it, reaching out to find ways to overcome basic obstacles in communication. While much of this communication can be accomplished by talking, we tend to forget that much of it must be accomplished by listening. In other words, it is not just a matter of telling people what libraries can do for them, or telling them what we have done, much less telling what they should do. It is rather a matter of listening to find out what it is they have in mind. For example, at faculty meetings, which some librarians attend sometimes sporadically, intermittently, or even inattentively, the librarian's first reaction and contribution tends to be, "Well, this is what I can offer you. This is what I have to say...." We do have much to offer as librarians, not just in terms of media resources, but in terms of human resources which we can offer through our own personalities, our ideas, and the support we can really provide. One problem, however, is that again we tend to think of the best that we have to offer and to measure that against the weakest that may be offered by someone else in a comparable situation. We are so conscious of what we have and we have so much to say about it, that we may not realize that much of the value of communication relates to finding out what people really want of us, and the answer to that is not always found by asking a direct question. It may be found only by listening to what is said, even when that may seem at first to be peripheral and meaningless.

The instances when teachers or administrators say most precisely what they want from libraries are not in the sentences that begin, "What I want from the library is ...," but rather in the statement where they indicate how they see their roles as teachers, their expectations for students, and what they see as realistic ways to achieve educational goals. We need to explore to determine, not by superficial listening, but by critical listening, what library programs may have to offer that is essential to those roles and expectations.

The Library Is a Classroom

Much of my own learning about what teachers and administrators want and expect from library programs came from my experiences with the Knapp School Libraries Project. It was necessary to visit a number of schools, and I learned that when I wrote or called ahead to say I wished to visit a school library, it was necessary to specify that I really wanted to see it in action, because one or two closed the libraries to students on the days I was to visit because they thought if I wanted to see the library, that was the way it could most effectively be seen. Yet it seems to me that the whole matter of climate of library programs, the feeling of relationships without unnecessary tension and yet sometimes with the exciting tension that goes with learning, were what I wanted to see. Accordingly, I usually indicated that I would like to visit not just the library facility, but also to visit classrooms to see how instruction related to the library. One of the most shattering experiences I had came during the third year of the project when I visited a senior high school, and received a schedule from the head librarian of the school who said, "Miss Sullivan, we noticed on your schedule you said you would like to visit classrooms, but I think it is because you are accustomed to working with elementary schools. You probably think there is a relationship between the classroom and the library, but now that you are dealing with secondary schools, I think you should know the library program goes on in the library." Well, if it goes on in the library exclusively, and if it does not go on elsewhere, I do not believe it is the kind of special unique library program which every school needs; it seems to me to be as simple as that.

This matter of territory for the library, the importance of the facility, is rather interesting. Some years ago, either gangs picked it up from educators, or educators picked it up from gangs, but there was much emphasis on the concept of, "turf." It was the place that had a particular meaning for a person at a given time as important.

We need to decide whether the librarian's concern is chiefly the library's turf or the library's substance. I believe that libraries should be places for active involvement of teachers, not just places to "send the kids." Teachers may advise on the selection of materials, deal directly with the librarian in the revision of the program of instruction, and welcome the opportunity for the librarian to get out, to be in classrooms, not just visiting or observing, but very often sharing in the teaching. There is much about this kind of program that is threatening, both to librarian and to teacher. We probably all have the feeling that if we stay where we are at least we can keep track of how far behind we are, but once we get out, we lose sight of that and therefore we may somehow feel that we are losing our grasp, simply because the job expands to whatever we can envision. Yet, we talk about librarianship as a profession for people of vision and people of creativity. We must talk about it as a profession for people who have the kind of vision to see what needs to be done even when they are not there and who can envision what needs to be done beyond their own four walls.

If I were writing for a group composed primarily of teachers, I would say, "It is up to you to take the first step in inviting the librarian to your classrooms. " But I also say to you, and I believe it is no contradiction to say it: "It is up to you to take the first step.... " The truth of it is, it is up to you, whoever you are, to take the first step, to be the first one to offer, the first one to listen, the first one to ask. Even then, nothing is simple. Too often we think that asking and answering is the end of something rather than the beginning. It is all too easy to get into the habit of thinking that the first thing a person asks is all he really wants. We respond by telling him what we have, offering it, and thinking that is the end, whereas it really should be the beginning. Let us say, for example, that a teacher comes in and says something like, "I would like five paperbacks for the ten students in my class who are ready to move into an independent study minicourse. " Click, click, click, click, click, we come up with five paperbacks. We may even find all of them in. We may even find them in duplicate so there are enough for ten people. That may sound ideal, but it is possible. But the continuation of that communication lies in listening, in getting reactions to how the paperbacks are used, not just from the teachers, but from the students. These reactions may be expressed in different ways to the librarian than they are to the teacher. These reactions may be some of the most valid judgments of our services and collections which we can obtain.

Access to Materials and Services

The whole problem of access to materials and to services is a major one in the relations among teachers, administrators, and librarians. Too often, this is because librarians have one view of access, and teachers have a strikingly different one. An interesting thing has occurred, for example, with the Reading is Fundamental Program, which has too often been competitive with library programs, rather than complementary. This is ironic, because RIF is a program that says, "We think books are so important that we want every child to have one." Librarians also think books and children are important. I believe it is wholly consistent for the library program to recognize the need to refresh and to re-evaluate collections at all times, to put in the best of what is new, to review what is outdated and inaccurate by reason of changes of history, even changes of time. I do not believe that access consists only in one book for one child forever, but it can be accomplished in a much stronger way through well-stocked, well-organized libraries. And yet, one person says, "By access, I mean every child should have a book every hour of the day and be able to take it home and keep it forever." Another may say, "By access, I mean that I want everyone to have equal opportunity to get everything." To some extent, we limit access to others every time we isolate even a small proportion of the collection and say, "This is for students in the advanced placement class only," or only for students reading at a given grade level, or something like that. I think we need to review our own philosophy of how much is appropriate in the way of channeling some parts of the collection to some audiences if our concern is total access. I once worked with a librarian who maintained that even to take a book from the shelves and place it on a display table was working against the individual who used the catalog to find what he wanted. Every time something was taken off the shelf and put somewhere else, this librarian believed it was taken away from the person using the library logically. I happen to disagree with his view, but at the same time, having seen many libraries with small collections and many limitations on the use of parts of it, I am more sympathetic to his view than I used to be.

This of course, relates to another problem that exists between teachers and librarians. It is the question of how much service can logically be provided by librarians. Where does service end and spoonfeeding (loaded term!) begin? What really seems to me important is to learn from teachers not just what an assignment is, but what the purpose of it is. Too often, what may seem to be efficient service may get in the way of the purpose of the assignment. Centralized access, certainly an ideal for school libraries, should mean that it is possible to find in one place the location of all of the services and resources that the library has to offer. It's not quite the same thing as to say that everything must be housed together. It often makes sense to have equipment to be used with some software located on different levels of a building that has several levels or wings, because that provides better access. The point is not where the materials are located but the ways in which they are accessible.

Other Considerations

One problem which comes up repeatedly, and which needs to be mentioned probably every time we touch on this subject is the problem that teachers too seldom have had opportunity to learn to use libraries as effectively as they can be used. One of the problems with being an adult, especially an educated adult, is that it is very difficult to get that opportunity again.

Everyone assumes that if you have reached this age and state of life, you know all about libraries. For teachers in a school library, this is further complicated by their sense that their students may be watching them all of the time, thinking that they should know how to find everything. It is important to find subtle, purposeful ways to assist teachers to make the most effective use of libraries and their services.

There is one kind of teacher who is a special problem. It is not the stupid or the unknowing, not the uncaring teacher, but the one who cares a great deal and who is unconsciously stimulating who really presents problems to libraries and librarians. It is the teacher who comes in and mentions something that was in today's paper or on last night's telecast who really creates problems. The one who never changes his notes from one year to another is great in the eyes of librarians because we can keep up with him, we can easily accommodate his needs because they do not change. But the stimulating teachers are probably the ones most worth serving, partly because they are the ones who students really want to please and they are the ones who really teach students. Therefore, they are the ones who are really helping us to do our work, which is education, even when they are making it more complicated. These stimulating teachers very often recognize that the library is the

center of instruction; they are the ones who will be reviewing books in order to evaluate them for the library collection, but they may make the terrible error of mentioning a
book enthusiastically in class and therefore stimulating a demand for it before it is back in the library collection. After
that they may lose it, or fail to finish reading it and returning it. They create these kinds of problems but they are
different, beautiful problems when one looks at it from another point of view. What we need sometimes is to remind
ourselves of what it is to be a teacher and what it is to
stimulate in that way.

One of the confusions or problems which relate librarians and their relations with teachers and administrators
is that very often, in the minds of teachers, responsibilities
for areas of the school, or responsibilities which cut across
the curriculum are associated with administrators. Very
often this can mean that they see librarians as a part of the
administrative team more than as a part of the instructional
team. Even such special knowledge as knowing how to un-
screw the top of the projector in order to reach the bulb and
knowing that it is desirable for the bulb to be cool before removing it can place one in a special category. That happens
to librarians, and that kind of knowledge can create a kind
of threat as far as other people are concerned. There is a
need not just for understanding between librarians and administrators but for total mutual respect, a recognition of
our own distinct abilities and those of administrators. There
must be a concern with consistent reporting to them of both
failures and successes. Very often what gets reported to
the administrator is the failure of what the administrator
has suggested and the success of what the librarian has
achieved. In my own visits to numerous schools, I have
frequently been in the company of administrators and I have
been embarrassed to realize that seldom does anyone on the
library staff come up to them and greet them saying, "Let
me tell about the great thing that happened in here yester-
day," but very often they will say instead, and in the presence of a visitor, "Well, it's about time you came; the plas-
ter has been wet for three days," and this is done without
even recognizing the purpose of our visit. It is tempting to
fall into that habit of seizing every moment with an administrator to register a complaint, but it is more realistic always to have something funny to tell them, something that
shows what goes on and that may never be recorded in written reports of the library. It may be subversive, but one
of the values I see in this is that then the administrator has

a "library story" to tell. The librarian has put him one up on other people. He tells that story again and soon it becomes his story and the next thing that happens when he meets with other administrators is that someone asks, "Well, what happened in your library this week?" In such simple ways one can create the "library-minded administrators" we are all talking about. He may begin as a library-joke-minded administrator but that is a great beginning and it is no small thing to overlook. My own belief is that library-minded administrators come from the places where we have smart-minded librarians.

TEACHERS AND THE SCHOOL
RESOURCE CENTRE*

Shirley Blair

If the school librarian is to serve the student through the teacher's program, the teacher becomes the most immediate and indispensable link to effective use of the school resource centre. Teachers, through planned design and encouragement, determine the effect the centre will have on students in their classes.

The teacher-librarian must, therefore, demonstrate to teachers how the materials and services of the centre can be used to improve the educational program of the school.

There is no area of the school's program that cannot be made more vital and varied through skillful use of the centre's resources. If the full potential of the media is to be realized, the teacher-librarian must show initiative in promoting the school resource centre, so that there is greater awareness of the contribution the centre can make. The power of media can be released only when one knows what is available. Since a school media collection is charged with fiscal responsibility and the realization of educational goals, the teacher-librarian must plan for active use of the centre's holdings.

The commandment for effective school librarianship must be: Thou shalt work closely with thy teachers.

There are obstacles that stand in the way of carrying out this doctrine, however. There must be continuous program evaluation through identification and appraisal of inter-

*Reprinted from Canadian Library Journal, vol. 35, pp. 93-100, April 1978, by permission of the author and publisher, The Canadian Library Association.

faces between teachers and media program components, to determine the degree to which operational design facilitates or blocks attainment of educational objectives.

Joe Smith may be willing, but Sally Brown may not, and no profitable, joint effort can be realized with an unready or uncooperative staff member.

The main factors affecting teacher use of the school resource centre are broad in nature, and contain many underlying, closely related factors. For the sake of clarity and expediency, only eight major factors identified in a review of the literature are mentioned here, but it will become apparent that a much larger list is being examined. Considerable overlapping occurs among the major factors, and by the very nature of their definition, various aspects of any one factor may be applied or related to one or more of the others.

The eight major factors identified as affecting teacher use of the school resource centre are cooperative curriculum planning; teacher in-service programs provided by the teacher-librarian; instructional programs of the school; professional and personal attributes of the teacher-librarian; administrative policies; physical facilities and tone and atmosphere of the resource centre; teacher attitudes, background and interests; and cooperative selection and evaluation of the collection.

Cooperative Curriculum Planning

The factor positively influencing teacher use of the resource centre most evident in the review of the literature was "cooperative curriculum planning" between the teacher and teacher-librarian. Repeatedly, researchers pointed to the significance of teacher-librarians working cooperatively with teachers in the development of instructional programs. In a study by Edward Barth[1] it was concluded that the librarian should become more involved in visiting classrooms and observing instructional programs. Robert Hardman[3] stated that "the media specialist is also a curriculum specialist, " a finding also supported by James Madaus.[16]

Hardman went on to say that the media specialist "must maintain contact with all aspects of the school's instructional program, including course of study, units of study, teaching objectives, curriculum guides, and experimental programs. " The media specialist should also assist educators in curriculum development and design of instructional systems, learning environments and learning experiences, he concluded.

Hilda Jay, [9] in a study about increasing the use of secondary school libraries, spoke of more librarian consultative assistance being needed by teachers. In a survey of problems, practices and conditions affecting the use of the library in instruction, Bennat Mullen[17] concluded that librarians generally were not participating in curriculum and course planning. Elton Tielke[21] found that classroom teachers have not realized the potential of the library as an integrative force with classroom instructional programs.

An investigation by Dorothy Hellene[6] also pointed out that integrating the school library/media program into the instructional program was rated high by school principals. David Loertscher, [13] studying media centre services, discovered that media specialists have yet to assume a partnership role with the teacher in the instructional program of the school.

A study by Margaret Ann Jetter[10] in 1972, which attempted to identify viable roles for the school library media specialist of the future, stated as its major conclusion that "the school library media specialist of the future (which is now as far as this study is concerned) will function as an instructional development specialist. " One important implication of this conclusion, mentioned by Jetter, is that different role expectations for the school media specialist of the future require changes in programs of professional preparation.

In Instructional Design and the Media Program, William Hug stated: "The purpose of the media program is to assist individuals in the attainment of both personal and program objectives; the media program and the curriculum are instruments for changing behavior. "[7:5] He continued that "media programs not only provide the information necessary for students to achieve personal and curricular objectives, but they also provide environments that encourage students to interact, confer, share, care, think, and challenge, " when planned and directly related to the ongoing teaching/learning program.

The expanding information base has obvious implications for teacher-librarians and media programs. Media programs must be designed to provide better ways of implementing a wide range of curriculum strategies, while also meeting the specific requirements of the school curriculum at any point in time.

The teacher-librarian must be actively involved in the whole instructional process by helping the teacher formulate educational objectives, assisting with materials in the classroom, helping the teacher select combinations of materials to introduce a topic, and serving as an extension of the teacher as students come to the centre to do individual study projects. The librarian's knowledge of the unit, including its behavioural and cognitive objectives, enable him or her to give effective guidance to the student. Throughout the unit development, the teacher and the teacher-librarian should cooperatively evaluate and modify the learning experiences.

As part of the educational team, teacher-librarians must be ready to discard the outmoded when better ways of meeting needs are found. Planning for meaningful change must be a professional way of life.

In our complex society, knowledge doubles every eight years. It is unrealistic to expect students to digest a text printed five to 10 years ago. The textbook instead must be used as a point of departure, leading each student towards a wide variety of print and non-print materials for a greater depth and breadth of understanding. To be an integral part of the school, the resource centre must be a place where the use of resources, facilities and services is not sporadic, unplanned and incidental, but purposeful.

New curriculum designs demand specialization in order for the theory to be translated into practice. As Hug stated, 7:37 standard university preparation programs for media personnel have produced a "basic professional, " leaving specialization for graduate level studies. These "basic professionals" have been trained in educational practices that were prevalent at the time they took their training. With the rate of change, their knowledge and learning strategies can become obsolete.

Teacher In-service Programs

Another major factor affecting teacher use of the resource centre revealed by a search of the literature was teacher in-service programs relating to library and media services. One of Tielke's conclusions was that there was an almost complete absence of in-service work emphasizing extensive use of library resources for librarians and teachers. Mullen[17] found that under half the school principals in his study reported some attention to in-service training for teachers in the use of the library, and concluded that in-service training was not systematic or well organized.

Hardman[5] noted: "The media specialist is a teacher. He is responsible for conducting workshops and other in-service education activities for teachers, supervisors and administrators on the full spectrum of educational media." Barth[1] also recommended that in-service programs should be developed to instruct teachers and paraprofessionals in the utilization and production of instructional materials.

A form of in-service program mentioned by Harlan Johnson[11] in a teacher utilization of libraries study refers to involving teachers in selection. He stated that "the policies and practices used by most of the librarians to encourage teacher use of the library was the involvement of teachers in selection and provision for classroom collections of library materials."

In-service programs were also dealt with by Charlene Swarthout[20] in her study, which sought to provide an approach to an in-service program for classroom teachers and library staffs that would develop the concept of the school library as part of the educational system. Her recommendations suggested that provision for staff planning had potential for in-service growth; that evaluation of the school library would include not only its collection, but also its program; and that pre-service education of teachers, school librarians and administrators would develop the concept of the school library as part of the educational system.

In-service programs for teachers can also be provided through disseminating and sharing information from professional journals. Phyllis Van Orden[22] suggested in the concluding statement of her study that this accepted means of communication with teachers was not being used to its fullest potential in the area of communicating the contribution of media and media centres to elementary education.

Conducting orientation for new staff members is important, as each school term brings some changes among the staff. The orientation session is an opportunity to demonstrate to teachers the procedures, services, materials, and equipment available for use. It must be emphasized that media services are not acts of kindness, but justification for the existence of the media program. Some teacher-librarians prepare a special handbook for teachers, or contribute a section to the general staff handbook used in the school.

Meetings with small groups of teachers may be on a single grade level or for a specific subject area. In a large school situation, where there are two or more teacher-librarians, each may be assigned to a subject department and attend regular department meetings.

The most sophisticated delivery system possible is useless if the school staff doesn't know how to use it well. Through in-service sessions with teachers, the teacher-librarian is able to interpret the role of the resource centre in the instructional program of the school, and to solicit suggestions that may make the service more effective. Continuous in-service education in the use of media should be carried on as a means of familiarizing teachers with new materials and improving instruction.

Instructional Programs

The nature of the school's instructional programs was also seen as a factor influencing teacher use of the resource centre. In studying the relationship of the behaviours of principals to the development of school library/media programs, Hellene[6] found principals in one of the well developed program categories rated higher in encouraging teachers to use media in individualizing instruction. Richard King[12] concluded that a positive relationship exists between well established educational media programs and teacher utilization of educational media. An important finding by Fred Welch[23] in this area was that innovative curriculum programs stimulated teachers to use instructional media.

Although traditional teaching methods may utilize the resource centre facilities and its resources, the instructional role of the centre is more effective when coupled with organizational patterns like personalized learning, interdisciplinary studies, team teaching, contract teaching, and independent study programs. Personalized instruction which requires learning experiences that are relevant, significant and appropriate in terms of each student's education and personal growth needs will depend more heavily on the resources of the centre.

Attributes of the Teacher-Librarian

The professional and personal attributes of the teacher-librarian also relate to teacher use of the resource centre. This factor was discussed by Madaus[16] in a study of curriculum involvement, teaching structures and personality factors of librarians. In material selection he found no single factor which emerged as predictive of high material circulation, but discovered that the best set of predictors was a high extroversion score on the Bernreuter Personality Inventory and a high degree of curriculum involvement on the part of the learning resources specialist.

Barth's recommendation,[1] cited earlier, which refers to librarians becoming more involved in visiting classrooms and observing programs, is an example of a necessary professional attribute of the teacher-librarian. Hellene[6] also found that poorly trained or motivated librarians in underdeveloped libraries prevented adequate program development. An interesting conclusion by Anthony Schulzetenberge[19] was that "the relationships between teachers and librarians must be developed, and it seems to be enhanced by a diversity of interests and a personality that tends toward extroversion." Johnson[11] found that policies and practices that had the greatest influence in teacher use of the library were informal conversation with the librarian.

As this review suggests, there are certain professional and personal characteristics of the teacher-librarian that contribute to success. Knowledge and expertise in the field are important, but also important is an understanding of the various subject areas that contribute to the school's educational program. A strong commitment to education and to the unified media concept is essential.

The teacher-librarian's competencies must be used in such a way to inspire confidence in his or her ability to make a valuable contribution to the learning program. If the teacher-librarian demonstrates that he or she is first and foremost a teacher, capable of handling an instructional situation, a great deal of credibility is achieved with the rest of the school staff.

The school resource centre program cannot be effective if the teacher-librarian is in any way isolated from school activities. The teacher-librarian must move as freely throughout the school as students move to the centre. As the articulation of the resource centre's services, the teacher-librarian must be a visible part of the total school program.

Administrative Policies

Administrative policies and the school principal's attitudes were also found to be major factors influencing teacher use of the resource centre. In Hellene's study, [6] it was found that behaviours essential to the school program were revealed as important to the school library/media program, and that principals must value and understand a program well in order to perform well. Tielke, [21] when referring to this factor, concluded that although principals were delegated the responsibility for developing library programs, they tended to shift this responsibility to the librarian. Mullen's[17] survey of problems showed that about three-quarters of the principals had no professional training geared to preparing them to assist teachers in the instructional uses of media.

Rutland[18] also noted the importance of administrative policies: "All unnecessary administrative controls regulating student usage of the library should be eliminated...."

Instructional changes take hold and earning is modified most significantly when a school staff (the administration and teachers, including the teacher-librarian) together redefine its educational objectives. There will be little visible change in teaching/learning strategies unless the staff understand the full implication of the change that is required of them. If, in the development of a media program, these changes don't occur through a support system of staff development, then an instructional program to foster individual potential will not materialize.

Failure to take into account the interdependence of curriculum design and organizational change explains why many sound educational proposals fail to be implemented.

The school's administrative policies can either enhance or inhibit the chances of success. The centre must provide prompt and efficient access to the resources of the school media program for teachers and students. The best means for achieving this goal is flexible scheduling, rather than scheduling that preempts facilities and staff to fixed periods of time. Open scheduling permits access by individuals and small groups at the time of need or interest and provides opportunities for teachers to schedule groups of students to the centre for special needs.

If students cannot move freely through the building, the school resource centre will have great difficulty in becoming totally integrated into the school program. If John, at the height of his enthusiasm and 20 minutes into his social studies period, cannot move to the resource centre quickly and without red tape, then a learning situation has been lost by the student and a teaching opportunity has been lost by the teacher/librarian. This way everyone loses--including the administration.

Physical Facilities

Physical facilities were also revealed as a factor influencing teacher use of the resource centre. Mullen,[17] in his summary showing factors which hinder library use, pointed to physical facilities, and Rutland[18] dealt with this factor exclusively in his study of the basic physical facilities and educational roles of secondary school libraries. A factor closely related to physical facilities, because of its dependency on them and administrative policies, is "time utilization," or "time available for the teachers to use media effectively, and adequate time made available for the teacher-librarians to work with teachers in cooperative curriculum planning."

A central location which offers optimum accessibility to users will encourage greater utilization of the facilities. Initial planning must provide facilities that are appropriate to the educational and media program goals and objectives. To permit adaptation to changing uses which result from developing educational technology and curriculum revision, provisions for flexibility of activities and services must be considered. Much efficiency of operation depends on a functional design, for the collection gains power with good facilities, equipment gets more use, and production increases.

The atmosphere of the resource center should be cheerful and friendly. This feeling may be partly produced by the physical surroundings, which should be inviting and

pleasant, and convey warmth and a feeling of hospitality.
The centre's staff should constantly re-assess the facilities:

--Is the general impression a favourable one?
--Is the furniture comfortable?
--Is it attractively arranged?
--Are browsing and reading areas provided that are condu-
cive to study, relaxation and enjoyment?
--Are the various parts of the collection clearly marked for
easy identification?
--Are display areas well used?

Teacher Attitudes

A seventh important factor discovered which affects
teacher use of the resource centre is the teacher's attitudes,
interests and educational and cultural backgrounds. Mullen[17]
found that only 41 per cent of the teachers in his study could
recall any professional course which in part dealt with the
library. Loertscher[15] noted that individual differences among
teachers accounted for as much variation in their utilization
patterns of media centre services as did membership in a
particular subject department.

With regard to educational backgrounds, King[13] concluded that having taken a college course or courses with an
instructor who utilized media effectively had a significant relationship to the frequency with which secondary school teachers utilized media. Chi Ho Lee[14] recommended that prospective teachers should acquire library skills during their pre-
service training, and an interesting conclusion drawn by
Saad Mohammed El-Hagrasy[2] relates directly to this factor.
He stated:

> The hypothesis that there is a measurable relation-
> ship between teachers' reading habits and library
> background (as predictors) and pupils' reading and
> library skills (as criteria) is substantiated for this
> example (a) when a teacher's reading habits and
> library backgrounds are significantly low then his
> class's reading and library skills are also signifi-
> cantly low; (b) when a class's reading and library
> skills are significantly high, then the teacher's
> reading habits and library skills have been at least
> relatively high.

Finally, with regard to teacher behavior as a factor influencing teacher use of the resource centre, Reginald Ginn[4] found that evaluators who judged the importance of the suggested elements of individualized instruction programs rated teacher behavior as the most significant factor in such programs.

Teacher attitude is one of the basic factors that must be considered when trying to encourage new and innovative practices in education. A quality resource centre program strives to create a new openness, a new awareness, to raise expectations, and to encourage teachers to experiment with different teaching/learning processes. Much of the success of the program will be contingent on the teachers' receptiveness to these ideas.

The Collection

Cooperative selection and evaluation of media, and the completeness of the resource centre collection, has been found to be another factor influencing teacher use of the resource centre. Rutland[18] referred to this factor in his recommendation that acquisition of all resources for the secondary school library should be guided and dictated by program need, rather than by prevailing standards. Mullen's statistical analysis[17] showing factors which create problems in library use listed instructional materials as one.

Hardman[5] also referred to this factor: "As a consultant, the media specialist assists teachers, students and educational leaders with the location, selection, production, utilization, and evaluation of educational media."

In noting policies and practices which have the greatest influence on teacher use of the library, Johnson[11] found that about 45 per cent of the teachers in his study cited involvement in selection of library materials. On the basis of his findings in this area, Barth[1] recommended that teachers and students should be given an increased opportunity to participate more actively in the review and evaluation of instructional materials.

Swarthout[20] summarized the general findings relating to this factor in her statement: "To ensure the full operational benefits of the library, each staff member should participate in a continuing activity of selection, utilization and production of library materials."

The size of the collection is, of course, important, but it may be a meaningless criterion unless the contents of the materials have been evaluated. Many teacher-librarians have clung to false principles concerning the building of collections, and have interpreted them to mean that an arbitrary percentage of books should be allocated to each subject area. A "balanced" collection is as much a myth as an "average" person. The only kind of balance that a centre can justify is one related to the instructional program of the school, and the interests and abilities of the students.

The second mistake is to believe that there must be an adequate book collection before a serious effort is made to build a non-print collection. The teacher-librarian, as a materials specialist, should be more concerned with the ideas and concepts presented than with the format used. Since the resource centre uses media not as "things" but as "ideas," there should be no need to question the necessity of having both print and non-print materials available.

The school's instructional program will be strengthened if the teacher-librarian builds a functional media collection appropriate to the unique needs of the curriculum, the community, the staff, and the students. To build such a collection, the teacher-librarian, working in conjunction with staff members, must evaluate media materials objectively, with care and discrimination.

In many cases, learning resources can be provided through local arrangements within the community. The importance of knowing what the community has to offer cannot be over-emphasized; the more positive, immediate and visible is the response to a need, the more the service will be sought. A carefully selected, articulated and readily accessible collection of information resources is essential for implementation of the school's curriculum.

Teacher and Student Use of the Centre

Laurence Wiedrick's purpose in his Canadian study[14] was to collect data related to the problem of integrating the resources of the school resource centre with the instructional program of the school. Two specific purposes were to describe how fifth and sixth grade students used resource centres, and to identify factors which might influence or explain student use of the libraries.

Two reasons accounted for most of the students' resource centre visits. To acquire free reading material constituted almost 40 per cent, and to obtain information for school studies was identified for slightly more than 26 per cent of visits. The findings of this study suggest that the major function of the resource centre was to encourage recreational reading, and that instructional program support was secondary.

Evidence from the study also supports the contention that the classroom teacher is the major factor affecting the use which students make of the resource centre. The teachers' perceptions of the role and function of the centre determine how their students use the resource centre. Therefore, Wiedrick stated, "to gain greater integration of the library with the school's instructional program requires increased understanding and acceptance by librarians, teachers and principals of the educational role of the school library."

Piecemeal attention to one or two components of the centre's program will not make the school resource centre an integral part of the total educational program. Innovative organizational changes can only be initiated, nurtured and expanded within a program designed in concert with both staff and curriculum development activities.

Much of the success for the program is dependent on the quality of leadership provided by teacher-librarians. They are the ones who ultimately must be held responsible for initiating and carrying out changes in their role as teacher-librarians, in their relationships with teachers, and in the management and use of learning resources.

References

1.   Barth, Edward Walter.   "The Relationship Between Selected Teaching Structures and the Activities of Media Centres in Public Senior High Schools in the State of Maryland."   George Washington University, abstract of Doctoral Thesis, 1971.

2.   El-Hagrasy, Saad Mohammed.   "The Teacher's

Role in Library Service, An Investigation and Its Devices."
Rutgers University, abstract of Doctoral Thesis, 1961.

3. Fadell, Frances. "Factors Influencing Teacher
Use of the High School Library." Chicago, Ill., University
of Chicago, unpublished M. Ed. Thesis, 1971.

4. Ginn, Reginald Alfred. "Individualizing Instruction Through the Elementary School Library Media Center."
University of Alabama, abstract of Doctoral Thesis, 1974.

5. Hardman, Robert Richard. "Philosophy of Role
and Identification of Critical Tasks Performed by Educational
Media Specialists in Elementary and Secondary Schools of
Iowa." Indiana University, abstract of Doctoral Thesis, 1971.

6. Hellene, Dorothy Lorraine Ingalls. "The Relationships of the Behaviors of Principals in the State of Washington to the Development of School Library/Media Programs."
abstract of Doctoral Thesis, 1973.

7. Hug, William E. Instructional Design and the
Media Program. Chicago, American Library Association,
1975.

8. Ishikawa, Kivoharu. "Teacher Attitudes Toward
School Library: An Investigation of Library Service Levels
Related to Teacher Characteristics." George Peabody Col-
lege for Teachers, abstract of Doctoral Thesis, 1972.

9. Jay, Hilda Lease. "Increasing the Use of Secondary School Libraries as a Teaching Tool." New York
University, Doctoral Thesis, 1970.

10. Jetter, Margaret Ann. "The Roles of the School
Library Media Specialist in the Future: A Delphi Study."
Michigan State University, abstract of Doctoral Thesis, 1972.

11. Johnson, Harlan Ray. "Teacher Utilization of
Libraries in the Secondary Schools of Tucson District No. 1."
University of Arizona, abstract of Doctoral Thesis, 1975.

12. King, Kenneth Lee. "An Evaluation of Teacher
Utilization of Selected Educational Media in Relation to the
Level of Sophistication of the Educational Media Program in
Selected Oklahoma Public Schools." University of Oklahoma,
abstract of Doctoral Thesis, 1969.

13. King, Richard Lee. "A Study of Selected Factors
Related to Variability in the Use of Certain Types of Instructional Media Among Teachers." University of Missouri, abstract of Doctoral Thesis, 1967.

14. Lee, Chi Ho. "The Library Skills of Prospective Teachers of the University of Georgia." University of
Georgia, abstract of Doctoral Thesis, 1971.

15. Loertscher, David Vickers. "Media Centre Services to Teachers in Indiana Senior High Schools, 1972-1973."
Indiana University, abstract of Doctoral Thesis, 1973.

16. Madaus, James Richard. "Curriculum Involvement, Teaching Structures, and Personality Factors of Librarians in School Media Programs." University of Texas, abstract of Doctoral Thesis, 1974.

17. Mullen, Bennat Curtis. "A Survey of Problems, Practices, and Conditions Affecting the Use of the Library in Instruction in North Central Association Schools in Missouri." University of Missouri, abstract of Doctoral Thesis, 1966.

18. Rutland, Thomas. "A Study of the Basic Physical Facilities and Educational Roles of Secondary School Libraries." University of Tennessee, abstract of Doctoral Thesis, 1971.

19. Schultzetenberge, Anthony C. "Interests and Background Variables Characterizing Secondary School Librarians Who Work With Teachers in Curriculum Development and Improvement of Instruction." University of North Dakota, abstract of Doctoral Thesis, 1970.

20. Swarthout, Charlene R. "An Approach to an In-Service Program to Develop the Concept of the School Library as Part of the Instructional System." Wayne State University, abstract of Doctoral Thesis, 1966.

21. Tielke, Elton Fritz. "A Study of the Relationship of Selected Environmental Factors to the Development of Elementary School Libraries." University of Texas, abstract of Doctoral Thesis, 1968.

22. Van Orden, Phyllis Jeanne. "Use of Media and the Media Centre, as Reflected in Professional Journals for Elementary School Teachers." Wayne State University, abstract of Doctoral Thesis, 1970.

23. Welch, Fred. "Relationships Between Curriculum Variables, Attitudes, Teacher Characteristics and the Utilization of Instructional Media." University of Southern California, abstract of Doctoral Thesis, 1974.

24. Wiedrick, Laurence G. "Student Use of School Libraries in Edmonton Open Area Elementary Schools." Unpublished Doctoral Dissertation, University of Oregon, 1973.

MEDIA SPECIALISTS WORK
WITH TEACHERS*

Nancy B. Pillon

The concept of the open school is one that has at-
tracted much attention in the past decade. The education
theory basic to open schools includes the concept that learning cannot be imposed by either teachers or well organized
materials. Instead, an environment must be provided which
will allow the learner to grow naturally into a person who is
curious, who can reason effectively, and who has acquired
processes for learning rather than a storehouse of remembered facts. In a rapidly expanding technology, specialized
skills become obsolete quickly. Students need flexibility,
and the ability to deal with change, and to make rapid ad-
justments. [1]

In considering successful ways that media specialists
have found to work with teachers in the open school, we
should begin by appraising the new role of materials in a
learner-centered open environment.

Open-concept education is based on individual and
small group interaction with resources, both human (teachers,
other students, the community) and material. The pupil is
no longer dependent on the textbook and the teacher as prime
sources for the information he needs. Instead the child enters into a dialogue with materials. [2] He does not wait pas-
sively for something to happen but rather reaches out, probes
for possibilities, takes meanings. [3] A greater part of the
teacher's time is therefore spent selecting and organizing materials, observing and assessing children-interaction with

*Reprinted from Drexel Library Quarterly, vol. 9, pp. 59-
69, July 1973, by permission of the author and publisher,
the School of Library and Information Science, Drexel University.

these materials, and planning the next encounter between the child, the materials, and the teacher. [4]

Teachers must work very closely with each other and with the media specialist to optimize materials use. A nongraded team-teaching program provides opportunities for each student to develop skills at his own rate. A team of teachers including the media specialist provides an opportunity to strengthen and enhance the students' learning experiences.

Teaming with Teachers

The teacher and media specialist form a team to teach the use of materials and the skills pertinent to the completion of learning tasks. This is effective teaching which enables the students to see the media center in relation to their present needs. The media specialist may spend as much time outside the center as he does within it. At times the media specialist will observe the teachers and students, evaluating the ways materials are used. At other times he will actively team with the teacher to completely integrate his talents and expertise with that of the teacher.

The main thrust of the media specialist's talents and time is work with students and teachers on a direct personal basis to improve the learning climate. The competencies of all will improve with interaction.

Media center specialists need to know what is happening in classrooms. Discussions between the teachers and media specialists of objectives and methods are fruitful. Media specialists should cooperate with teachers in actual instruction, setting up collections, and guiding utilization. When all of the materials available in the collection for a unit have been gathered, the media center specialist should assist the teachers to design and produce additional materials. In order to do this the media specialist needs an understanding of learning theory, curriculum design, and evaluative techniques.

Community Resources

The media specialist utilizes media that are available in the school and outside the school. Many open schools make extensive use of community resources including public libraries, social agencies, and individuals. Children and adolescents find themselves continuously bombarded by a deluge of information. Barriers are imposed by the complexity of society which makes direct involvement with learning difficult. [5] Thus we find students protesting the inhumanity and irrelevance of their educational experiences. [6] Utilization of the community as a resource can help fill this gap. [7]

Prostano and Prostano expressed very well how communications could be improved by saying, "If the media specialist has developed the means of successfully working with teachers on a continuing basis--through membership on the principal's advisory committee, through the L. M. C. committee of teachers, through the media selection committee structure and through the reading guidance structure--then dealing with teachers is facilitated. "[8] (L. M. C. refers to learning materials center.)

Human Relations

The nature of the open school requires that the media specialist concentrate on human relations. A freer relationship exists between media specialists, teachers, and students in the open school. The environment of mutual trust and respect that is found in open schools provides for optimum learning. Furthermore it permits students and teachers to be themselves.

Robert M. Hutchins believes that the proponents of the open school want the school to have an atmosphere of warmth and friendliness. He said, "They want children treated as human beings. They correctly believe that there are many ways to learning, and that those which are pleasanter may also be more productive. "[9]

Interviews with Open School Personnel

In order to learn more about the services in the open school media center, this investigator visited several open schools and interviewed school personnel in an elementary school which was in its first year of operation and a middle school which was in its third year of operation. Portions of the interviews are presented in an attempt to compare the reactions from the two schools toward the media center. (Quotations in this section, unless otherwise indicated were

taken directly from the Interview Form used by the author
with school personnel. The interview questions appear as
an appendix to this article.)

When the investigator asked about the advantages of
the open school, the principal of the elementary school replied, "Pods feed into the media center, which makes it accessible and gives a feeling that it is the focal point of the
school. Children are more involved in the use of the media
center.... The media specialist must keep in constant touch
with the staff. "

When the media specialist was asked about the advantages of the open school, she replied, "The students can come
any time. There is room for two or three classes. Or they
can come alone or in small groups. They don't have to wait
for the next library class to come. Kids don't feel that a
visit to the media center is an interruption, and they enjoy
the open school so much that they don't want to miss a day
of school. "

Summarizing the advantages of the open school and the
way in which the media center of an open school is utilized,
a teacher responded, "Since the media center is in the center
of the building, the children see it more often. They pass
through on their way to lunch or to the office, and they feel
more at ease in going. The materials are more easily seen.
They (students) are no longer scheduled to go to the media
center, but they can go when their interest is greatest. One
of my students said that she wanted to go right then because
she saw a book that she wanted. I personally like it better. "

Some of the comments of a third grade teacher are
as follows, "The students can come for reports, for pleasure,
or for viewing and listening at the time that they are the
most interested in coming. I have more contact with the
media specialist in receiving help than I would in a traditional school. The unscheduled use of the media center is a
strong point. "

A teacher of the upper levels seemed enthusiastic
about the improved services of the media center when she
said, "The additional services of the media center are much
more than I anticipated. There is no question about the fact
that the students have benefited in terms of working more
independently. The media specialist brings to our attention
appropriate materials and asks for suggestions in selecting

new materials. Furthermore she has been helpful in teaching library skills. It is great that students can go to the media center when they really want to go."

A teacher of the youngest children replied to my interview questions by saying, "The media center is centrally located, which is an advantage for children and teachers. I think the children feel freer to use it, and I think there is something special about the informality. This fact makes the children relax and enjoy it more. We feel closer to the media specialist, because we get a chance to talk to her at various times, whereas if the media center was isolated we wouldn't have as many opportunities. I think the parents are much more familiar with the open media center than they were with a traditional library, because they have to pass through the media center for numerous reasons. Of course, we have more materials here than I ever dreamed we would have in the elementary library. I feel free to give my suggestions to the media specialist, because she makes every effort to order the things we are interested in. Usually, when we get new materials, the media specialist makes sure we see them or know they are here. At the beginning of the year we had in-service training and learned how to use many new kinds of equipment. The children use the media center a lot more by being able to visit it when they want to find something. I would be a little reluctant to send my age group if it were way down at the end of the hall or upstairs."

A parent, serving as a para-professional in the media center, used personal experience to show the value of the open school and media center. She observed, "Students are learning to use the media center, and they are doing more recreational reading. In browsing they find books on subjects they are discussing in their classes. Teachers enjoy having a say in what is purchased. I had a terrible time getting my daughter in the fourth grade to read until she came to this school, but now she is reading much more pertaining to school subjects and for recreation as well. By continually passing through the library the students see materials they want. The students are getting proficient in using the equipment themselves. Books are not enough now that they know the variety of other materials that are available."

One of the teachers in the elementary school was especially impressed by the services to children, and she commented, "Basically the children can come at any time, and more children can be accommodated. The atmosphere is more relaxed and the students like the media center more. The ability for students to work on their own has increased, since they are taught to look for themselves. This experience gives them confidence. When we need help with library skills, we can arrange it with the media specialist. The media center is opening a whole new world to the children."

Many similarities were observed in the enthusiasm shown toward the media center in both schools. It seemed that the media specialist in the middle school had found more time to become involved in curriculum planning. But then, her program is in its third year. She seemed very adept at communication and motivation.

When asked if she ever had problems with supervising so many students, and whether teachers ever failed to come with their classes, the head of the media center at the middle school replied, "It just isn't done. This has never come up. The teachers always come and stay with their classes. We don't want a hush-hush atmosphere. There is a lot of learning going on and kids like to be here. I tell the teachers personally about new materials, and all of them have a map of this area. The place is almost jumping in the morning because there are so many students in here."

In the middle school each pod has a curriculum coordinator. One of the curriculum coordinators indicated the value of the media center to the instructional program by pointing out that the students like the relaxed atmosphere, the freedom, the friendliness, and the warmth. She said, "The media center is not closed in." She was generally enthusiastic about the integration of the media services with the overall curricular program of the school.

In response to my questions about services, a teacher who was busy making plans for team teaching replied, "I cannot say enough about the length to which the media specialists will go beyond the call of duty. I have had a wonderful response to anything I have requested, even if it is on the spur of the moment. When we turn in a request for materials, it is filled almost immediately. There is nothing that the media specialists are failing to do. The media specialists have done a lot to acquaint the students with the center, and there is no problem in students going there without advanced scheduling. We coordinate all types of media because this gives the kids the idea that we can learn through many devices."

The other member of the team said, "The media specialists will do everything they can. They will organize materials for you or they are willing to go to your room and be a resource person. At teachers' meetings, the media specialists tell about new things in the media center. I don't know how it could be used more, and by the middle of the year most students are ready to work on their own, but they are never afraid to ask."

One teacher seemed impressed by the media center's great accessibility when she responded. "As a teacher I check on little things and pick up material whenever I pass through. It is favorable to students who have the ability to work independently. The atmosphere is friendly for all and not forbidding as it was in my school library. The physical plan and people make it accessible."

The guidance counselor said, "The open plan breaks down walls that have surrounded bookshelves for so many years. This is needed in this day and age when too many people are depending on television for their information. The open school does it as well as anything. It gives students opportunities to work independently that they wouldn't have otherwise. There may be better media specialists, but I haven't run across them yet."

The attitude of the faculty and administrators toward the media center in the open concept school as well as in the traditional school is the key to success of its program. A brochure from one of the schools visited indicated the attitude often taken in open concept schools toward the media center:

> The heart of the new building is an instructional materials center which is situated so that students naturally pass through it many times a day, entering, leaving or moving around the school. Such constant contact is designed to create interest and invites the student to avail himself of readily accessible books, magazines, audiovisual and electronic resources. 10

Guidelines for Operating Media Services to Teachers

Based on visits to open schools the following guidelines

are suggested for making the media center more viable to the needs of the teachers. The media specialist should realize that times have changed and that teachers and students have changed also. Therefore, the media specialist must adjust to what is happening in education. This involves accommodating the procedures of the media center to the needs of the teachers.

The media center specialist needs to participate actively in faculty and team meetings by showing the teachers and administrators the materials and services that the media center has to offer. This may be done formally or informally. It will often be necessary for the media specialist to demonstrate his worth before he will be fully accepted as a full colleague. At times the facilities of the center may be utilized by teams of teachers for planning sessions and for faculty meetings if they do not interfere with services to students.

The media specialist must not always be cast in the role of ex post facto reactor to innovation but rather must anticipate the function and contribution of the media program to the total school program, present and anticipated. In order to do this it is necessary for the media specialist to be a part of the administrative team.

Scan journals such as Learning: The Magazine for Creative Teaching, The Bulletin of the National Association of Secondary School Principals, Educational Leadership, and The National Elementary Principal as well as subject journals. When implications for media services are seen in these journals he calls the attention of the administrator to these. (This also demonstrates the media specialist's interest in the teachers' or administrator's specialty. -- Editor)

The media specialist should familiarize himself with the total curriculum and know the materials the teachers are covering now and what they are planning to do tomorrow. In the future take time to visit classrooms in order to talk and listen to the teachers in their rooms. Volunteer to share responsibilities in particular classes, especially those related to the use of the library. Attend team meetings, contribute the unique preparation which the media specialist has on materials, their utilization, and the ways students interact with them.

The media specialist should encourage teachers to participate in the selection of materials. Ordering procedures should be as simple as possible. The media specialist must be able to react to demands for new materials immediately. At times this will mean sacrificing discounts obtainable from jobbers and using the local drugstore, bookstore or paperback dealer.

As soon as materials arrive in the media center they should be taken to the teachers who recommended them. Teachers should be kept informed of additional materials that have arrived through lists of new acquisitions. Academic librarians have been using "pathfinders," annotated lists of materials on special topics to keep their clients up to date.[11] It is important for teachers to be allowed to keep materials as long as they need them. The media specialist should be willing to go outside the collection to procure resources and be responsible for getting needed materials from not only other libraries but also other sources.

Faculty members are equals. The media specialist should not make the mistake of sending directions to teachers or of expecting teachers to do the media specialist's work. Most teachers will be "turned off" if the media specialist asks them to take care of the overdue notices during home room period or during class.

It is important for the media specialist to know the teachers personally. He should know their interests, hopes, and aspirations. This implies discussing not only library services but additional topics as well. Contacts within and outside the school will facilitate communication.

The media specialist should be friendly, dependable, accessible, and dynamic. The media specialist cannot wait for teachers to come to him and should get out and work with the faculty members. That approach will give teachers a more positive attitude toward the media center and its program.

The open school demands cooperation of media specialists with teachers if a successful program is to result. Media specialists who combine imagination with the use of current materials and equipment, who can listen to teachers and students, who can spark the initiative and creativity of students and then wait for their productivity will have media centers that are "learning centers."

Paul Goodman in advocating the discovery approach said, "Perhaps the chief advantage of incidental educating rather than schooling is that the young can then carry on their movement grounded in experience and competence."[12] An "open" media center in an open-concept school can promote and enhance this process.

Appendix

Interview Questions

1. What grade or level do you teach?

2. What are some advantages that the media center of the open school has over the traditional library?

3. Give examples of how helpful the media center specialist has been in:
    a. Introducing you to new materials.
    b. Providing you with new materials.
    c. Assisting with the designing of instructional experiences or programming for individual students in your class.
    d. In-service programs for acquainting the faculty with recent educational developments and the effective use of equipment and media.
    e. Bringing about innovations in the curriculum in the classroom.

4. How effective are each of the following phases of media center services in relation to your work in the classroom?
    a. Unscheduled use of the media center.
    b. Participation in evaluation, selection and ordering of materials.
    c. The media specialist acting as resource person in the classroom when requested.
    d. The media specialist serving on teaching teams.

5. Are there any additional services which you think the media center should provide for teachers?

6. What is the effect of improved accessibility of the media center for student use?

7. How much do you think the media center has increased the student's ability to work independently?

8. Do you think the media center is effective in leading students to self discovery?

Notes

1. Alvin Toffler, Future Shock (New York: Random House, Inc., 1970).

2. Tony Kallet, "Some Thoughts on Children and Materials," Mathematics Teaching, Autumn 1967, p. 38.

3. Ibid., p. 39.

4. David Hawkins, "I-Thou-It," Mathematics Teaching, Spring 1969.

5. James S. Coleman, "The Children Have Outgrown the Schools," Psychology Today, February 1972, pp. 72-75.

6. John Birmingham, Our Time Is Now: Notes from the High School Underground (New York: Praeger Publications, 1970).

7. Raymond W. Barber, "The Open Media Center" (Unpublished, Tallahassee, Florida: Department of Educational Administration, Florida State Univ., 1972).

8. Emanuel T. Prostano and Joyce S. Prostano, The School Library Media Center (Littleton, Colo.: Libraries Unlimited, Inc., 1971) p. 242.

9. Robert M. Hutchins, "The School Must Stay," The Center Magazine, Vol. 6. January-February, 1973, p. 12-23.

10. Metropolitan School District of Perry Township, Meridian Middle School (Indianapolis: The Township, [1970]). For copies write to: Mr. Morris Beck, Principal, Meridian Middle School, 8040 S. Meridian St., Indianapolis, Ind.

11. Charles S. Stephens, Marie P. Canfield, and Jeffrey J. Gardner, "Library, Pathfinders: A New Possibility for Cooperative Reference Service," College and Research Libraries, January 1973, pp. 40-46.

12. Paul Goodman, "The Present Movement in Education," New York Review of Books, Vol. 12, April 1969, pp. 14-21, 24.

ACTION ACTIVITIES*

Mildred Laughlin

The 1969 Standards for School Media Programs had a good deal to say about professional staff services. Specifically, they called for resource specialists who are capable of "Working with teachers in curriculum planning," and who know enough about education "to design instructional experiences."[1]

Virtually all states now require secondary school librarians to have teaching certificates. Similarly, today's media specialists usually consider themselves to be teachers, and, as evidence that they are carrying out an educational function, most of them point to their involvement with instruction in use of the library.

At the same time, many librarians slight their teaching role in doing their daily work. Sometimes they do this inadvertently, but more often it is through lack of teacher-librarian planning, especially the kind that leads to learner-centered activities.

An example of this is apparent in the way media people gauge the value of most student work. In many cases resource specialists don't even bother with evaluation. In others, they may do little more than conduct pencil-and-paper tests which have little importance to the student. Usually the questions are superficial, and almost never are they interesting.

But even when this is not the case, such testing still serves little purpose. This is because the whole examination

---

*Reprinted from Learning Today, vol. 7, pp. 69-72, Winter 1974, by permission of the publisher, Library-College Associates, Inc.

procedure destroys the "freedom to choose" image that a resource center should project.

When asked why skills activities are isolated from individual and/or classroom needs, the librarian often defends her teaching with complaints about scheduling problems, lack of time, or teacher disinterest. While such comments usually contain some truth, the real problem is just as frequently a lack of conviction, or a feeling that she--as "just a librarian"--is not really an expert in educational matters.

In short, too many librarians seem to think they should play only a minor role in designing curriculum experiences.

Unfortunately, waiting in the library for teachers to seek out services if not fulfilling an educational responsibility. It is, in fact, the opposite, for librarians who do this are refusing to assume any initiative of their own. In today's education, of course, initiative should be accompanied by a basic understanding of how to carry out evaluations that enhance a unit of study. When this unit deals with the teaching of skills, an instructor can avoid much frustration by establishing certain objectives before he begins.

According to writers such as Mager and Blough, a teacher's success in using this approach depends on analyzing those things he wants to achieve. In helping a student develop skills, one thing the teacher/librarian wants is for the learner to see how he can utilize his skills in various situations. Because of this, Mager favors the use of objectives, for he feels they "help us to see where we are heading and tells us how to know when we have arrived."2

Skills teaching lends itself to the writing of behavioral objectives because most of the outcomes are subject to measurement. Here, for example, one needn't worry about such elusive terms as "enjoy," "appreciate," or "realize." The building of skills concerns such things as selecting, comparing, classifying, and preparing. As a result, the learner should always be able to measure his gains.

Ideally, skills teaching is on a one-to-one basis according to needs that a student displays. This, of course, implies much individual attention, for one student may feel a need everytime his class group begins a new unit which requires problem-solving ability.

With this caveat in mind, a teacher-librarian team may begin its study of a unit by having the class gain an overview of the <u>Readers' Guide to Periodical Literature.</u> In this case the following plan illustrates one behavioral approach that a team could follow with considerable success.

Objectives: The student will be able to

1. Locate five articles on a given subject in the <u>Readers' Guide;</u>
2. Prepare a bibliography of these articles; and
3. Locate one of them in the appropriate journal.

To help the student achieve these objectives, the librarian can introduce the <u>Readers' Guide</u> by using transparencies that show appropriate entries. In doing this, she should encourage participation of the entire group, particularly as the class builds up skill in identifying articles, periodicals, volume numbers, and other bibliographic points.

The next step may be for the students to acquaint themselves with accepted bibliographic form. As a way of building skill in this area, it is well for members of the group to complete missing items that appear on overhead projections. This technique has several advantages, for it enables everyone to discuss all problems which the group has under study.

As a final step, each class member should research a topic through study of the <u>Readers' Guide.</u> Here, each student can--with the aid of his teacher/librarian team--prepare a bibliography, locate various periodicals, and decide if given articles are pertinent to his topic. The advantage of this approach is readily apparent. The student works out his problem while he simultaneously fulfills the objectives of the unit.

In an approach such as this, behavioral objectives contain a built-in evaluation procedure that is more personal, original, and action-oriented than what one finds when using paper-and-pencil tests. In addition, they are open-ended and allow for continuous growth.

Notes

1. American Association of School Libraries, <u>Standards</u>

for School Media Programs (Chicago: American Library Association, 1969), p. 8.

  2. Robert E. Mager, Developing Attitude Toward Learning (Palo Alto: Fearon Publishing Co., 1968), p. 13.

AGENDA FOR ACTION:
TEACHER- LIBRARIAN PLANNING*

Alma Ruth (Ferguson) Hess and Karen Harris

"I hate to go to the library. I can't ever find what I'm looking for. "

"Our library isn't any good. It never has anything I need. "

"I'm not about to look through all those magazines just to find one article on _____.
We're not even supposed to read it after we find it. "

"The library scares me. It's so big and everyone looks so busy. "

"I answered all the questions but I still got an 'F.' "

"I'm graduating this year and I've never even been inside the library. "

"I don't even know where to begin to look for this stuff. "

"Who did you say our school librarian is? She had to go to college to be a librarian?"

How often have we shunned such comments and thought to ourselves: "How lazy can a student be?" "He should know better; the books are cataloged and he knows how the system works, let him find his books himself. " "If the teacher doesn't care enough to put the materials on reserve, then. ... "

The comments students make about the library can be very instructive. Even though generalizations abound, careful study of them can reveal causes of frustrations, sources

*Reprinted from Louisiana Library Association Bulletin, vol. 36, pp. 81-84, Summer 1973, by permission of the authors and publisher.

of difficulty and areas where adjustment in library practice or teacher-librarian planning can lead to more fruitful and satisfying experiences for the students. Considering the vast resources school libraries of today possess, students should be able to find and make effective use of relevant materials to meet their needs.

What do the above comments reveal? If sufficient material is available and students cannot find it, this would probably indicate that students don't know how to use the library and need considerable guidance in using the appropriate library tools to locate information. If material is not available, then the fault may be in the collection, or it may be in the assignment. Often assignments demand such esoteric materials that only a specialized research library could provide them. Others require whole classes to consult the same few sources. Latecomers are out of luck completely. If advance notice is given, sources could be put on reserve. Even so, thirty students clamoring for three books is a surefire recipe for frustration. In either case, some variation in the assignment would have yielded an experience of equal educational validity but without built-in assurances of failure for some. Insufficient materials or lack of material to complement the curriculum indicate a lack of awareness on the librarian's part of the particular needs of her school's faculty and students.

Some student comments denote confusion about the purpose of the assignment and how to satisfy it. There are many points along the path to the completion of an assignment which can reveal a lack of understanding, or a misunderstanding, a lack of skill, a confusion of purpose, or an inability to interpret either the requirements of the assignment or the content of the materials.

Again, the problem could very well be in the assignment itself. It could be too vague or it could simply be too difficult for some students. The students may be insufficiently informed about how to find materials which will satisfy their needs. They may just need more time to explore and browse so that they get the "feel" of how different sources can be used. They may not be sufficiently skilled in making qualitative decisions, scanning, interpreting information, taking notes, or preparing a finished project or paper. The librarian, by observing student behavior in the library, can often be of assistance. Most desirable would be a closer working relationship between the teachers, librarian and students so that the many frustrating and discouraging experiences can be either avoided, or diagnosed and remedied.

The key to the problem is obvious. Librarians must go beyond simple knowledge of the curriculum; they must become actively involved in providing sound professional service to the educational process. Responsibilities do not end with selecting, processing, circulating and counting books. The main reason for existence is to select and organize the materials needed for a richer educational experience for students, to assist students in finding such materials, and to encourage and cooperate with teachers in creating ways to make the library and its materials valuable to the instructional program.

Following is a list of questions which the librarian needs to have answered before students begin work, and a series of steps the teacher and librarian must take for effective planning.

1. What is to be studied? Civil rights movement in the 60's? The future tense of regular French verbs? How to budget for a family of six? The history, development, production and sale of nail polish?

2. Who are the learners? Are there some generalizations about the class or groups within the class that can assist the librarian in planning? For example: Is this the first experience of its type for these students? What basic skills are needed by these students for the successful completion of their assignment? Are there any students who need particular attention? Is there a student for whom books in large type should be provided? Are there students with physical disabilities who must not be allowed to overexert themselves? Are there students for whom high interest-low ability materials must be found, or conversely, students who need more intellectually challenging materials? Are there foreign-born students who may need reference materials or books in another language?

3. What pedagogic approaches will be used for each part of the unit? Will the whole class participate in some activities? Will there be small group instruction? Will individual students be expected to work independently? Which activities will take place in the classroom? Which in the library? Will some students be working in the library while

others are involved in classroom activities? Will more than
one teacher or one class be involved with this same project?
Will the same approach be used for all?

    4. <u>What specific attitudes, skills, or information are
to be learned as a result of this assignment?</u> If students
are working independently, is there any core of experience
that all of them should or do possess?

    5. <u>What measures are to be used for student evalua-
tion?</u> Testing? Observation? Written or oral reports?
Is the librarian to be involved in any way in evaluating these
students?

    6. <u>How much time is to be allocated?</u> Any amount
from one hour to one semester may be the answer. The implications for how deeply a subject is to be covered can
easily be seen from the time allotted to it. The types of
materials will have a direct relationship to this factor. If
the librarian has a schedule and sees that students are still
searching for data when they should be starting to write
their papers, then intercession in time to prevent a disaster
might be in order.

When these questions are answered, the librarian's
work begins. First, a calendar needs to be developed so that
materials can be prepared on time, lessons can be developed,
and activities can be planned so they do not conflict with other scheduled events. The librarian must make sure that appropriate materials are available in the school itself. If
there are deficiencies, loans should be made from the local
public or state library. If sufficient appropriate materials
cannot be made available, then the assignment should be reexamined and, if necessary, completely changed. The school
library should have the bulk of materials needed for the completion of assignments. The availability of the school librarian as well as the collection of materials is critical for student success.

The librarian may need to provide special services.
Bibliographies may have to be developed. In addition, the
creation of audio-visual materials may be necessary for use
by the reader or as a vehicle for presentation by students
of what has been learned.

The librarian should be available while students locate materials. Students can be expected to need encourage-

ment and assistance in using reference sources, locating information, assessing its relevance, evaluating its credibility, and integrating it with other information already found. Some students will not know how to handle conflicting opinions. Some will not be able to differentiate between fact and opinion. Some may find materials that are too complex for them to handle. The teacher and librarian need to provide assistance in the solution of all these problems. Only by active involvement with the students for the duration of their work are librarians able to spot those students who are having difficulties and to provide help when needed. The librarian can cooperate with the teacher and provide additional learning situations.

Although it may sound as though a schedule of this kind places unbearable burdens on the librarian's time and energy, it does not work out this way in actual practice. The time a librarian spends with students and teachers in planning turns out to be profitably spent. There is less demand for reteaching of the same skill to the same student year after year, and, in time, the students become increasingly independent. Advance planning in no way implies rigid scheduling. The library can and must be open to students and faculty. Flexible scheduling assures the availability of the services of the librarian in the initial stage of a library learning experience.

Evaluation is necessary to measure the full impact of the services provided. Questions that must be asked include: Were there adequate and relevant materials of sufficient variation in complexity? Which students had difficulty in completing the assignment? Why? How could this assignment have been improved? Which students still need help in using the library? Was enough or too much time allotted? How did the students react to the assignment? What materials should be recommended for future purchase?

Teachers as well as librarians are responsible for programming successful library experiences. Students do not automatically become independent or sophisticated library users. Carefully planned activities are essential to achieve such an end result. Too often the librarian expects the teacher to be responsible for skill development without the availability of a laboratory. The teacher often expects the student to possess all the library skills when he enters the classroom. The student feels that no one really cares and he might as well just copy his report anyway.

Library activities are not necessarily successful. Only when teachers and librarians cooperatively plan a systematic program of learning will students begin to feel success in library-related activities and ultimately approach the library with confidence.

MINIGUIDE MEDIA CENTER SERVICES FOR TEACHERS*

Rita Ziegler

Services that a media center can and should provide for teachers are an integral and essential part of the educational program of the school. The media specialist supplies these needed services by keeping in touch with classroom activities and assisting teachers in the planning of units of work. This is done through individual conferences, by compiling lists of materials, and by promoting the media center for the individual teacher and student use by providing reading, listening, and viewing guidance.

In-service Training

In-service education in the use of multimedia and the demonstration in the use of equipment must be part of the school and media center's function. These sessions should be planned only after direct input and consultation with the teachers. Workshops should be planned by the administration with the teachers and media specialist involved in planning.

The N. J. State Library is available to conduct many of these in-service training sessions along with the Educational Improvement Centers who will send speakers with expertise to conduct one or two day workshops. The programs are many and varied. In-service training should be: self motivating, relevant, continuous, flexible, and individualized as much as possible.

*Reprinted by permission of the author and publisher from NJEA Review, vol. 50, pp. 84-85, Feb. 1977. Copyright 1977, New Jersey Educational Association.

Organizing Materials

Cataloging and organizing instructional materials facilitates the use of the collection and makes it more readily available. Systems for publicizing materials start with the first essential, namely, the catalog. There are two basic kinds of catalogs, the card catalog and the list type catalog. To assure maximum use of media, there is a necessity for both types.

The card catalog lists all book and non-book materials in the center by author, title, and/or subject heading. However, teachers need to know in a convenient and comprehensive way what audiovisual material is available. One of the most effective ways is to provide each teacher with a booklet containing a list of audiovisual software arranged by subject area and grade level. This booklet should be revised and reissued every other year. It should be kept up to date by an annual supplement and by listings in news bulletins. One of the chief advantages of this type catalog is that it can be used anywhere, anytime.

Two basic factors must be considered when preparing this booklet. It must be reasonably economical to produce and be sufficiently informative as to content, grade level, and index. The circulation of nonbook media will increase dramatically when each teacher has his or her own catalog.

Resources for Curriculum Planning

The media specialist should assist the curriculum planners in selecting and adapting learning resources. Such services may require the media center to supply lists of materials, manuals, outlines of resource units, and other related resources.

The media center should supply forms to teachers to make recommendations for the possible purchase of media. Media specialists should devise a form that will suit their own situation yet be sufficiently informative for selection decisions.

A service of the media center that has been very successful is the supplying of multimedia units on a specific subject area to the teacher for intense classroom use. This is loaned for a designated time and includes books, filmstrips, magazines, records, maps, tapes, etc. A listing of these borrowed materials is prepared and three copies are made, one for the teacher, one for the center, and one filed for future reference. In addition to using these learning resources in the classroom, the student comes to the media center for other reference materials.

Instructional Resources

There is no one method or technique for using instructional materials effectively. Good teachers, working with others, sharing experiences, combining ideas, and plans will be a force to stimulate more and better use of media. Another good source for ideas and rich learning experience lies in the pupils themselves and interested people from the community.

An effective media specialist will stimulate and assist in experimental tryout and evaluation of media and learning procedures by involving teachers and students whenever possible. A routine school experience can take on new life through the use of a field trip, a new book or map, or a resource person used at the right time.

Media center newsletters can be sent to each teacher and administrator several times a year. They can contain information about the addition of new media to the collection, announcements of coming events, book fairs, and exhibits etc.

Community resource files listing persons with expertise on specific subject areas willing to share their knowledge with students is also part of the media center. When the 7th grade here at the E. A. Tighe School in Margate had a unit on the "American People, " a genealogist on the staff of the Atlantic City Public Library came to the school and discussed with the students the early background of most of the immigrants to this country. This proved to be a really worthwhile learning project and served as a motivating force for the students to learn about their own racial heritage.

Providing Clerical Services

Media center personnel, working closely with the teacher, prepare multi copies of reading lists to be distributed to students.   Lists are graded and categorized by type.   Special lists can be prepared that are of high interest for the reluctant or slow reader.   These are usually annotated.

Compiling an annotated bibliography of publications in the professional library can be a real service to teachers and administrators if the collection is not too large.

There are many ways, if time and personnel permit, to perform clerical services.

Producing Simple Teaching Materials

Valuable learning media is sometimes a simple object produced by a teacher and/or student to meet a specific need. Common examples are models, handmade slides, posters, and tape recordings.   Basic materials for the production of these materials should be housed in the media center.   Production services are provided as needed to duplicate materials, to prepare transparencies, laminate pictures, or make recordings.

Assisting with Instructional Equipment

The purchase, maintenance, and use of AV hardware is administered through the media center.   All media equipment is inventoried in the center's records whether or not it is housed there.   Some items are distributed to classrooms for an extended period of time.

Training and organizing interested students in the operation of this equipment is usually the function of the media specialist with the assistance of interested teachers. Effective scheduling, correct operation, and proper maintenance assure the maximum good use of such equipment.

The key role of the media center to the school is one of service.

Part VI:

INSTRUCTIONAL DEVELOPMENT IN
THE CURRICULUM

THE ROLE OF THE LIBRARY MEDIA SPECIALIST
IN THE INSTRUCTIONAL PROGRAM*

Johanna S. Wood

Instructional development is a term that is being used increasingly in elementary and secondary public school education. Certainly, the term and the process itself are not new. The literature in the area of educational technology is replete with references to the instructional development process. These references provide us with a variety of definitions of the process. However, for our purposes, let us define instructional development as a systematic, data-based process for designing, developing, implementing, evaluating, and revising instruction. Three key characteristics of the process are it is learner-focused, data-based, and systematic in approach.

In instructional development, the basic questions are the same as those faced in the development of curriculum. These questions remain the critical ones:

1. What is to be taught to learners?
2. How will it be presented to learners?
3. How are learners to be evaluated?

The instructional development process coordinates and combines four basic elements in a highly organized way to create an instructional systems approach. These elements are:

1. The instructional objectives which express in specific

*Reprinted by permission of the author and the Maryland State Dept. of Education from a paper presented Feb. 1977 at the School Administrators and Library Media Personnel Conference, School Media Services Office, Maryland State Dept. of Education.

terms what the learner will be able to do at the end
of the learning sequence/instructional unit;

2. The instructional strategies which specify the activities
the learner will engage in to achieve the objectives
and which employ a variety of learning modes in order
to accommodate differences in learning styles of students;

3. Evaluation (assessment) which measures the degree to
which the objectives have been achieved; and

4. Revision of the instructional program based on the data
derived through the valuation process.

When we take a close look at these four elements, we
see that the instructional objectives represent the desired or
intended outcomes of instruction while student performance
and student achievement represent the actual outcomes of instruction. The second element, the instructional strategies,
provides the ways students can learn whatever it is that they
are expected to learn. Evaluation, the third element, is
used to determine whether or not there is a gap between the
intended outcomes and the actual outcomes--as well as the
extent of the gap if it does exist. Revision, the fourth element, continues in the instructional development process until the stated objectives are achieved.

One of the effects of utilizing the instructional development process is that it helps us to measure at the classroom level, the building level, and at the system level the
degree to which our programs are effective or ineffective.
Data collection for this reason is an important part of the instructional development process. However, we can reason
that the smaller the gap between intended and actual outcomes, the more effective is the instructional program. Conversely, we can reason that the larger the gap between intended outcomes and actual outcomes, the more ineffective is
the instructional program.

Another effect of utilizing the instructional development
process is that it brings about changes in roles. For example, the traditional role of the teacher that we all know is
that of "knowledge-dispenser" and "information-teller." However, in the instructional development process, the teacher
becomes a classroom manager and a learning facilitator who
carefully structures the learning environment to guide students
toward the achievement of objectives. This is done through
the development of carefully-planned learning activities which
use various media and which relate very directly to the instructional objectives.

Certainly, the pertinent questions that we must address here are those that relate to our roles as librarians. Is there a place for the school librarian in the concept of instructional development? Does it necessitate a role change for the school librarian? Is there a new role for media? What is the place of media in instructional development? What is the function of the media program within the context of the instructional development process?

A simple, direct answer is "yes, there is an important role for the school librarian, for media, and for the media program in the process." However, its use, as with the utilization of many other newer approaches to learning and teaching, is bringing about great changes to the traditional school library. Instructional development requires an increased use of media for instructional purposes. However, the term "increased use" does not convey the full meaning, for in the concept of instructional development, the media carry the content and, thereby, become the transmitters of information and the instruments of learning. In other words, media are central to the concept.

As a direct result of the newer approaches to learning, school libraries are being transformed across this country into library media centers in which library and audiovisual materials are fused into unified media programs. The traditional school librarian is disappearing quickly and is being replaced by a newer model who carries the title "library media specialist."

Who are these library media specialists? First, they are full members of the instructional team who work in partnership with teachers to help students achieve instructional objectives. Moreover, they are persons who possess competencies in media design, development, and evaluation.

Now, let us identify the potential contributions of school library media specialists to the instructional program at each stage of the instructional development process.

Stage I--Setting Instructional Objectives
Stage II--Constructing Learning Activities
Stage III--Evaluating the Outcomes of Instruction
Stage IV--Revising the Instructional Program

Setting Instructional Objectives. This is the planning stage. Not only do library media specialists work with the team to determine appropriate objectives through the assessment of student needs, but they can also help identify the learning styles of students. They can purchase or locate materials which are appropriate to varied curriculum needs and student needs. When library media specialists are involved at the planning stage there is greater assurance that varied media will be fully integrated into the learning sequence and the instructional program.

Constructing Learning Activities. It is just as important that library media specialists be involved in determining the instructional strategies that are to be employed to help students attain the objectives. Planning conferences with teachers is necessary in designing the instructional strategies which utilize media. The library media specialists can help to determine what kinds of media are best suited for specific instructional strategies. Additionally, library media specialists can assist teachers in the production of media such as transparencies, learning activity packages, mediated instructional modules, films, filmstrips, and slide-tape presentations.

Evaluating the Outcomes of Instruction. In the instructional development process, evaluation is ongoing. It is important that the evaluation plan be in performance agreement with the instructional objectives. Library media specialists can help gather data and analyze feedback about student progress through the use of such methods as testing, observation, and interaction with students. Testing is an essential element in the instructional development process. It is obvious why this is so. The performance tests administered to students provide the data needed by the instructional team or the classroom teacher to determine if the individual learners have achieved the objectives.

Revising the Instructional Program. If the objectives have not been achieved by learners, then the teacher's role is to route new learning paths by identifying alternative strategies and media that the learners can utilize. This becomes the feedback loop that provides for the revision of the instructional plan if the learners have not achieved the objectives. The school library media specialist can assist in the identification of alternative learning paths and media.

A critical question is "how can administrators and teachers help the library media program become the vital force that it should be in the instructional program?" The attitudes and actions of building principals are key factors here. As the instructional leaders of their schools they can:

1. Bring teachers and library media specialist together in planning groups;
2. Support adequate budgets for their library media centers so that the needed materials in varied formats will be available in the school;
3. Seek to provide clerical and technical assistance for the library media specialist, with a realization and an understanding that with support personnel as a part of the media team, students and teachers will have greater access to the professional services of the library media specialist for instructional development activities;
4. Encourage the library media specialist to conduct inservice workshops for teachers on newer techniques of media utilization for more effective presentations of content matter;
5. Utilize the planning expertise of media specialists in preparing programs for parents and community groups;
6. Give active, visible support to the library media specialist and the media program by participating in media program activities.

Teachers, also, can help the library media center fulfill its potential as an instructional force within the school. It is important that they perceive library media specialists as instructional personnel and as vital members of the instructional development team. When teachers have this perception, they involve the library media specialist in planning the instructional objectives, in designing the instructional strategies, in evaluating the instructional outcomes, and in revising the instructional design, wherever necessary.

Finally, it is imperative that librarians, as media specialists, view their roles in an instructional context as they go about their tasks of selecting, acquiring, organizing, coordinating, retrieving, designing, evaluating, and revising media.

Today's library media specialists see themselves as instructional leaders, as educators, and as vital members of the instructional development team.

INSTRUCTIONAL DEVELOPMENT IN MEDIA PROGRAMS*

Janet Sullivan

What is instructional development and what does it have to do with media specialists?

Instructional development involves solving an instructional problem by utilizing all available resources in designing a program to accomplish stated objectives. The process of instructional development, adapted from models which have been successfully used in business, industry, and government, is a process which has received considerable attention in professional journals. The process should be visible in the daily activities of school media specialists.

By exercising the process of instructional development, library media specialists can demonstrate that important link between media and curriculum, between media and learning, between media center services and classrooms, and between media specialists' expertise and teachers' needs.

Most media programs offer a variety of services to teachers and students. For some media specialists, adding instructional development procedures to the library media program may require updating of their skills through independent study, workshops, or courses offered at summer sessions. Media specialists are in a position to encourage innovative teaching and learning practices. They possess a unique knowledge of curriculum, available materials, and learning theory to provide an invaluable service to teachers. However, because their role in the process of instructional development is relatively new, teachers are often unaware that this type of service is part of the media specialist's

*Reprinted by permission of author and publisher from School Library Journal, vol. 25, p. 24, April 1979. © R. R. Bowker Co. /A Xerox Corporation.

teaching strategy. Therefore, media specialists must initiate activities that involve their capabilities as integral components of the educational program.

The concept of instructional development has been endorsed by the American Library Association and the Association for Educational Communications and Technology (ALA and AECT). The process of instructional development has been defined in articles and books, yet the widespread implementation of instructional development is not a reality. The problem may be found in the following imaginary conversation.

> Query: "What instructional development model do you find most effective?"
> Reply: "I don't use any instructional development model. I'm a media specialist in a public school."
> Query: "Certainly you must have some means for attacking learning problems."
> Reply: "Sure, I provide resource lists and suggest alternative approaches of instruction, but what does that have to do with instructional development?"

Perhaps resource lists and suggestions for alternate approaches to instruction have everything to do with instructional development--perhaps nothing. Media specialists at the in-service and pre-service levels of education have not established a formalized approach to the application of instructional development. And yet, when a teacher voices a concern over a student's inability to learn, the media specialist quickly provides resource lists and suggests learning alternatives. Media specialist/teacher consultations are common occurrences. Aren't these consultations, in essence, the beginning of the process of instructional development? For example, see Figure 1.

Although this example of planning is generally informal in nature and may never be evaluated, revised, or documented for further use, it parallels the instructional development process.

Instructional development in public schools is, at best, at a rudimentary level of development. However, the potential for a more formalized, more effective approach does exist. Whether resource lists and suggestions for alternate approaches have everything to do with instructional develop-

Figure 1.

A teacher voices concern . . .

about a student's ability
to learn . . .

certain specified content.

The media specialist sug-
gests resources and alternatives . . .

which the teacher utilizes
with the student . . .

to see if the student then
can learn the content.

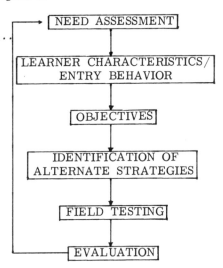

ment or nothing to do with instructional development depends
on the support and understanding each media specialist develops with administration and staff. An informal consultation with a teacher, if taken to a formal level, is only the
first step--not necessarily a large step. It may be as
simple as sitting down with the teacher and, using the more
formal headings listed on the flow chart, documenting the
process of instructional development. By formalizing and
identifying the steps, the media specialist provides the teacher with an understanding of the complete process to the solution of an educational problem not just resource lists and
alternative approaches. Schools, professional organizations
can heighten an awareness of instructional development
through their publications and through continuing education efforts. Colleges and universities are now beginning to include training in instructional development specifying the role
of media specialists in this process in their pre-service education programs.

When the process and application of instructional development is more fully understood by educators, media specialists who are in positions to provide leadership will be
making a more meaningful contribution to the education of
all students.

THE LIBRARIAN AND INSTRUCTIONAL PROGRAMS*

Kevin J. Swick, Frances Carr, and
R. Kim Driggers

Too often the elementary school librarian is considered to be a "keeper of the books." Yet in our ever changing educational and social world, the librarian like all educators, has taken on new roles and new challenges. No longer does he or she sit behind the library desk watching the children read or quietly sit by while children do not become involved in the instructional center. For the library, the resource center, or the learning center are the hub of the school today. The librarian, the instructional resource person, media specialists, or learning center coordinator play varied and significant roles in the instructional program.

The librarian is a coordinator of materials, a resource person, an information disseminator, a teacher, and a consultant to all involved in the learning process in and out of school. Let us examine some of the roles the librarian performs in today's elementary school setting.

A Coordinator of Materials. Vital to the effective implementation of any instructional program is the coordination, organization, and use of the learning materials that support the educational process. This is not "keeping the books" but pulling together available materials for their maximum use in and out of the classroom. For example, the librarian can organize reference and resource materials to complement a unit of study being conducted in the classroom, and when needed, the librarian can implement new materials so as to enrich the unit of study. In the same respects, it is the librarian who acquires new materials or

*Reprinted from Reading Improvement, vol. 12, pp. 32-33, Spring 1975, by permission of the authors and publisher, Project Innovation.

loans these materials so they can be integrated into learning units and modules. The classroom teacher's instructional program is made more meaningful via this coordination.

A Resource Person. To whom do you go (or to whom should you be going) for making your teaching units or class assignments contain the kind and quality of information necessary for meeting excellence in learning? Who can help your children develop adequate library skills such as learning how to use the dictionary or how to select useful reference materials? Of course, it should be the librarian. Beyond providing assistance and resources in the library, the librarian can be an effective in-class resource person. He/she can tutor children, teach children to tutor each other, listen to teacher needs, and help the teacher acquire and organize their learning environments. For who better knows the available materials, media, and resources to help you make your learning setting an exciting and worthwhile place than the librarian.

An Information Disseminator. Without current and relevant information the classroom teacher will do a less than adequate teaching job. Yet, the classroom teacher, the curriculum coordinator, the school principal, and parents do not always have the time to preview, critically judge, and select the kind and quality of information they need at hand. The librarian makes delicate decisions in selecting and disseminating information to meet the educational needs of the school. In addition, the librarian can contact resource people in your community to visit the classroom and enhance your unit of study. He/she can send you materials after they have been previewed for use in your instructional program. Indeed your best friend in keeping abreast of current materials is the school librarian.

A Teacher. No teacher can teach everything! A good example of this is the teaching of library skills. Every teacher would like to do this job adequately but may not have been trained to do it. Your librarian has been trained (or should have been) in these skills, uses them daily, and can teach them in a relevant and enjoyable way to young children. In the same respects your librarian is probably looking for the chance to work with small groups of children in story time or to share with them some new films, games, books, or interest activities. And of course you have always wanted more peer learning in your instructional program. Now you have the chance, ask your librarian if the both of you can team on developing a tutorial program which can be housed in the library. You see the librarian is a teacher too!

A Consultant. Above all the school librarian is a consultant who holds new worlds for the teacher, the child, the parent, and the community. He/she can keep the community abreast of new reading materials and worthwhile learning activities for home use. He/she can (if relevant to the times) initiate a school-community library program where shared use of materials enriches both libraries. Or, he/she can develop programs such as mother aides for providing more individual attention in the classroom and library which is so related to the child's success in school.

Summary. Let us move beyond complaining, talking, wishing that our library and librarian were more involved in the educational setting. Take a look at your instructional program and if you have not begun, start now to integrate the librarian and the library into the overall curriculum.

Part VII:

DIFFERENT SCHOOL SYSTEMS' NEEDS
IN CURRICULUM DEVELOPMENT

HOW ELEMENTARY SCHOOL TEACHERS AND LIBRARIANS COOPERATE IN INSTRUCTION*

Mary Lathrope and Margaret Dees

"There goes our book keeper!" said a primary child as one of our librarians got into her car which was parked by the school playground. It took a few seconds for the librarian to realize who was the "book keeper." We have come a long way since the president of Harvard asked the librarian how things were going in the library and received the answer: "Just fine. There are only two books out and I'm on my way to get one of them right now."

In Urbana elementary schools, most of the librarian's time is spent in teaching. With the help of the librarian, children learn how the library is organized and how to use the card catalog. Even elementary school children become accustomed to using the Abridged Readers' Guide and the National Geographic Index. They learn how to use encyclopedias, dictionaries, almanacs, and atlases more effectively.

Teachers know that they cannot possibly give children all the knowledge that they will need. They can teach children how to find out and give them a zest for learning.

If the school has a rich storehouse of materials in a centralized library, children will enjoy a wealth of superb children's books, both fiction and nonfiction, beautifully illustrated and covering almost any subject, some as timely as masers and lasers. The availability of all kinds of audiovisual materials, such as films, filmstrips, records, transparencies, charts, maps, and models, is also a necessity.

*Reprinted from Illinois Libraries, vol. 48, pp. 285-91, April 1966, by permission of the authors and publisher, the Illinois State Library.

It is impossible for busy classroom teachers to keep up with the job of selecting the best of these materials so the role of the school librarian in this area is vital. However, this is an important field of cooperation for teachers and librarians with teachers contributing their suggestions of materials to purchase and informing the librarian of their needs. Occasionally, a book that is not especially outstanding in itself becomes the springboard to an exciting adventure in learning in the hands of a creative teacher.

A few of the activities that were found to be worthwhile and which capitalized on the usefulness of the library in our elementary schools will be described in this article. We do not claim that these ideas are original with us; they are ways in which the librarian and teacher worked together successfully in using the resources of the library for instruction.

Important occasions in the school year are celebrated by inviting students from the Storytelling class at the University of Illinois to tell stories in our schools. A schedule is set up for Book Week, Christmas and National Library Week each year. The university students and their teacher go from school to school putting on a program of stories for a class, several classes or even half of a small school assembled together. Occasionally, teachers request storytelling for a special unit, such as some of the Greek myths when a sixth grade is studying ancient Greece.

When fourth graders have been reading folktales as part of their library activities, we have invited the Campus Folk Song Club to send representatives to visit the classes and sing some of the old folk songs. One of the young men who came last year was interested in all kinds of folklore, including the chants and phrases children use in their games. The children ended up giving their kind of folklore to him, and were amazed to discover that they were a part of the transmittal of a folk heritage. In one school where the folk singers appeared, a child who had probably never been singled out for any distinction before sang the ballad of John Henry with a high sweet voice to the accompaniment of the guitar and the applause of the whole school.

In addition to the storytellers and folksingers, local authors enrich the experience of our children. During Book Week this year, Mrs. James Ayars (Rebecca Caudill) visited with all third and fourth graders at one school. All of the

children had prepared for this visit by reading some of the
books for their age group.   Many had read all of them.
They were full of questions about her life on the mountains
and so immersed in Mrs. Ayars' childhood family life that
one felt that they had almost lived it.   One class learned in
music class the ballad "Barb'ra Allen" mentioned by Mrs.
Ayars in one of her books, and sang it to her for a surprise.
Other local authors such as Natalia Belting, James Ayars,
Sidney Rosen, Larry Kettlekamp, and Ruth Painter Randall
have participated in the library program in Urbana schools.

Some fourth graders are going to be reading poetry
in the library just before Christmas.   This will turn into a
Christmas poetry reading time and the language arts teacher
plans to have them write Christmas poems in class.

After the librarian had read poetry to a second grade,
the children listened to John Ciardi reading his poetry in the
record "I Met a Man."   When the children returned to their
room, they produced the following poem and sent it to the
librarian:

The Write Man

> There was a man so skinny and thin
> He had a face made out of tin.
> He had a rubber-colored hat
> Now what do you think of that?
> His biggest size he'll never stay
> For he grows shorter every day
> His wooden body ends in a sharp foot
> That grows again after it goes
>   KA-PUT!

A fourth grade class seemed to enjoy discussion of
books of fantasy in the library.   These children were tre-
mendously enthusiastic about such books as A Wrinkle in
Time, Time at the Top, The Teaspoon Tree, and C. S.
Lewis' Narnia tales.   We decided to call this project "The
Possible Impossible," and each book was evaluated in terms
of whether this book was "The Possible Impossible" or "The
Impossible Possible."   The children were delighted to play
with these terms, and the teacher carried out the project in
their language arts period by having them do creative writing
in "The Possible Impossible."   By the time we were finished
all the children had read a great many of the finest fiction
books in the library.

For several years, a sixth grade teacher has had her class make a rather ambitious book on the Middle East. After introductory lessons on how to do library research, how to make bibliographies and use the Abridged Readers' Guide, the librarian reviews the different parts of the book and sets up committees to be responsible for various parts, such as the title page, table of contents, glossary, and index. The librarian always ends up on the acknowledgments page.

In addition to the storytellers, folk singers, and authors, other talented individuals in the community have been drawn into the educational program in one elementary school where the librarian has developed a Human Resources File. This is a listing on three by five cards by subject of people who are willing to contribute their time to share hobbies, vocational specialties, travel experiences, and other interests with the children. Parents are asked at the open house held in the beginning of the year to list subjects which they are interested in sharing or to suggest names of other experts in a certain field.

By consulting this file, teachers can secure the services of a mother who has lived in Thailand for several years and who can come in to show slides, lecture on life in the country, and supply magnificent exhibit items. The file provides access to experts in the fields of architecture, city planning, homes around the world, printing, the textile industry, Vietnam, and even four different geologists. Some children come in and sign up their own parents, who generally acquiesce gracefully.

One elementary school owns nine filmstrip previewers that are used by pupils as sources of information as readily as they consult reference books, the vertical file, pamphlets, and magazine indexes. In one library, where there was only one previewer, the librarian had to leave numbered cards by the previewer the way that supermarkets do so that children can know when their time has come to use it. This has prevented a long line of children from wasting their time lining up behind the child using the previewer. Fortunately, four more previewers have now arrived which may be checked out to classrooms. Each school library owns a small number of filmstrips and in the District Curriculum Library, there are 1,670 filmstrips available to the children and teachers. Daily mail service makes it possible for a teacher to call the Curriculum Library in the morning and have her materials at the school before noon. As soon as a full-time librarian is provided in each elementary school library, the district's filmstrip collection will be decentralized.

After the children preview a filmstrip, they decide if parts or all of it would be useful and when the time comes to present their reports to the class, they project the filmstrip with their own comments. Some teachers encourage children to use films in the same way. After previewing the film, the children prepare an introduction for the film, alerting their classmates to look for important aspects of the topic being studied, and then make a list of follow-up questions to stimulate discussion.

Teachers are becoming quite ingenious in making book reports more palatable. After the librarian has given a book talk, the children will give their own book talks, attempting to describe the book so attractively that other readers will want to read it. The children always enjoy taping their book talks for future study and enjoyment. Ways of Reporting on Books Read is the title of a list of suggestions given to the teachers by the librarians.

A reading record in the library is a simple device to learn how much and what the child reads. Especially for the reluctant reader, this works well. Each child writes down the title of a book when he finishes reading one. At the end of the year, these are sent to the room teacher who may give them to the children. The children seem very interested in having these lists of books they have read during the year; however, they could become a part of the child's cumulative folder. For those children who read two hundred books or more in a year this seems to lack the value that it has for the less avid reader. Volume usually insures a catholic selection and a mere suggestion by the librarian of a book that might interest a reader like this is enough to sell a new title, author, or subject. For those who do not find much that they can read and enjoy, the reading record is a source of useful information for the librarian and teacher. All that is needed is a box and a stack of five by eight cards.

Another cooperative effort involved a sixth grade class where the teacher was interested in the linguistic approach to the children's writing activities, and the librarian was hoping to teach the children to write book annotations. The children read annotations of various kinds in The Horn Book, the Bulletin of the Center for Children's Books, Wilson cards, the blurb on the jacket, New York Times, Chicago Tribune, Children's Catalog, and even The Saturday Review of Literature. The librarian encouraged the children to do critical thinking about the book, as well as to use the correct bibliographic form they had learned, while their teacher watched for use of fresh, unhackneyed words. They were to be "word watchers." The results were put on a transparency so that the children could criticize their own annotations.

This class, also when studying Europe in social studies, read books selected by the librarian that had been translated from the language of the country they were studying. In the library, the children discussed such questions as whether or not the book read helped them understand the country or the people, if it differed from books written for American children in theme or subject matter, or if they noticed any peculiarities in the translation.

A project on "Understanding Others Through Books" was planned by the teacher and librarian in cooperation for a class that was intellectually gifted, but socially at odds with each other. They had great difficulty in working cooperatively together and it was the hope of librarian and teacher that reading and discussing books about other children with problems would help develop their sensitivity to others.

We started by having the librarian read Eleanor Estes' short book, The Hundred Dresses, which has the theme of the left-out child. In addition to the little Polish girl who is not included in the group, there is the girl who makes fun of her and the best friend who is uncomfortable about the tormenting, but is too insecure about her own position to speak out. This gave us an opportunity for much discussion and gave us a point of reference for the whole project in which we said we were trying "to get underneath someone else's skin."

The children were given copies of the questions we wished to consider in relation to the collection of books which was selected by the librarian and placed in the classroom for easy access.

The librarian prepared a card for each book with an annotation on it, enabling the teacher who did not have time to read all the books to have some idea of the pertinent ideas involved.

The children reacted with enthusiasm and a great deal of seriousness to the project. With both teacher and librarian interposing questions and comments, themes covered included the problems of the child who is not accepted, minority groups, courage, growing up, identification with parents, understanding the other side in wars, and discovering one's own identity. For the most part, one topic ran into another as different books were introduced. The children reacted in a most natural manner, coming in with comments like, "Well, I read a book like that, but in this book, they--. " Even in the summing up, they were still coming in with comments from books they had read and which we had not been able to cover.

One of the difficulties encountered was that the children were so carried away sometimes by their feelings about the books that they occasionally mentioned or tried to mention actual children in the class that fell into some of these categories. The most devastating comment was from a girl who, filled with great brotherly love, declaimed (before we could stop her)--"A lot of the children in this class don't like _____, but I do!" This does not show that they really were incorporating these ideas into their day-to-day experiences, but being a very verbal group were unable to be discreet about it. Before attempting such a project again, we will have to do more preparation in this area.

There is no way to evaluate the success of this effort. We hope that it increased the children's sensitivity to each other. The children did read a great many books that they would not have ordinarily read and their own evaluation was that the books they had read were excellent. As this was incorporated in their language arts period, all their reading was done in library books rather than in a reading textbook, which was much more challenging for these children.

We taped the last two sessions of the class. The tape is technically very poor, but does give some of the feeling of the discussion. We played it this year for these children as sixth graders and they criticized their discussions. To the librarians' amazement, the children were still interrupting the tape with ideas and points that they felt they still needed to make. We can only infer that they found the discussion stimulative.

Another activity, which requires the interest and cooperation of a teacher and a librarian is the Read-a-Story project. Intermediate grade pupils who are good oral readers are assigned to a primary grade to read to the children at a specified time each week. The middle-grades child is responsible for getting a suitable story to read, practicing reading it until he can do a good job, and then going to his assigned primary room at a particular time each week. This provides a real audience situation for the older child who is interested in oral reading, the children enjoy their contact with "one of the big kids," and the teacher has an opportunity to observe her own pupils without being personally involved for a few minutes.

The librarian is not only involved with the children and teachers in cooperative projects. In Urbana, because our evolving elementary school library program cannot as yet hire enough clerks, we utilize the interest and time of hundreds of parent volunteers. Each P. T. A. has a library chairman. This is, according to one principal, the most important office in the local P. T. A. This parent is responsible for scheduling a mother helper in the library at all times. In large schools, each parent serves the school in this way one half day a month. In small schools, the mother may work a half day each week. Mothers (and a few fathers) feel an involvement that they did not feel before in the school's program, children feel that they belong more surely when mother is helping in the library, and the library parents are some of our most enthusiastic supporters for more librarians and larger budgets.

In a second grade class, the librarian read Sesyle Joslin's What Do You Say, Dear? and the teacher and children followed this reading with creative art and writing activity inspired by the book. The teacher discussed with the pupil the idea that the situations presented should make it possible for both characters to show good manners. Typical stories that were dictated to the teacher in the Joslin style included the following:

> You are out enjoying your regular Saturday afternoon hippopotamus ride when you come to a big mud hole. "Let's jump in and take a cool bath," suggests your friendly hippo. What do you say, Dear?
>   Answer: "I'm sorry to disappoint you, Sir, but I just bathed a few minutes ago."

> When you get home from school one day, you hurry to the kitchen to greet Mother and get a snack. When you get to the kitchen, you are surprised to see a dinosaur instead of Mother. It is cooking

noodle soup for your supper and says Mother has
gone on a vacation. It asks, "Will you please
set the table for me?"
What do you say, Dear?
Answer: "Yes, I will. My, that soup smells
delicious. "

The children illustrated these stories and then put
their stories and pictures into a book with a title page.
(Project from Leal School, Alvera Knox, librarian; Susie
Hayes, teacher.)

As a member of the teaching team, the librarian
works closely with teachers in planning the intermediate program. She conducts classes once a week as a member of the
team. Library instruction given during these periods is integrated with homeroom activities. For a class studying ex-
plorers and needing practice in using the encyclopedia, the
librarian prepared a series of questions on this subject and
the results were taken back to their social studies teacher.

It is almost impossible to say when a library activity
becomes a class activity and when a class activity spills into the library. We do know that a stimulating teacher, a
class full of curious and eager children, and a librarian with
all the resources of a modern school library find each other
and learn.

PEOPLE--THE INGREDIENT WHICH FORGES THE DYNAMIC RELATIONSHIP BETWEEN MEDIA CENTER AND SCHOOL*

Martha S. Angevine, Marion A. Bond,
Charles F. Christensen, and Richard J. McKay

Abstract

   The article discusses the process by which a school's
media center becomes a vital part of its instructional programs. Faculty involvement is the key. The model is a
new media center at the Junior High School East in Arlington, Massachusetts, created as part of an extensive renova-
tion and building project in 1964. The efforts of this school's
media specialists to assess the needs of the teaching staff
and to maintain a professional dialogue with them are traced
through the center's planning stages and first year of operation. The organization of the East's teaching faculty into
interdisciplinary teams called clusters is shown to aid this
process. Concrete suggestions on how to develop lively communication and directions for the future are offered.

   Books and boxes, scattered software, shelving in
   disarray, open space, bright colors, new furniture.
   How to convert a one-time auditorium into a new
   media center?

   It was January, 1975. Junior High School East
   in Arlington, Massachusetts, was returning to its
   newly renovated and expanded building. Some four
   hundred and fifty seventh and eighth grade students
   were wondering what the staff of forty, including

*Reprinted by permission of the authors and publisher from
International Journal of Instructional Media, vol. 3, pp. 237-
42, 1975-76. © 1976, Baywood Publishing Co.

two media specialists, had in store for them. The task was to make the new media center an integral part of the learning process for these students.

Item: The physical education teacher is concerned about accommodating students who lack athletic skills; he also needs space for rainy day activities. He works with media specialists to develop and teach a media production unit through which students demonstrate visually the principles of the techniques they cannot physically perform.

Item: An art teacher, invited to drop by the center to see new materials, learns about the football unit and is encouraged to try a similar approach with her classes. She decides to have her students work in the media center on assignments dealing with heraldry and astrology, taking advantage of materials and production facilities. Results will be displayed in the center.

Item: A student with a reading disability is engrossed with audio visual hardware. His interest leads him to the center, where he reads manuals and writes appropriate information on inventory cards, erasing his efforts several times until he is satisfied that they are neat and legible. Media specialists work with his teachers to direct his activities in the center toward skills he needs to acquire.

In these examples communication between people is key to developing the vital function of the media center in the learning patterns at Junior High School East. There is a dynamic interaction in which teachers and media specialists, each expert in their own field, respect, listen to and learn from each other. The media specialists involve faculty members in the decision making process regarding center use. Each is excited by the other's ideas. A quantum leap in problem solving and the development of practical teaching techniques results as each suggestion leads to another. Isolation between staff members is replaced by the excitement generated from team effort.

How to foster such interaction is the pivotal question educators, particularly media specialists and administrators, should be asking. At the East several factors contribute to the process.

Planning and Early Involvement

When it was determined that the Junior High School East would undergo a major building program to update and expand its facilities, a media center was primary in the thinking of the central administration. Planning involved the administration and teaching staff with the architects and Permanent Town Building Committee. The new center was envisioned as a germinal resource area supporting and enriching the various instructional programs in the school. What had been a traditional library occupying a space of 750 square feet was to become a true media center housing both print and non-print materials. The new center would encompass 4,500 square feet. Storage and circulation facilities for hardware and commercially produced software, as well as expanded space for the growing collection of print materials, were included. In addition, equipment and space for producing audio visual materials, a photographic darkroom, and recording and previewing rooms were incorporated into the planning.

Several instructional programs were actually located in the center. The learning disabilities and reading specialists would teach there, which would allow easy access to the wealth of center materials. Foreign language classes and tutorial sessions would meet there for similar reasons. The location of these teachers in the center would encourage an interchange of ideas between themselves and the media specialists and would draw other faculty members to the center. Their programs would bring most of the school population to the center on a regular basis.

During the disruption caused by the building project, the East's staff and students were temporarily housed at the High School on a split session basis. The East faculty formed itself into four working committees in anticipation of the completion of the building project and the new learning spaces to which they would return. These committees explored the instructional possibilities inherent in the new facility. The largest of these was the media center committee which involved teachers from a variety of disciplines. The goals and directions identified by this group developed enthusiasm and set the tone for the early use of the center. Increased production and use of multi-media materials were evident even during split sessions. So successful was that period of planning that the notes from those committee meetings are still used in developing budgets and in assessing faculty needs and expectations.

The Cluster Concept

Concurrent with the planning and implementation of the building project, administrators and consultants were developing a new organizational pattern for the East's teaching staff. Teachers were closely involved in this planning process which resulted in the formation of "clusters." Clusters would group together in a specific learning space one hundred students and four teaching specialists from the areas of English, Mathematics, Science, and Social Studies.

The cluster system returns to teachers the responsibility of structuring the learning programs for their students. The cluster teachers together determine approaches to scheduling, grouping of students, curriculum content, and methods of dealing with special needs students in the classroom. Working in interdisciplinary teams counteracts the isolation felt by many teachers who are otherwise confined to four walls and a departmental structure, or who are not involved in the decisions which affect their teaching. The team provides a basis for consistent communication and supportive interpersonal involvement. [1]

Cluster teachers are provided with joint planning time on a regular basis. Sessions may include teachers from other curriculum areas such as art and music, or media specialists, who might support and enrich the learning activities developed by the cluster team. Media specialists attend cluster meetings to learn from teaching specialists their curriculum directions. The media staff brings to the meetings ideas from other teachers, suggestions regarding materials to implement curriculum ideas, techniques concerning the use of these materials, and knowledge about the availability of space and equipment. By working with the cluster teams throughout the school, the media specialists gain on-going knowledge of the school's curriculum direction and keep the center's services responsive to the current needs of teachers.

Throughout the early planning stages with the architects and in the discussions of the faculty media center committee, the goal was to make the East's new center an integral part of its instructional programs. Concurrently, the organization of the East faculty on the cluster concept helped reinforce the communication between the media center and other learning areas necessary to reach this goal. In order to maintain the momentum generated by these early efforts, concerns focused on faculty involvement in charting the direction of the center during the first year.

Impact: The First Year

Upon their return to the renovated school members of the faculty were excited about using media-oriented activities in their teaching. Specifically, the center was a valuable aid to the techniques of individualized instruction and an inquiry approach. Thus, the teachers needed the center, and several were not shy about saying so. That was good. Center use was increased; media specialists became less defensive about their "empire," more open to change and suggestions.

After four months in the new school, the principal requested faculty members to complete a confidential questionnaire which provided insights into the needs and expectations of the center. Media specialists and the principal analyzed faculty responses to the questionnaire during a summer workshop, and used them as a basis for discussion with the faculty.

During the first week of school in September, two workshops were held in the media center, each lasting two and one-half hours. These were devoted to an intensive assessment of needs with the faculty. Attempts were made to identify objectives for the media center, the services it should offer to accommodate a variety of teaching styles, the use of center space, its environmental quality, and role definitions of media specialists. In short, the faculty was directly involved in decisions concerning the best use of the new center.

On an early release day later in September, media specialists arranged a multimedia exhibit for the faculty. Software and print materials were categorized by subject and displayed throughout the center, so that teachers could incorporate them into their planning for the year. Appropriate machines were available for listening and viewing. A teacher-produced video tape was played to demonstrate the potential of this medium. An art teacher made signs to designate the various categories, and a group of students under the direction of the foods instructor, provided refreshments.

At the exhibit a blueprint of the center was displayed showing the rearrangement of space and the environmental changes that had been made as a result of faculty suggestions at the earlier workshops. The blueprint also illustrated projected changes to meet the faculty's expressed needs for use of the center. Both the workshops and the exhibit could not have happened without vigorous administrative support.

Media specialists are members of such groups in the school as the Faculty Council and the Language Arts Study Committee. These groups are other important sources of information regarding faculty expectations of the center; they also provide an opportunity for educating the faculty to the center's potential. Materials selection is another vehicle for interaction between the media center staff and the faculty. The center budget must be defended to the administration in terms of the teaching program. Materials are suggested and evaluated by faculty and media specialists against the criteria of appropriateness to curriculum and quality. Informally, media specialists have learned the following practices encourage communication:

> Get out of the center
> Take coffee breaks with teachers
> Stagger eating times in teachers' room
> Encourage invitations to observe classes
> Keep a pot of coffee in the media center
> Locate duplicating facilities there.

It is noteworthy that the principal's questionnaire, the exhibit, and the other avenues of communication involved all faculty members, not simply Social Studies and English teachers, who are traditional media center users.

Evaluation and Potential

Attempts to develop a media program that is based on faculty needs and to involve the faculty directly in decisions concerning center goals must be continuous. There are problems and frustrations. There is never enough time or money to provide ideal services. Equipment breaks down at crucial times, and there is never enough. Personalities grate, and there are communication breakdowns. Materials still have to be cataloged and processed. Energies are constantly divided between the program and the administration of the center. There is an immediate need to offer more training in uses and production of media to faculty and students. More interaction with teachers is desirable. Various subject areas could be highlighted with speakers and programs based on a community resource file. A two-year media curriculum could be developed. More cooperation with the public library, the immediate neighborhood, and nearby elementary schools would be beneficial. The use of computer terminals to strengthen individualized instruction should be considered.

In his preface to the Aims of Education, Alfred North Whitehead states his central theme as follows: "The students are alive, and the purpose of education is to stimulate and guide their self-development. It follows as a corollary from this premise, that the teachers also should be alive with living thoughts."[2] Our thesis is that media specialists not only have to be alive with living thoughts; they also have a unique opportunity to generate the exchange of these thoughts and to foster enthusiasm for teaching and learning.

References

1. R. J. McKay and A. Ansara, "The Cluster Organizational Pattern as a Model for Continuing Education for Professional Staff in Public Education," International Journal of Career and Continuing Education, I, January, 1976.
2. A. N. Whitehead, The Aims of Education and Other Essays, The Macmillan Company, New York, 1929.

Bibliography

American Association of School Librarians, ALA, and Association for Educational Communications and Technology, Media Programs District and School, American Library Association, Chicago, 1975; Association for Educational Communications and Technology, Washington, 1975.

Davies, R. A., The School Library Media Center; A Force for Educational Excellence, 2nd ed., R. R. Bowker Company, New York, 1974.

Gillespie, J. T. and Spirt, D. L., Creating a School Media Program, R. R. Bowker Company, New York, 1973.

Prostano, E. T. and Prostano, J. S., The School Library Media Center, Libraries Unlimited, Inc., Littleton, CO, 1971.

Wittich, W. A. and Schuller, C. F. Instructional Technology; Its Nature and Use, 5th ed., Harper & Row, New York, 1973.

<u>Direct reprint requests to:</u>

Richard J. McKay
Assistant Superintendent
Arlington Public Schools
Arlington, Massachusetts   02174

TEACHER UTILIZATION OF
INSTRUCTIONAL MEDIA CENTERS IN
SECONDARY SCHOOLS*

Harlan R. Johnson

In today's curricula, the focus is on the library media center, the instructional media center, the materials center, the educational materials center, the learning center, or the learning resource center. "Center" is the word that receives the emphasis. The media center is very much involved in the curriculum, and the importance of the teacher's utilization of it would seem to be without question.

The teacher needs to be involved in the media program, working with the media specialist and the students, promoting discussion, answering questions, and directly relating library skills to classroom activities. Whenever entire classes come to the media center, the teacher's presence is imperative. [1]

The importance of teacher use of the instructional media center is upheld in the study of El-Hagrasy in which he stated the hypothesis that there should be a measurable relationship between teachers' reading habits and library backgrounds and pupils' reading and library skills. He found the hypothesis acceptable. When the teachers' skills are high, the pupils' reading and library skills are high. The opposite is also true. [2] This author found nothing in recent professional literature to refute these findings.

Ways in Which Teachers Utilize the IMC

Teacher utilization of the instructional media center

*Reprinted from The Clearing House, vol. 51, pp. 117-20, Nov. 1977, by permission of the author and publisher, Heldref Publications.

is an important part of instruction in the secondary schools, and it encompasses the use teachers make of the materials, services, equipment, and facilities of the media center, whether they themselves use them or direct their students to use them either for study or for pleasure.

Many teachers use the services, materials, equipment, and facilities of the instructional media center every day in a variety of ways. They bring classes to the center to work on a specific assignment or involve them in independent exploration, and they work with classes in cooperation with the media specialist either in the media center or in the classroom, or perhaps in both. The teacher briefs the class before a visit to the media center so that the class enters with purpose. 3

A teacher may work individually with students who are in the media center, or he may be involved in some personal use of the facility, such as reference, research, pleasure reading, professional reading, previewing a film or filmstrip, listening to a recording, selecting materials to be used in a specific unit, or simply browsing.

Teachers are users of services as well as users of things. They involve themselves in the selection of materials, they use classroom collections of media center materials on loan for a particular unit, and they use bibliographies prepared in cooperation with the library staff. The offer from the media specialist to provide orientation in use of instructional materials and equipment to students and teachers is accepted. Teachers use media center equipment for the production of teaching materials, and they work with media specialists in developing curriculum units.

Although teachers use the instructional media center for these activities and more, media specialists are faced with the problem of non-use by some teachers and little use by others. Often only the teachers in certain departments or subject areas use the media center to a great extent and sometimes just a few teachers within a given subject area will avail themselves of what the center has to offer.

Services Which Teachers Expect from the Instructional Media Center

The media specialist provides teachers with whatever

services will aid in their teaching. [4]   He needs to know what
is happening in classrooms, [5] and, if media centers are ever
to be used, media specialists are going to have to abandon
the center long enough to get into the classroom. [6]

Only when teachers and media specialists cooperatively
plan a systematic program of learning will students begin to
feel success in library-related activities and ultimately approach the library with confidence. [7]

Expansion of service is one of the keys for teacher
utilization of the instructional media center.   As service is
expanded and new materials and equipment are acquired,
teachers must be made aware of what is available to them.
There must be communication between the media specialist
and every individual teacher in the school.   There needs to
be more than written communication; the media specialist
should strive to meet and to talk with every teacher and determine what he needs and expects through the media program of the school.

Teachers expect that media specialists will provide
such services as compiling bibliographies for individual teachers, delivering materials and equipment to the classroom,
presenting book talks and exhibits, distributing lists of recent acquisitions, working with teachers in developing curriculum units, routing materials selection aids to teachers,
holding library in-service programs, producing audiovisual
materials for teachers, and demonstrating how to use audiovisual materials and equipment.   The list could go on, but
the point to be made is that the media specialist has the responsibility to offer whatever services, materials, and equipment are feasible in relation to budget, staff, and desirability, and then communicate the availability of all services,
materials, and equipment to the individual teacher.

A random sample of secondary school teachers in one
large school district was asked, "What changes do you think
are necessary to further encourage your use of the library
or the use made by other teachers in the future?"   Teachers
of every subject area taught in the secondary schools of that
district were represented in the response, and here are some
of their suggestions: [8]

- Offer more audiovisual materials and equipment in the individual school libraries.
- Stop allowing students who are not interested in using it
  into the library.

- Offer more assistance to students sent to the library by teachers.
- Inform teachers about what services are available.
- Keep audiovisual equipment in working order, and check it before delivery to teachers.
- Establish decentralized learning labs.
- Provide more clerical help for the librarians.
- Provide more reference materials for specific subject areas.
- Prepare bibliographies in specific subject area.
- Make students and teachers feel welcome in the library.
- Take the librarian out of the role of disciplinarian.
- Establish closer informal communication between librarians and teachers.
- Provide audiovisual production services for teachers.
- Provide as much attention to the needs of other departments as is given to the needs of English and social studies.
- Let teachers know that the library staff is eager to help them.
- Establish personal contact between the library staff and new teachers in the fall.
- Provide in-service training for teachers to learn how to use audiovisual materials and equipment.
- Involve teachers more in the selection of library materials.
- Conduct training sessions to show teachers what the library has available for specific subjects and how the available items might be used.
- Present more book talks to classes.
- Provide the opportunity for teachers and librarians to work together in the classroom.
- Establish a professional library.
- Facilitate teacher and librarian cooperative development of course guides.
- Keep the library open longer hours.

Some of the above suggestions would be the responsibility of the media specialist, some would be the responsibility of school administrators, and some would involve joint responsibility; the media specialists, however, should be concerned with every one of them.

Even though the suggestions come from a particular school district, many of them can be applied universally. What do your own teachers want from the media program? Ask them.

The Role of the Media Specialist in Improving Services

Before considering steps to be taken to stimulate and to encourage teacher utilization of the media center, the media specialist needs to determine answers to the several questions that follow. Once he has examined answers to these questions, he is in a better position to determine his role in improving services.

1. Do teachers see any need to use the media center? It is a question that cannot often be answered in general terms. Individual contact with teachers is essential so that they may be shown how the media center relates specifically to the subjects they teach. For the home economics teacher, what specific materials are available which will facilitate and enrich the teaching of home economics? What particular services is the media specialist able to offer the industrial arts teacher to help him in his teaching? How can the media center provide growth in mathematics beyond the current use of the textbook? Each teacher in the school needs to see how the media program can help him individually, and the media specialist works toward that end on a continuing basis.

Few teachers possess the sophisticated media skills that media specialists have acquired through their professional training. [9] Because of this, in-service training should be offered by the media center staff on a continuing schedule throughout the school year. The American Association of School Librarians and the Association of Educational Communications and Technology include conducting orientation and in-service education in media for the school media staff and teachers as one of the responsibilities of the school media program. [10] From the general approach of in-service, the media specialist goes on to a more personal contact.

2. Are teachers aware of the services, materials, and equipment available to them? In-service training sessions provide a base for making teachers aware. Such practices as distributing lists of especially helpful materials and lists of recent acquisitions, setting aside displays of new materials, putting up bulletin boards, promoting the media center through faculty handbooks, distributing flyers describing services, concentrating on working with teachers all help to make teachers aware of the media program, but individual communication between teacher and media specialist remains the key to awareness.

3. Does the media center offer the services, materials, and equipment that the teachers really want and need? As many people in the school as possible should be involved in the selection process. 11 The media specialist involves the teacher in the selection of materials. The media specialist helps the teacher select by providing periodicals, review literature, bibliographies, and selection aids. If the teacher does not request materials, the media specialist goes to him. The media specialist consults with teachers to find out what equipment and services will be most helpful to them.

4. What image do teachers have of the media specialist and the media center? Image will often have a direct bearing on use of the media center. Image might be traced back to awareness, or lack of awareness of what the media center has to offer. How often have you heard people complain about a media program, when you know through an acquaintance with the program that the complaints are unfounded? If there really are shortcomings in the program, as far as teachers are concerned, how do you resolve those shortcomings? A start is to discuss the program with each teacher.

The continuance of a high level of teacher utilization of the instructional materials center and an increase in utilization in the future is a significant goal. A part of the role of the media specialist is to determine what the teachers want from a media center and to work with them cooperatively to develop the program in the proper direction. Individual communication with all teachers is not only desirable, but necessary for the meaningful media program. It is too easy to work with teachers who are already media users and to ignore those who are not. The role is clear: Communicate!

Notes

1. Martha Olson Condit, "If Only the Teacher Had Stayed with the Class," Elementary English 52 (May 1975): p. 666.

2. Saad Mohammed El-Hagrasy, "The Teacher's Role in Library Science; an Investigation and Its Devices," (Ph. D. diss., Rutgers University, 1961).

3. Martha Olson Condit, op. cit., p. 666.

4. Russell G. Stauffer, "A Reading Teacher's Dream Come True," Wilson Library Bulletin 45 (1970): 287.

5. Nancy B. Pillon, "Media Specialists Work with Teacher," Drexel Library Quarterly 9 (1973): 60.
6. George O. Eisenberg and Virginia B. Saddler, "Dear Principal; Dear Librarian; a Dialogue on the Heart of the Matter," Wilson Library Bulletin 48 (1973): 55.
7. Alma Ruth Ferguson and Karen Harris, "Agenda for Action: Teacher-Librarian Planning," Louisiana Library Association Bulletin (1973): 84.
8. Harlan R. Johnson, "Teacher Utilization of Libraries in the Secondary Schools of Tucson District No. 1," (Ph. d. diss., The University of Arizona, 1975).
9. Shirley L. Aaron, "Teaming for Learning," School Media Quarterly 4 (1976): 215.
10. American Association of School Librarians and the Association for Educational Communications and Technology, Media Programs: District and School (Chicago: American Library Association, 1975), p. 14.
11. John T. Gillespie and Diana L. Spirt, Creating a School Media Program (New York: Bowker, 1973), p. 135.

MEDIA SUPPORT SYSTEM FOR
THE SECONDARY SCHOOL*

Frederic R. Hartz and Herman Elstein

The twenty-five years from 1945-1970 span a concentrated period of economic, political, social and technological
change never equaled in history.   In the remaining third of
this century changes will accelerate; propelled by the "ex-
plosion" of population and knowledge.   The control of population and information are formidable problems, and there is
every reason to assume that technology will play an increasingly important, if not dominating role in our future.   Considering the philosophical question of whether man will become the slave or master of the machines he creates does
not forestall the inevitable.

If the past is any indication of the future, the benefits
of technology will accrue most to those who are best organized to use them.   This is not only true of those inves-
tors and corporations who profit in immediate material ways,
but for all children, even those in the most isolated schools,
who will have access to information; to the most skillful
teacher and teaching tools.   But wishing won't make it happen, nor will the adoption of a "wait and see" attitude.   The
implications for education are clear.   Organizational patterns
and structures within the educational community must be
modified, or adjusted, if the promise of technology is to be
realized with a maximum efficiency.   This is apparent at
all levels from elementary school to the university.

No longer can we afford in time and money to "grow
like Topsy" in a haphazard, piecemeal, fragmented, and unplanned program of technological development.   As technology

*Reprinted from Journal of Secondary Education, vol. 45, pp.
31-39, Jan. 1970, by permission of the authors and publisher,
the Association of California School Administrators.

develops in sophistication and complexity, the need for a well planned integrated system increases. Likewise, the "lead-time" to develop and implement a system increases.

The planning and development of an integrated instructional support system would enhance the potential of meeting the following objectives:

1. improve the educational effectiveness of the respective services.
2. increase the efficiency with which the various services are provided.
3. minimize the relative cost of providing the services.
4. encourage inter-agency communication and co-operation.
5. reduce unnecessary duplication and waste.
6. stimulate planning and development.

Chapter one of the new publication Innovation in Education: New Direction for the American School[1] opens by concentrating on the problems of instruction as the precondition for better schooling. The first reason given is: "We are convinced that a most pervasive problem in American schooling is the need for improving instructional techniques and processes."

Technology has begun to impose changes of monumental import on the basic character of education. These changes can best be described by saying that in the past, institutions were attempting to provide the greatest good for the greatest number. Today, through instructional technology, increasing emphasis is being placed upon providing the best for each. The new tools make this possible.

The overpowering drive of education is to improve instruction and facilitate learning. To fulfill this drive, greater coordination and application of technology will be necessitated. We would hypothesize that one approach should be to marshall our technological resources in an integrated instructional support system designed to help the teacher to teach and the student to learn.

The core component of such a system would be the Instructional Materials Center (I. M. C.). It is recommended that the various services be housed here in common, adjacent, or nearby facilities. The major emphasis of the center

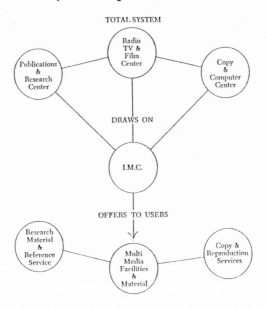

TOTAL SYSTEM

would be to provide instructional support for faculty and students.

The sketch (above) presents components of an I. M. C. in a functional manner:

The school's I. M. C. may be linked to a central source and other I. M. C.'s by any or all of the following: telephone lines for transmitting data from closed channel TV and computer outputs; receiving radio/TV signals; teletype or Xerox copy (Xerox device at each end of telephone). The school's center may have very few of its own materials in hard copy. Through its own microfilm collection and through its channels, however, it could supply more books, journals, etc. than the school library can do now. For the user the I. M. C. is not only a source of information, but a place where the techniques of discovering and assembling information is learned.

Because of their instructional relationship with specific services, curriculum research and development, AV services, and the EDP center of the school system will be most heavily involved with the I. M. C. All schools in the area covered would have access to the staff, equipment, materials, facilities, and services provided by a central unit directly or through other I. M. C. centers.

In relation to the total educational system, the diagram (page 210) represents a possible organization scheme for a large network:

Building or local school I. M. C. personnel organization is represented by the diagram (page 211):

Components of the Media Support System

Curriculum Development and Research Center: There is constant need for active research which is ignored for lack of time, staff, or experience. When it is attempted, research too often is poorly designed, inefficiently executed, and ineffectively disseminated. A separate division to service the whole system encourages and facilitates active, on-going experimental studies and research projects which develop new teaching tools, techniques, and re-evaluate current material. Such a division should be found in all large school systems.

Professional staff, non-professional aides and clerks, data processing equipment, all would be brought to bear on improving the quality of curriculum materials. The services of the research center would be available to administrators and faculty. Activities would be closely coordinated with other units, especially the computer center and the publication center. Evaluation of tools and practices would be the other essential activity of the research center.

Audiovisual Center: Many school systems have developed some centralized means of fulfilling needs for audiovisual equipment and materials. Such services can be wastefully duplicated if fragmented and uncoordinated. The establishment of an audiovisual center to service the entire school system could streamline this area of instructional support.

Professionals, and their aides can provide for member schools the services involved in ordering, distributing, cataloging, maintaining, and replacing a variety of AV equipment and films. Laboratory technicians and photographers could fill requests for "live shots," photo-copy work, developing, printing, enlarging, encartridging, soundstriping, and mounting. Graphics specialists would produce transparencies

ORGANIZATION CHART

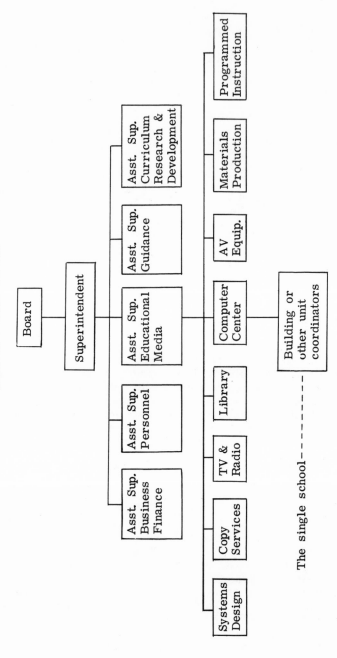

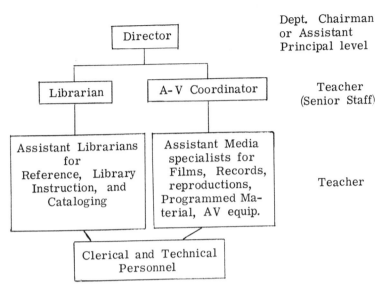

and instructional aids. The services would be provided to the staff in support of the instructional process.

Radio-TV Center: Except for the confusion with the previous center this too could be called an AV center (audio-video). In many cities individual schools and the central administrative unit operate radio and television studios and transmitters.

In addition to functioning as a training facility for students or as a public information service, the radio-TV center would directly aid the faculty. Practical application in the classroom setting and for independent study in the I. M. C. with video tape imply an increasingly potent role for television.

Publication Center: The staff of the center would coordinate the writing, copy development, revisions, submission, and actual printing of publications. The center staff would normally work with the research center and utilize the computer, the audiovisual center, and the copying and duplicating service units.

Computer Center: The potential of the computer in providing and improving services in the beginning stages of development. The storage and retrieval of information is the most complex and sophisticated of the technological support systems for instruction. The establishment of a computer center can provide services to a system in such areas as statistics, payroll, student records, purchasing records, scheduling, grading, and computer assisted instruction.

Copying and Duplicating Center: Promptly supplied copy services never seem able to keep up with demand. New processes and equipment have not only increased production but have created greater demands.

It is often desirable and practical to have localized facilities for copy and duplicating work. But, a need also exists to share some facilities and centralize when more expensive copy and duplicating equipment is involved. Such services would be available to the faculties of the various schools as an aid to the instructional process, to the administration, to other centers of the support system, and to the students for certain projects.

Services to the faculty might include the production of such items as course syllabi, final examinations, etc.; by using electronic stencil cutting, microfilm printing, spirit ditto copies, Xerox copies, and multi-graph copies, to mention a few. Some new copy devices can, from any original, produce a master copy which can be used to run quantities. Size, color, clarity, and quantity are all variables in copying and duplicating which for maximum efficiency require a trained staff and specialized equipment.

In summary, instruction has been criticized as being lecture dominated and the shortage of teachers requires new methods. The multi-media approach has the potential for meeting needs in many subject areas by providing the following kinds of support technology: CCTV, rear screen projection, automated devices which are programmed to synchronize TV, 16mm film, 8mm film, slides, filmstrips and studio tapes. Student involvement through a built-in electronic response system could be linked to a computer for scoring, recording, and storage of individual and group responses. A staff of professionals and non-professionals would work with the teaching staff to encourage and aid development and application of such multi-media programs.

The I. M. C. in the school would serve specifically as the core unit for the instructional support system and for the individually oriented teaching-learning process as a whole.

The school is philosophically committed to encouraging the maximum development of each individual student by providing proper facilities, staff, and programs. Good conditions of learning are met when the human learner is made the central part of education as a system. Carl Rogers has written that "the only learning which significantly influences behavior is self-discovered learning and that such self discovered learning can not be directly communicated to another person."[2]

The acquisition of knowledge has always been an individual matter regardless of the size of the group where it takes place. Two factors have combined to focus attention on the individual act of cognitive learning. First, a comprehensive development of independent study programs have provided a logical extension of the classroom and the concept of individualization. Staff, materials, and facilities aiding the student in his pursuit of knowledge carry the concept of "homework" to new levels of sophistication. Second, the technological advent of equipment geared to individual use has provided an easy to use, efficient, and effective means of presenting information. The I. M. C. combines traditional printed materials with new and varied resources in an accessible storehouse of information. Therefore, the I. M. C. becomes an intellectual learning laboratory designed to facilitate self-discovery by the individual. What better expression of the concept of the I. M. C. than these words, again, from Carl Rogers:

> "The only man who is educated is the man who has learned how to learn; the man who has learned how to adapt and change; the man who has realized that no knowledge is secure, that only the process of seeking knowledge gives a basis for security."

Internal Structure and Facilities of the I. M. C.

If we assume that an adequate traditional library already exists, the I. M. C. is built near, adjacent, or around the existing library. In many respects the I. M. C. can appear similar to the traditional library with table areas, open stacks, card catalogs, reserve shelf, check-out desk, book trucks, displays, wall shelving, dry carrels, locking research carrels, informal reading areas, offices, storage areas, and conference rooms. In addition the following will be available:

Small Group and Individual Viewing Rooms: A number
of rooms will be available to students for viewing and/or
listening to programs. Each room will be connected to
CCTV, dial access audio, and dial access video.

Portable AV Equipment: Wet carrels for students will
be available near an equipment check-out desk. Portable AV
equipment including reel, cartridge, and cassette tape recorders, slide and filmstrip projectors, 8mm silent and sound
cartridge projectors and other similar items will be checked
out by students. Compatible software programs (film, slides,
tapes, filmstrips, etc.) for a great variety of courses will
also be on reserve for use in the center.

Stereo Listening System: Individual stereo listening
stations can be used by students who check-out headsets
from the area mentioned above. At least two programs will
be scheduled each day; an outline and description of which
will be available at the check-out counter. Stereo FM classical music will be presented on one channel whereas the other will carry stereo tapes of show tunes, light classics,
chorale music, marching bands, big bands, etc. While some
programs may be required of students for certain courses,
to most students, this facility represents an opportunity for
enrichment and enlightenment.

Typing Rooms: A series of practice typing rooms
will be provided for students for use. Several typewriters
of different types and manufacture will be located in each
room.

Dial Access Video Carrels: Individual dial access
carrels will be available for video viewing. Programs will
feature some live presentations from commercial or local
productions, but more often, timed start film chain programs,
slide selectric programs, video tape playbacks, etc. Programs will reflect required viewing for some students and
enrichment for others.

Computer Terminal Carrels: Space is provided for a
number of computer terminals. The installation will include
both typewriter keyboard and cathode tube-light pen terminals.
Terminals will have direct access to internal programs at
the computer center, but on-line capability with other software resources nationally.

Dial Access Audio Carrels: Connected with other car-

rels in the library and the language laboratories these facilities will probably be dominated at least initially by the foreign language department. Other programs can be expected
to develop rapidly from local production, commercial sources
and participation with other tape banks. In addition to foreign language, many audio programs are currently available
in the areas of fine arts, English, and social studies.

Microfilm Reader-Printers: Periodicals should be
available on microfilm or microfiche in addition to original
form. Initially, at least, 3 readers and 2 reader-printers
should be available. As with the other equipment, hardware
can be expanded as software develops and usage demands exceed availability.

Copy Machines: Several kinds of commercial copy
machines are available for a small fee to students using the
L. M. C.

The comprehensive and sophisticated media support
system, just described, will require several years of planning, construction, and implementation. Key staff members
and subject specialists should be engaged at the outset to
plan cooperatively. Such a complex system will initially create more problems than it will solve. Overcoming the problems will be the job of the support system team working in
three areas simultaneously.

First, and most obvious, with the construction of a
new facility comes the opportunity to change the structures
by radical modification of the environment in which teachers
and students function. This first emphasis on structure can
be illustrated by establishing new systems and procedures,
differentiating the size of learning groups, revising the schedule, and providing time and space for independent study.

A second front of attack of innovation represents the
most critical of all--personnel. Major emphasis must be on
in-service training. Everyone has to grow by learning how
to make the new structures function efficiently and effectively.
Change is uncomfortable for many people. Innovation drains
energies and taxes reserves; some educators prefer security.
Instructional advantages of the new systems must be stressed
with staff members involved in planning. This phase requires
sustained effort and leadership. In-service is not self-
propelled.

The third effort of planning and implementation must be directed toward changing the program. Emphasis here needs to be on the modification of the curriculum and the acquisition of appropriate and sufficient individualized learning materials. Where commercial materials are unavailable they must be produced. Every effort must be made to see that no teacher is denied an important teaching tool. Every teacher with a constructive and creative idea should be given time and materials.

Notes

1. Committee for Economic Development. Innovation in Education: New Direction for the American School. New York, The Committee, 1968.

2. Rogers, Carl R. On Becoming a Person: A Therapist's View of Psychotherapy. Boston, Houghton Mifflin Co. 1961.

MEDIA SERVICES IN THE OPEN SCHOOL:
AN OVERVIEW*

Judith K. Meyers

In considering the topic of media services in the open school, it seems important to explore the concept of openness at the very start. The literature provides a bewildering variety of definitions. Each reading brings out a different shade of meaning. Yet, when one reflects upon all that has been written, then remembers the unfailing enthusiasm with which various practitioners of openness speak, and finally recalls the happy and relaxed children caught up in learning through the open process, it becomes apparent that the kind of openness most essential to education, schools, media centers, classrooms, and learning is not an architectural openness, nor a structural openness, but rather an intellectual and emotional openness.

This openness permits the free sharing of resources and self with all in the school community. It requires flexibility in working with many kinds of people and multiple sets of equipment and materials in an astonishing array of ways. At its foundation is confidence in one's knowledge, skills, and abilities; respect and trust in one's colleagues; and complete dedication to the principle that each child shall have the opportunity to learn in keeping with his own special needs, at his own pace and in his own way.

What we are saying is that it is the resourcefulness of the media specialist that is the most essential ingredient in media service programs for open schools. Several writers have developed rather complicated and elaborate rationales

*Reprinted from Drexel Library Quarterly, vol. 9: pp. 9-26, July 1973, by permission of the author and publisher, the School of Library and Information Science, Drexel University.

for what this person does and what he should be called. It
seems unnecessary to echo their thoughts here. Note well,
however, that it is the action words, the verbs, rather than
the nouns, that are most intriguing. Elenora Portteus,
Cleveland's (Ohio) Directing Supervisor of School Libraries,
put it something like this recently in a bulletin to her staff:

> The media specialist should expand, like, utilize,
> learn, face, back up, appeal, conflict, practice,
> listen, hear, speak, decide, participate, cooperate,
> communicate, function, interest, commit, join, give,
> see, suggest, pledge, recommend, plan, organize,
> grow, struggle, create, inspire, think, live, direct,
> visit, know, teach, administer, disagree, unite,
> hope, want, manage, devise, expect, believe,
> dream, report, confront, review, present, guide,
> command, use, value, facilitate, interface, struc-
> ture, strive, encourage, evaluate, build, counsel,
> account, schedule, be, face, design, vary, make,
> tolerate, contribute, risk, assist, weld, welcome,
> study, experience....

Functions of the Media Specialist

... as medium

It is difficult to discuss the media specialist's function in the open school without taking the opportunity to point
out three rather fascinating plays on the word "media" in relation to this function. Certainly one of the most important
aspects of the media specialist's work is that of medium in
an anticipatory and divining sense. It is his power to pre-
dict what his clients will need far enough into the future so
that the materials and equipment have been acquired and processed into the collection ready for use when called for.

... as medium of communication

Unlike many of his fellow librarians, the educational
media specialist does not hesitate to function as a medium
of communication when the situation warrants. In this sense,
he is a part of the formal educational organization of people
and resources by which society transmits its values and
knowledge from one generation to the next. Not content with
a role as sentinel at the storehouse of information, he is
also an instrument for communicating information. In most

states he is by law a teacher. In some school districts
teaching experience is a prerequisite for the position of media specialist. More and more frequently the media specialist has had formal training and experience in audiovisual
media and methods as well. It is understandable then that
he does not blanch at his role as a presenter of information
or as a consultant to colleagues and students on their information presentation and communications problems.

... as mediator

This last thought provides a logical transition to the
third play on the word "media. " The media specialist is a
mediator between man and his graphic records in both a man-
agerial and manipulative sense and an interpretive sense.
He is comfortable in taking information originally presented
in one format, restructuring it, and re-presenting it in another format, as teachers and students may require. He
understands what it is to facilitate learning by restructuring
the learning environment. Regarding the various graphic
records in the media collection as possible events in the
learning environment, he selects all or parts of them, re-
orders them, and places them in new juxtaposition. By presenting these graphic stimuli in either printed or audiovisual
formats in such a way that they tend to elicit desired responses from his users, he has taken a giant step beyond
his more traditional library bound colleagues. Their perception of their role as mediators between man and his graphic records tends to dim after they have created physical and
intellectual access to the desired information, and given in-
nocuous and noncommital levels of interpretative assistance
to their clients.

The media specialist is knowledgeable about learning
theory. He has studied Pavlov, Skinner, Glasser, Maslow,
Piaget, Thorndike, Dewey, James, and others. He knows
about the behavior modification model, developmental models,
and information processing models. He has thought through
the relationship of behavioral principles to the school media
program, and does not hesitate to apply these theories. A
quarter of a century of audiovisual research has shown no
significant correlations between learning behavior and different media. He is therefore suspicious of claims about the
superiority of any one medium over another. Rather than
betraying his annoyance or impatience with the hundredth student who has failed to use the card catalog in his quest for
information, he accompanies the student to the catalog and ob-

serves his work, providing positive reinforcement in the form of praise, encouragement, and whatever additional clues are required, until the student has experienced success in his information quest.

The media specialist does not regard his responsibility as being fulfilled once he has assured himself that the student has found the item requested. He continues to provide his assistance until he is certain the student is having no difficulty in interpreting whatever information is required. Further, if he and his teaching colleagues wish to provide for some sort of behavioral change in their students through media, he and they keep working together until the desired change is observed. Likewise, if students wish to share their newly found information with others or to create a multimedia presentation as part of the process of psychologically internalizing their new information, the media specialist will advise and assist them until they do. The media specialist in the open school has come a long way from the librarian who holds his clients at such distances that service is rarely extended beyond the bare bones of information. Yet, he is motivated by the same basic respect for freedom and privacy in learning that characterizes the information scientist, but which produces among some a more formal and conservative stance.

Earlier in this discussion a statement was made to the effect that the media specialist in the open school works with a wide variety of materials and equipment. One of the common complaints against open education is that it does not give enough attention to the "basics." In librarianship, a parallel claim continues to rise from a still rather vocal and excitable minority who believe in all sincerity that "books are basic" and to whom non-book materials and electronic or mechanical equipment seem beyond the pale of their profession.

Conscience and duty compel one to gently reassure the critics in both camps that the importance of books, reading, and other basics are not overlooked either in the open school or its media center. The basics are recognized as the backbone of education, in both media centers and open schools, and both assign considerable emphasis to all of the basics within the structures of their programs. What has happened, and is happening in reading and the other basic skill areas, is that, by the combination of the best from both the media movement and the open education movement, a multiplicity of approaches to learning has been made available to each child. Further, each child has many more opportunities to read and learn from more sources, about a greater variety of subjects, in more depth, and more frequently than in traditional schools.

For well over a quarter of a century educational leadership has been advocating the abandonment of the single textbook approach to learning. Media centers and open schools have done much to banish this restrictive educational tool in the last several years.

In the late 1950's and early 1960's some heady ideas were bursting upon the educational scene. An ex-admiral martialed hoards of better-than-ever-educated citizens to direct their volleys of unending criticism toward the schools. A leading economist advised us that we lived in an age of affluence, and a prominent social philosopher put forth some important notions about the kinds of excellence toward which we should be aiming (Admiral Heyman Rickover, John Kenneth Galbraith, and John W. Gardner, respectively). When the Elementary and Secondary Education Act was introduced many librarians had already done some dipping into the trough through the National Defense Education Act. This enabled them to set an exciting and fast-paced course toward some of the excellence about which they had dreamed. NDEA had brought them close enough to the audiovisual movement for them to begin to examine some of the benefits which might be derived from moving along with the flow.

One of the old ideas which quickly wore thin was that school library collections needed to stop growing after they had reached the standard numbers of trade books, reference books, periodicals, and newspapers. Vision was broadened to include the instructional materials horizon, and acquisition habits changed. There was an increased understanding of, and tolerance for, all kinds of instructional materials. A practice which is particularly strong in the open schools is the utilization of multiple sets of texts. Instead of buying several hundred copies of one text to be read by all students at the same time, increasing numbers of schools were buying several copies of many different texts to be used by children at any grade level when they were ready for them.

School administrators were quick to find out that school librarians had a well developed set of routines which could easily be adapted for the handling of these many ma-

terials.   More and more often they became part of the library collection.   The librarians, on the other hand, didn't
protest.   For the first time in history they were receiving
substantial amounts of revenue to support their programs.
The increased availability of more and different kinds of materials had made it inevitable that change overtake them.
One more change didn't matter that much, once the momentum had built up, especially as it enhanced their status
within the school community and was often accompanied by
increased clerical and technical staff.

Meanwhile the crafty school administrator, who quite
often had started out increasing his support of the "library
cum media center" as a means of getting a knotty problem
out of his office, discovered that he was getting more from
his equipment and materials dollars than at any time in the
past.   Media and equipment organized into a fully integrated
program, with someone devoting full professional time to its
promotion and use, paid off an unanticipated dividend in
terms of better instruction and therefore increased learning.
Not only was he pleased with this bit of serendipity, but when
he looked around his own office, he found that he had delegated the responsibility for much of the nitty-gritty that had
hampered his own mode of operation to a team of people who
were coping with it most competently.   He was free to upgrade his own contribution to the educational program.   He
was able now to spend more time in the supervision, evaluation, and the improvement of instruction.

The Media Specialist in Administration

The new relationship between the media specialist and
the school administrator is worth further attention.   As a
group (with the possible exception of those administrators who
are managing store front schools, guerilla schools, and similar operations where some very acute social and economic
needs in the community currently have justifiable priorities
in their programs) administrators in open schools appear to
have a much better grasp of the media center concept and to
be much more active and aggressive in supporting programs
than administrators in traditional schools.

Some rather provocative things are occurring which
to this writer's knowledge hitherto have gone unreported.
In one school the media specialist has been given the title
and is functioning as an administrative intern.   In another

school, in a city where the general policy is to provide space and materials but no staff for media services, an assistant principal has been assigned the task of implementing the school media program. While the assistant principal does not perceive herself as a media specialist and is most humble about her lack of professional background for the job she is doing, the program that she has developed exhibits most of the earmarks of a good one. Only the technicalities of some of her improvisations are disconcerting. She is doing a commendable job of bringing together teachers, children, and resources, and it is administrative skills, not media skills, which have enabled her to function successfully in this assignment.

In a third school, one in which efforts to move ahead with the media center have been blocked by firm district-wide teacher-pupil ratio formulas, the principal has scheduled himself to work in the media center for a portion of every day along with a professional staff member, an aide, and a large number of volunteers. Students in this school use the media center on an average of more than once a day, while the district-wide average attendance in media centers is about one and a half times a week.

In a very large and complex high school the assistant principal for curriculum recently confided that they didn't know quite what to do with their media person, but they were including him in their administrative council meetings because they could not function as effectively and efficiently as they would like without him. In several open schools the media specialists have standing appointments to work with the principals one or more times a week.

Dr. Edythe J. Gaines, Superintendent of the Community School District No. 12, Bronx, New York, in an article in Nation's Schools asserts that, "Media specialists are beginning to assume new responsibilities in education's middle management."[1] Many media specialists, if they had time to analyze their media programs and their role within the school, would find that they have administrative responsibility for time, space, materials, equipment, and people in the process of getting the job of education done. In some schools this new role has caused conflict between the media specialist and the principal.

In many of the open schools this problem has either been formally identified and dealt with, or both principals and media specialists have worked it out on a more intuitive level, drawing upon some of those extraordinary human-relations abilities that all the authorities recognize as essential for working in the open schools. Almost without exception, where the media program is functioning as it should in the open school, there is evidence of a much higher level of media specialist involvement in administrative activity with the principal, particularly in goal setting, program and fiscal planning, curriculum design, and evaluation. After the human resourcefulness of the media specialist, which has already been cited as the prime ingredient for success in the media program, this new relationship with school administrators comes forth as the next most important ingredient in an open school operation.

Materials--Selection, Production, & Dissemination

A media specialist, learning from his education colleague, does not hesitate to balance out the collection with some controlled vocabulary materials and guide those children to them who might otherwise have a difficult time with a book valued as literature. He does not stop here but includes games based on basic vocabulary lists in the collection, and makes up flash cards or language master cards that can be borrowed and used by children who need lots and lots of practice with these very basic sets of words before they can move on to more complicated reading skills and activities.

Similarly, the media specialist has brought himself to ask the question, if children are reported by literary experts to enjoy and identify strongly with much of the repetition in the folk tales, then why is repetition in beginning reading materials ridiculed? Classroom experience has demonstrated repetition to be one way in which some children learn best. It is also the best way to learn certain selected tasks. Materials with a high repetition element have their place in the spectrum of learning tools. The media specialist includes a representative selection of them in the collection and puts them to good use when they are needed.

The nature of the textbook is itself changing. Quite often a textbook is no longer a textbook. It has been superceded by a program. A program may consist of any one of a number of things, but quite often it is a package of many different kinds of media which are to be used together as a text. Such a package might include multiple copies of a paperback that would pass as a text, but it might also include 16 millimeter films, filmstrips, recordings, games, replicas, or facsimiles of primary source materials, manipulative objects, sometimes even balloons for blowing, or biological specimens of something as far out as planeria, which students may borrow long enough to teach to run a T maze. You name it, and it just might be part of one of the new learning packages.

One of the best ways of disbursing these new learning packages, generally too expensive for the individual classroom, is to put them in the media center. They actually get more use when they are centrally housed and made available to all instead of being hidden away inaccessibly in one classroom.

Another category of instructional materials that is playing a vital role in the opening-up of education is programmed materials and other empirically developed materials. There are still any number of traditional librarians who regard programmed texts as non-books and who refuse to have any part of them, even though many are printed and come in hard bindings. Other programmed materials incorporate audiovisual media. Some are stored into computers as in the famous project PLATO. Others are the products of some of the regional educational laboratories, such as the aesthetics program developed by CEMREL. These materials are popular with some students in that they let them learn in small stages and do not necessarily require that they have to encounter a live teacher to learn what they wish. Mathematics materials seem to be highly successful in these kinds of formats. They are reliably successful with a high percentage of students. Sometimes brighter students claim that the programs are dull. Perhaps they are. Perhaps the brighter students might have been placed into programs where the objectives were broader in scope and more complicated in nature.

At any rate media specialists are attuned to this movement in the development of materials. When confronted with such a package they ply its sales person with questions about the developmental testing which was done on their programmed products. They check to see if pre-tests and post-tests are included and whether or not they are actually parallel tests. They look into validity and reliability quotients. If necessary, they can perform a task analysis, design and edit a program, complete its developmental testing, and establish the validity and reliability data themselves. More often though, the media specialist serves a teacher in an advisory capacity when the teacher wishes to develop a program of his own.

At a lesser level of sophistication, media specialists create or help others create simple learning packages such as a jigsaw puzzle made of tear sheets laminated to poster board, a slide-tape presentation on the local fire department, transparencies, a math lesson worked around a food ad from the local newspaper, a nutrition lesson based on a menu from a local restaurant, a map reading lesson from a country map, a word wheel, a simulation game, or a shoe box science experiment. Sometimes the learning packages are deposited in the media center and shared by the whole school. Sometimes they become part of a classroom learning center. They are almost always something which children especially look forward to using.

More important than the commercially prepared materials and the materials prepared by the very best of media specialists, teachers, and technicians, are the materials made by students themselves. They are both the product and process of learning. This stands out over and above all other kinds of media utilization as the most effective and exciting part of the modern media program. Yet many schools hold back when it comes to adding the production component to their media services programs. To be sure, production can be messy, but children can and should be taught to clean up after themselves.

To those who claim that production is too difficult, the answer is that anyone who has ever grilled a cheese sandwich can laminate. The instamatic type camera makes picture taking about as simple, enjoyable, and fool proof as any bit of technology on the market. The hardest thing about getting started is wangling the copy machine from the school secretary.

Community Resources

One more set of resources needs to be discussed before the topic of materials is left behind. These are the resources within the community. Human beings as resources seem to take on more importance in open schools than in conventional schools. The open schools are more likely to

use field trips and community service projects as learning
experiences. Ecology projects, consumer education projects,
trips to local governmental units, public service agencies,
businesses, industries, and cultural centers are more frequently arranged. The incidence of resource persons as
visitors and instructors in the open schools is also higher.
Again, the firemen, policemen, and other public servants
are favorites. Some schools have scheduled coffeehouse-
type seminars with local artists, writers, and craftsmen participating. Vocational and career days are popular in the
secondary schools. High school and college students are
often called upon to work with children in the open schools,
sharing their guitars, their interests in astrology and the
occult, magic acts, and so forth. One of the favorite vari-
ations on the in-school use of people as resources is to have
minicourses developed by persons both inside and outside the
formal school organization. Another is to have free choice
days for which the students decide what they shall study for
the day, identify and invite whomever they wish to be their
teachers, and then spend the whole day with whatever local
talent they have invited. This often gives a chance for students to see their teacher's avocations. Students are sometimes surprised to learn that the football coach is an excellent cook, and the little old Latin teacher holds a brown
belt. Mother might come to school to teach macrame for
the day, and father might offer a short session on the repair
of simple home appliances, or better still, vice versa. Media services personnel frequently do much of the organizational work on these various programs. A community resources file or handbook often evolves out of such projects,
listing people and places that have been successfully involved
in the open school program and are willing to be called on
again. [2]

Volunteers

The media center volunteer is a very special community resource. While some media specialists still protest their
presence in the media program, their use in the media center is really one of the most popular applications of the volunteer movement in the schools. Many media programs
simply could not function without volunteer assistance. Even
those staffed according to ALA-NEA standards find that some
of the new learning programs and packages, require an ever
higher adult-pupil ratio in the school. The functions of the
volunteer are usually at the paraprofessional level. They

perform many of the same tasks that paid aides and technicians perform. We often find retired teachers, librarians,
and student teachers in the act. The teachers and student
teachers make excellent tutors for remedial work. Often
they set up their "clinics" at a media center table or in one
of the media conference rooms. They are quite often given
responsibility for carrying out small-group enrichment activities. Student teachers especially like to work with audiovisual media. Librarians tend to work on the catalog, generate special indexes and bibliographies, or work out special
storytelling and book talk programs that the regularly assigned staff might not have time to develop. The media center in the open school probably has had more participation in
the utilization of differentiated staffing patterns than any other unit within the organizational structure.

Evaluation and Selection of Materials

To a greater extent than his colleagues in public libraries and in more traditional schools, the media specialist
in the open school serves to coordinate the selection process,
rather than carry out all the selection. The selection process may be said to be moving in two different directions at
the same time, depending on the type of media. Insofar as
printed materials are concerned, the effort is in the direction
of broadening the decision-making base. The involvement of
students in the evaluation of printed materials and more extensive efforts to get teachers involved in evaluating and
recommending printed materials stand out. Success with students has been remarkable. Involvement of the busy teacher
has moved along more slowly.

Teachers have traditionally been far more involved in
and more autonomous in their selection of audiovisual materials. Here the trend is toward centralization, upgrading,
and increased control over the selection process by the media
specialist. Centralization of audiovisual collections where no
previous pattern of centralization existed has probably been
a slower and more painful process than the centralization of
book collections. Teachers tend to view audiovisual materials as stronger teaching aids than printed materials. It is
harder for them to perceive of audiovisual materials as alternate information formats suitable for individualized and independent research and study. A common complaint is the one
formerly heard in connection with books--teaching isn't as effective as when the students have been exposed to the materi-

als beforehand. Research bears out the fact that students sometimes remember more and longer that which they have seen and heard than that which they have read. The basic issue, though, is whether the teacher's desire to teach in a given manner precludes the student's right to learn what he wants to learn when he is ready to learn it. Authorities are generally agreed on this subject. The learner's rights are basic. The teacher facilitates the learning process. That's what the opening up of learning is all about.

Finding time for previewing audiovisual materials is becoming as difficult a problem as finding time to participate in book selection. Several locales are experimenting with over-the-air previewing via their local educational television set-up. While there has been some squabbling about broadcast rights, breakthroughs are being made with the cable and ITFS installations. This writer knows of no one who is currently experimenting with the compressed speech machines for cutting down preview time for audio materials. However, it stands to reason that this should be one of the applications of the compressed sound technology that should soon be forthcoming. Likewise, the writer is not aware of any case where time for evaluating media has been a central issue in teacher contract negotiations, but rest assured that before long it will be.

The upgrading of the selection of audiovisual materials and the resulting improvements in utilization continue to be a problem, but not so severe as it was perhaps five years ago. As librarians have entered strongly into the audiovisual movement, they have been articulate and aggressive in setting high selection standards and criteria. While the production of audiovisual materials does not seem to have tapered off, the quality of the products is gradually getting better, especially among the larger and well established producers.

The librarian's insistence on better and more widespread reviewing of materials has resulted in the expansion of the reviews section of Book List and Subscription Books Bulletin. Previews has outgrown its parent publication, School Library Journal. The new bulletin from the University of Chicago is also promising. Multi-Media Reviews Index creates access to a surprising number of evaluative statements. The reviews themselves still tend to be descriptive at the expense of being comparative and generally do not give enough detail about possible utilization. It would appear that many of the reviewers do not have enough access yet to large enough collections to be able to make truly sound comparisons. As libraries enlarge their non-print media collection this aspect of reviewing should improve. Utilization is tricky, too. The use and increased precision of behavioral objectives should assist us in making judgments concerning utilization. Many improvements have been made in the reviewing of 16 millimeter films and filmstrips. There seems to be room for improvement in both disc and tape recordings. More widespread attention might be given to non-musical recordings. Also someone might start to give more serious attention to sorting out from the classical music reviews those recordings which are particularly appealing to, and appropriate for, children and young adults as listeners. The reviewing is least effective when it comes to transparencies, study prints, art prints, posters, other graphic materials, and of course, the large learning packages which border on text materials.

Cataloging and Classification

There is much more cause for optimism about the improvement in the selection and evaluation of materials for learning than there is about their cataloging and classification.

Cataloging and classification of printed materials has been a relatively settled issue for many years. The system is working fairly well. Yet, one sometimes wonders why media specialists are not making more demands of it. The question which follows has arisen mostly from experiences with children, books, and computers, and is more directly and readily applicable to printed materials, but does have application to both printed and audio visual materials. Why haven't we asked for a finer level of subject analysis than is currently available? One of the reasons for the alleged decline of the book's popularity is that quite often the book provides too much information in a larger and longer package than the user needs. Schools that have moved to modular scheduling usually work on a 15 minute module. The learning activities that can be fit into a 15 or 30 minute time period are close to the length of a chapter of a book. Learning objectives also tend to be narrower than the scope of an entire book. Filmstrips and recordings seem to fit more readily into the abbreviated temporal patterns. It seems appropriate that we suggest a reconsideration of what levels of access it is possible and desirable to achieve for children's learning materials. When we consider the power of computer technology and the fact that the spectrum of juvenile publishing is about 2,500 new titles each year, the suggestion to expand subject access from 3 or so headings to 15, about the level given in an average table of contents, or better still, to the level of the index, may be worthy of serious contemplation.

Better subject access to audiovisual materials is often even more important. First, the negative aspects which closed shelving practices present must be considered. Open schools have tended to lead in open shelving of audiovisual materials. Integrated shelving of both print and non-print materials has been tried in several locations.

Accessibility to audiovisual materials is further limited by the format characteristics of the very materials themselves. Browsing through a film collection, for example, is next to impossible. The technology to permit something akin to browsing is not too remote. Fast forward mechanisms have been developed for projectors. Footage counters might be adapted to serve as place indicators. Second sound channels might provide a specific access point in much the same way they currently provide the change signal for sound filmstrips and slide-tape presentations. Yet nobody has quite got it all together. Also, the demand has been slow in growing. If we may consider the catalogs of most of the largest university film libraries in the country as typical of the state of the art, there is vast room for improvement. [3] In the light of the cost of film footage compared to the costs of some of the other audiovisual formats this helter-skelter approach is particularly difficult to justify. The user is more dependent on the audiovisual cataloger to provide access to audiovisual collections than on the book cataloger to provide access to printed collections since audiovisual materials do not usually possess indexes or tables of contents. The inadequacies in the present system cannot all be attributed to the slow merging of the vastly different approaches to cataloging developed by librarians on one hand and audiovisual specialists on the other. Nor can they be entirely excused on the basis of the rapidity with which new developments are occurring in the audiovisual field. Catalogers themselves must assume part of the responsibility.

A related suggestion is that in many cases similar improvement needs to be made in providing title access to children's recordings. Standard cataloging rarely gives title access to long playing recordings where perhaps 15 to 25 nursery rhymes, short songs, or poems are included. Quite often more refined and more direct access to titles is genuinely needed too.

When commercial cataloging agencies are pressed for better services on audiovisual materials, their reply is that they cannot afford to do any better and that the market has not standardized enough to permit the increase or expansion of service. Even though there are several widely recognized sets of guidelines and handbooks for audiovisual cataloging, none have apparently been sufficiently comprehensive and clear to be adopted by enough media centers to have affected the level of bibliographic control over audiovisual materials that would enable the much needed commercial cataloging services to develop to their fullest potential. High professional priority needs to be placed on the solution of this problem. Library of Congress information on 16 millimeter films, filmstrips, and recordings needs to be disseminated more rapidly and more widely adopted. Much more serious attention needs to be given to slide sets, transparencies, study prints, art prints, games, and audiovisual media other than that cataloged by the Library of Congress. The large learning packages and programs are truly complicated cases in point. One currently on the market has over 1200 different items, not counting consumables, which are to be purchased in conjunction with its use.

If this criticism seems strong it is because service to over 50 million school children is at stake. This fact should carry enough weight in itself to motivate better efforts on the part of the profession. When one considers that this group of school children comprises the largest single group of actual library users in the country, the case for reassessment and realignment of cataloging priorities gains strength. Much progress has been made during the last ten years, but even after we've been as generous as we know how in judging all those who have participated in these high level conferences and deliberations, the bald question still remains--just what are we prepared to do about that planeria that learns to run a T maze?

Behavioral Descriptors

As the behavioral sciences mature and behavioral technology builds, the kinds of descriptors or subject headings

used to describe materials seem to become less and less
relevant to the user's needs. Behavioral technology, and its
off-shoot, educational technology, are predicated on behavioral change. Change is an action or a motion occurring
across time. Subject headings do not project this dynamic
potential. If media centers in the schools, and other types
of libraries, are to keep pace in a technological society,
some new dimensions are going to be necessary in our catalogs. Materials need to be described in terms of the changes
in human behavior which can be reasonably anticipated as the
result of human beings having interacted or interfaced with
them. Education is at the forefront of the applications of
behavioral technology. Why aren't the media specialists asking this question and making this demand of catalogers? How
do we move from description of materials as static objects
to description of materials according to their power to elicit
behavioral or social change? Librarians have believed for
a long time and spoken out most eloquently about the power
of books to change the world. Why then are there no serious efforts afoot to index this power?

Yet another question is, Should we not also be seriously seeking non-verbal ways of accessing visual materials?
This question is far from simple. It is based upon the evidence which seems to indicate that certain levels of visual
literacy precede language development. It is also related to
the impact that the visual element in television has had in
the shaping of behavior over the last several decades and the
power of this and certain other audiovisual technologies to
present more of certain kinds of information to vastly larger
audiences in much less time than can ever be expected of
printed materials. In addition the question is tied to the notion that when presented with concrete objects or their equivalent, in one or another of the visual formats, the response
is believed to be far more general across all classifications
of human beings than the response to verbal stimuli in either
oral or written codes. There is an intriguing connection,
too, with the experiments which give rise to the claim that
human intelligence may begin in the development of visual
responses to moving objects.

Today it is a quantum leap from these scattered ob-
servations and bits and pieces of research and theory to the
question that has been posed. Twenty-five years from now
that distance may have narrowed considerably, and perhaps
one or another of the possible paths suggested above may
take on considerably more importance. It is nevertheless in-

teresting to speculate about the direction such probes might take. Might the ultimate answer be the kind of visual matching activity that presently occurs in the mind's eye when using one of the catalogs of art prints which presents a postage-stamp size black and white reproduction of the work of art under consideration? Or is it closer to some of the sensing devices developed by the Department of Defense for their robots to explore the moon and planets?

Out of a little bit of chaos a great good has come. To be sure, open schools are such busy places that they appear to be pretty messy and unorganized much of the time. The media center is no exception. Since it is where much of the action takes place, it tends to be even a bit more chaotic in appearance than some of the other parts of the school. Some anonymous wag immortalized it this way:

Barely Visible

My desk is always piled with work.
I do not understand the jerk
Who keeps his nasty-neat and bare
How can he work with nothing there?

The media specialist serving in the open schools has to be one of the best organized persons in the world. His schedule and the demands upon his time and talents are unbelievable. If he hasn't gotten around to putting the catalogers on notice that they need to be considering better ways of describing and organizing multi-media collections for open education, it is to his credit that he has been much too busy serving children to analyze some of the issues in the depth they deserve.

As we conclude this discussion it is with a great deal of respect for the media men and maids who have pioneered the way. They have been regarded as the illegitimate children of the profession by far too many, for far too long. It is probably much more accurate to characterize them as professionally free souls who have dared to dream some rather impossible dreams about what schools and libraries ought to be, and who had both the good luck and good sense to be able to do something about them. Through their example and their spirit they are opening the way for many of the rest of us. Therein we find the greatest value of media services in the open school.

Notes

1.   Edythe J. Gaines, "Accountability: Getting Out of the Tangled Web," Nation's Schools, October 1971, pp. 55-58.

2.   Sylvia Marantz, "Turned On, Not Punched Out: People in a Human Resources File," School Libraries, Winter 1969, pp. 49-53.

3.   John S. Whyde, "Comparison of the Subject Headings Assigned by Eight Major University Film Libraries with Those Assigned by the Library of Congress and an Analysis of the Deviation of the Former from the Latter," (unpublished master's thesis, Kent State University, 1973).

THE OPEN-CLASSROOM CONCEPT
AND ITS EFFECT ON THE SCHOOL
LIBRARY (MEDIA) PROGRAM*

Elsie L. Brumback

What is a person who teaches all grades from kindergarten to sixth grade, does remedial work in various subject
areas, directs enrichment activities for normal and gifted
pupils, and sorts, displays, and catalogs all kinds of equipment and materials from multi-media social studies kits to
science models and realia?

The title may be librarian or media coordinator of an
elementary school that has adopted the open classroom, individualized (or personalized) approach to learning.   Yes,
schools have finally begun to recognize what many librarians
have long known--that learning is indeed a personal thing.
I can't learn for you and you can't learn for me.   Both my
purposes and my prior knowledge differ from yours as well
as the speed with which I can accomplish my task.   It is
sometimes frustrating and inefficient for us to try to learn
together.

With emphasis being placed more on individual needs,
the self-contained classroom of thirty students has dissolved,
losing first doors and then walls.   So to have the library
walls dissolved until it is totally fused with the whole of the
school environment.   As one Fairfax County Principal so
aptly stated: "It is hard to ascertain where the classroom
ends and the library begins.   It's as though the library is
just an extension of the classroom, " and that's the way it
really should be in an open concept.

*Reprinted from Virginia Librarian, vols. 18-19, pp. 3-4,
Fall-Winter 1971/Spring 1972, by permission of the author
and publisher, the Virginia Library Association.

If the child is to develop a spirit of inquiry, self-motivation, self-discipline, and self-evaluation, it is important for all school instructional personnel to assist in shaping his learning environment and the design of instruction. The skills of reading, listening, observing, speaking, and writing, once taught as "Library Lessons" by the librarian are now developed through the cooperative efforts of the librarian and teaching team. One of the most popular library skills program of the moment is the individualized "learning centers" approach.

The real key to the open classroom and open library concept is accessibility. Resources are to be used, so materials and equipment must be easily available and accessible to both students and teachers. It is not enough for the library doors (and perhaps walls) to be open. There must be an open-concept in attitude and atmosphere!

Even in the older schools with traditional facilities, when the total staff is committed to the personalized approach to learning it is not unusual to see the entire school become "media-activated," with walls between the classrooms and library appearing to be diminished, and learning spaces extended. All areas (classrooms, library, halls, etc.) begin to show visible signs of what can happen when teachers and librarians plan together. But perhaps the most visible sign is the student freely involved in his own learning process, permitted access to various learning areas and a variety of new exciting equipment and materials.

Just what would you expect to see students doing in one of these so-called learning areas? It varies from: wearing earphones, attentively listening and following directions from a pre-programmed unit; peering through individual filmstrip viewers while preparing reports; grouped around an 8 mm projector and screen while participating in unstructured discussion; browsing through book and audiovisual catalogs to locate materials; thumbing through study prints and transparencies; using an overhead projector to give a report; interacting with a small group of other students in dialogue, dramatization, and interpretation; preparing experiments; working with maps, charts, globes, and atlases; color-lifting pictures for group projects; using cameras to record action and develop sequential skills; listening to taped cassettes and disc recordings for both pleasure and assignments; using language masters, tachistoscopes, and opaque projectors; viewing instructional television or video tapes; and tape recording thoughts, ideas, and impressions for a report. Close by is a team of teachers, including the librarian, planning, directing, challenging, encouraging and assisting students individually, in small groups, and in large groups as determined by student needs.

Contrast this view with the traditional setting where teachers worked with one group at a time while the other group worked at desks in rigid rows, reading questions and directions from blackboards and mimeographed sheets, writing their answers, drawing pictures, or reading a library book, while awaiting their turn with the teacher. A similar approach could have been seen simultaneously in the library; a group of thirty or more students marching into the library and sitting in hushed silence while the librarian used her dog-eared chart to teach the Dewey Decimal System from beginning to end in one sitting. Innovative teaching would have been difficult in this setting without upsetting established school routines and time schedules, or hoarding materials which were scarce, ineffectual and not readily accessible.

Schools wishing to embrace the open classroom-open library concept must first really wish to do so, and the entire school community must commit itself to this goal. The total school staff must be committed to work together and the school environment must be conditioned to the change. Each staff member must exercise his full responsibility. The principal must take a leadership role and provide the personnel, space, financial support and evaluation. Too many times, the open-concept has failed due to the lack of administrative support.

The teacher has the responsibility to:

● plan in advance with team members and librarian
● use various media for specific teaching purposes
● select each teaching moment according to student needs,
● and provide orientation and follow-up activities.

It then follows that as a resource person, the librarian has the responsibility to:

● provide a variety of curriculum related materials, centrally catalogued, efficiently administered, and readily accessible
● plan continuously with teachers for meaningful activities
● give instruction in the selection and use of all forms of media and equipment

- arrange spaces to facilitate all types of media use, and
- evaluate constantly the effectiveness of the use of media in personalized learning.

Since students are most often motivated in the classroom to use the library for individual or group research, it is imperative that librarians know what is going on in the various subject areas so they can correlate book and nonbook materials with the curriculum and recreational interests of students. One librarian selected representative study prints and books and prepared an audio tape of seasonal sounds to enhance a unit being studied by a second level group. While using these materials, students were learning to use reading, listening, viewing, and identification skills the "painless" way.

Everyone agrees that each child is entitled to the best education possible to meet his specific needs and capabilities. The educational experiences which will enable this must be identified and the necessary resources and personnel made available. No longer should a child be restricted to one classroom with one teacher dominating the teaching-learning environment with only the resources of that room available. The child must be able to rely on all instructional personnel and materials in a variety of formats to find the media and instructional modules best suited to fulfilling his needs. In view of this, why do we, as librarians, not rise to meet the challenge?

In talking with librarians, I find that many of them are afraid of the "open door" policy. It is not just the older librarians but even those who are chronologically younger in years and experience. They seem to have two fears. First, they fear they will be left alone in the library with no patrons if they don't have their thirty students marching in every thirty minutes as in the past. Second, they seem to be afraid of the other extreme and being bombarded by everyone at once!

Librarians possessing these fears should visit several schools that have adopted the open classroom-open library concept. Immediately, their fears will be allayed and they will be converted--never to return to the closed door, thirty minutes, lockstep approach again!

THE MEDIA CENTER AND
CONTINUOUS PROGRESS*

Robert J. Dierman

"Individualized instruction, " "continuous progress, " and "non-graded learning" are all currently used terms that emphasize a pupil's ability to learn specific things at his own rate with varying degrees of independence and with many options of materials and activities. A school that puts these ideas into practice presents specific challenges for a media center.

Learning Activities Packages

In a secondary-level continuous progress program, teaching utilizes a learning activities package. This package gives the student a specific behavioral objective to be attained in measurable terms, a series of both required and optional activities, and a list of materials for those activities.

Good instructional packages, like good "traditional" teaching, use multi-media extensively. The difference, however, lies in the mix and timing of the multi-media used.

The Converse County Junior-Senior High School is located in the county seat of a lightly populated, rural area in eastern Wyoming. Some five years ago, the school district embarked upon a continuous progress mode of curricular design, which eventually came to be built in the junior and senior high school around learning activities packets. Because of this change in instructional format, certain changes had to be made in the format of the media program.

*Reprinted from NASSP Bulletin, vol. 59, pp. 47-50, Sept. 1975, by permission of the author and publisher, the National Association of Secondary School Principals.

Since the total enrollment in the school, at that time, barely exceeded 500 pupils, the media collection remained centrally housed in the resource center with the addition of both wet and dry carrels for individual pupil usage. Hardware items for single students were also added along with microfiche reader-printers, programed calculators, and a television cassette system.

Increased enrollment due to the district's mineral wealth has necessitated recent building renovations and additional facilities. With the school firmly committed to individualized progress, library floor space has been increased by over one third to provide three main student work areas and greater audio-visual storage space.

Making Space Allocations for Media Activities

One area in the library has been set aside for individual student stations for written, computer, and viewing activities. Another section contains tables for more conventional group or individual study areas, while a third area provides facilities for leisure reading and group discussions.

A science suite is being developed that will include a small resource area with film loops, cassettes, and tapes and television materials. Because of the nature of the science program, written source materials remain in the central collection, housed in the media center along with the more esoteric and expensive hardware items.

Almost all of the English materials are being moved to a departmentalized media center adjacent to classrooms to provide easier access. The content of the collection has undergone extensive revision into materials that can easily be replicated and are programed for individuals to use on their own.

Resource center personnel sit in on all curricular planning sessions, providing the faculty with materials evaluations and literature regarding projected program revisions.

Moving to a continuous progress mode of instruction, then, creates for the media center certain decisions and tasks. First, the collection of hardware and software items must be sufficiently increased and diversified to permit student accessibility, regardless of where he or she is on a given program continuum, at any time.

Second, location of media facilities and materials must be considered. If the overall collection is to remain centralized, provisions must be made for rapid student access, traffic patterns and usage, which may entail redistributing spatial allocations and developing specialized areas for differing kinds of work. If locations of certain kinds of materials are to be throughout a building to service specific curricular areas, decisions must be made as to the cataloging, inventorying, controlling, and issuing of materials needed for each program.

Students will require tapes, film loops, filmstrips, and cassettes at different times, depending on their location in the instructional continuum. To serve a continuous progress curriculum well, several alternatives must be taken into consideration. First is the housing of the media collection itself. In a large school, sending students to the library to use media software may create a continual flow of pupils with continual requests for materials and equipment. Additionally, the teacher will be separated from his students and thus be unable to render immediate individual assistance.

One alternative is the decentralization of the software collection along subject area lines into departmentalized media collections more readily available to pupils in specific areas of the building. Another way to approach this alternative would be to provide audio-visual facilities in each classroom and to duplicate software for simultaneous use by several faculty members. The number of software items required will, of course, depend upon the scope of a particular program and the number of students participating in it.

While decentralization can be costly, it does make materials more immediately available to students under the direct supervision of a teacher in charge of the course, while, at the same time, it frees the library for use by more traditional programs and needs. Also, more space would be available for materials and items such as reader printers and television recorders.

The media collection will have to be increased. More individual viewers, projectors, recorders, headphones, and viewing and listening spaces (or areas), will be needed to accommodate individual students using many different kinds of materials. Perhaps a physical rearrangement of the media center will be necessary to accommodate a continuous progress program.

Responsibilities of Both Students and Center

Learning activities packages place a heavy emphasis on a student's ability to handle his own materials through an ability to read and to comprehend. Obviously, this imposes certain expectations, which an exceptional child might be unable to fulfill. Because of this, any learning package must contain, or provide for, alternative materials geared to the exceptional child and designed to help him achieve those particular objectives for the package. Since these materials, most generally, will be of an audio-visual nature, the media center will, again, come into focus.

The center should become responsible not only for the housing and cataloging of these materials, but also for assisting in their development, construction, and collection. Personnel should provide resource information to the teaching staff on those kinds of materials most suited for various types of children in various learning situations.

Part VIII:

RESEARCH

DO MEDIA SPECIALISTS SEE THEMSELVES
AS OTHERS SEE THEM?*

LaMond F. Beatty

What role do media specialists fulfill in school media centers? A recent follow-up study of 50 graduates of the University of Utah was conducted to answer this question. To better understand the media specialist's role, 16 of these graduates, representing eight urban and rural school districts in several states, were selected for indepth interviews.

Task Performance

In the first part of the interview the media specialists were asked which of the 11 tasks shown in Figure 1 they performed, the percent of time spent per week on each task, and whether these duties were self-initiated, assigned, or requested. They also were asked how, based on their philosophy and desires, and under ideal conditions, they would rank the 11 tasks in importance.

The responses indicated that tasks 1-4 and 7-10 were performed by all 16 of the specialists. The research task was performed by only nine, a resource and consultant center for the community was provided by five, and professional associations were supported by thirteen.

The specialists reported spending varying amounts of time performing these tasks each week. The greatest amount of time (16 percent) was spent on curriculum development, and the least (1 percent) in providing a resource and consultant center for the community.

*Reprinted from Audiovisual Instruction, vol. 21, pp. 44-45, Nov. 1976, by permission of the author and publisher, the Association for Educational Communications & Technology.

FIGURE 1

1.	Supervision	Determine staff requirements and participate in the selection, training, and supervision of para-professional, professional, clerical, or technical personnel.
2.	Selection	Coordinate selection and evaluation of instructional materials to be used in the curriculum of the school.
3.	Utilization	Conduct workshops and other inservice education activities for teachers, supervisors, and administrators in the use of technology to improve the methodology of instruction.
4.	Curriculum Development	Work with teachers, students, administrators, curriculum specialists in the design, selection, utilization, and evaluation of teaching materials to be used in the curriculum of the school.
5.	Research	Conduct experimentation and evaluation of media programs and projects within the school or school district.
6.	Community Resources	Provide a resource and consultant center for the community. Center will include community inservice programs, special presentations to service or church groups, etc.
7.	Equipment Operation, Distribution, & Maintenance	Manage the organization, distribution, and maintenance of instructional materials and equipment, including the training of students and teachers in operation and use of equipment.
8.	Production Services	Work with teachers, students, administrators, curriculum specialists in the production of teaching materials (may include television, photography, duplication, and graphic arts production) to supplement those commercially available.
9.	Budget & Facilities Planning	Develop the media budget; monitor its expenditures. Plan for space and facilities required to house media services; include these needs in the budget.
10.	Information Processing	Maintain liaison and coordination with district-level media services. Keep school administrators and teachers informed of new technology developments related to teaching and instructional communication.
11.	Professional Association Activities	Belong to and actively support professional associations such as UEMA, AECT, ALA, etc. Attend meetings, conventions, serve on committees, read papers, or write articles for publication in professional journals.

Table 1
Rank Order of Importance

Order	Task
1st	Curriculum Development
2nd	Utilization
3rd	Selection
4th	Supervision
5th	Equipment Operation
6th	Production
7th	Budget Planning
8th	Information Processing
9th	Research
10th	Professional Activities
11th	Community Resources

The specialists' ranking of the tasks in order of importance is shown in Table 1. This also reveals that curriculum development is seen as most important, and community resources as least important.

The majority of the 11 tasks were performed on a self-initiative basis. The two exceptions were equipment operation-distribution and maintenance, and budget and facilities planning, both of which were assigned tasks. Few duties were requested.

Leadership Role

Comments of the media specialists regarding behaviors that demonstrate their leadership role are shown in Table 2. They felt it was important to display an image of service and willingness to help teachers and students, to provide inservice programs, to assist in the development of curriculums, to plan and spend budgets wisely, to provide accurate and up-to-date reports, and to display a knowledge of the current literature and programs in the field.

Self-Image

In assessing their role in the staff organization of the

Table 2
Behaviors Media Specialists Feel Demonstrate Leadership

Behavior	No. of Times Mentioned
Display image of service and a willingness to help students and teachers.	14
Ability to provide inservice programs for teachers, students, and administrators in the proper selection and utilization of instructional materials.	20
Ability to assist teachers in the development of curriculums for their subject areas.	7
Ability to effectively disseminate new information to teachers, students, and administrators.	6
Ability to wisely plan for and spend budgets.	5
Ability to provide accurate and up-to-date reporting of activities of the media center.	4
Display a current knowledge of the field gleaned from reading available literature.	3
Must be a qualified expert in the field of instructional technology.	3

Table 3
Rank in the Staff Organization of the School

Classification	Above	Same As	Below
Classroom Teacher	10	6	0
District Curriculum Specialist	1	10	5
Assistant Principal	3	4	9
Department Head	10	6	0

school, ten specialists indicated that they consider their role to be above the rank of classroom teacher, and six considered their rank to be the same. None of them considered it below that of a classroom teacher (see Table 3).

Responses regarding the role of the media specialist on a curriculum revision committee indicated that they saw themselves as consultants in the design, selection, utilization, and evaluation of instructional materials. They also indicated that they had a responsibility in helping to develop specific objectives and components of the curriculum, and in serving as a communications specialist.

A COMPARISON OF ROLE PERCEPTIONS OF THE SCHOOL MEDIA SPECIALIST AMONG ADMINISTRATORS, CLASSROOM TEACHERS AND LIBRARY MEDIA SPECIALISTS*

Margaret A. Pemberton and Earl P. Smith

In recent years the school library has greatly expanded in scope and function as part of the total school program, especially in public elementary schools. Both the American Library Association and the Association for Educational Communications and Technology have been instrumental in promoting this evolvement.

The concept of a "new" profession espoused by Howard Ball has tended in some minds to create more confusion than clarification regarding the new found responsibilities of school library/media specialists (used interchangeably with school media specialist or LMS). Neither administrators, classroom teachers or school media specialists themselves are clear on the precise identity for the media specialist in today's changed institutions and programs.

In the Southeast the standards committee of the Southern Association of Colleges and Schools (SACS) in the early 1960's recommended in their guidelines for accreditation that schools with twelve or more full-time teachers employ a full-time library/media specialist. As a result there are presently more positions for professionals in school/media programs of public schools than ever before. The problem that confronts many school people is how to make the most effective use of the school media specialist in the context of changing programs and facilities and with new arrangements for teaching and learning.

*Reprinted from Southeastern Librarian, vol. 28, pp. 92-95, Summer 1978, by permission of the authors and publisher, the Southeastern Library Association.

Research requires much greater clarification of the role and function of the school media specialist. Some further interpretation to those in charge of school programs could lead to much better use of the services of the adequately trained media specialist.

Increased numbers of jobs has also necessitated the development of alternative training programs which lead to special certification for media professionals in many states. There is evidence of considerable variability in these programs as well as in state standards for certification and licensure.

In the light of these developments it is no wonder that there is confusion for many in education regarding the primary role and service tasks for the school media specialist in public elementary schools.

This study collected information from administrators, classroom teachers and school media specialists regarding the perceptions of role and expectations of these varied educators toward what the school media specialist does within the elementary school program. A comparison of these expectations among the three groups should help to confirm or refute varied hypotheses regarding assumed differences in outlook and help to dispel misconceptions about the current practices of the school media specialist.

The major question posed in this study was whether the perceptions of role of the library/media specialist differed among groups of administrators, (ADM) classroom teachers, (CTR) and library/media specialists (LMS) sampled. The four subsections of the test were to provide information related to varied sub-tasks of the library/media specialist, namely: (1) the development and management of physical facilities, (2) the development and management of the collection, (3) the curricular, teaching and faculty relationship role, and (4) the personality and student relationship of the library/media specialists. The sub-tasks were determined by dividing the test items into four logical categories which in the investigators' judgment represent fairly distinct role dimensions of the library/media specialist in public school setting. Though these do not completely overlap the functions described by other writers, these were judged to be realistic dimensions for those in the schools sampled.

The role expectations of the library/media specialist

were determined by the administration of a thirty-five item
Likert type scale in which the respondents checked one of
five responses to role statements varying from strong agreement to strong disagreement with each statement. The
sample groups were taken from the whole populations of
teachers, administrators and library/media specialists in
several schools of two school districts in West Georgia.
Among the sample were 43 media specialists, 48 administrators and 140 classroom teachers.

Little can be provided in the way of justification for
the selection of these several schools except that the authors
were dealing with the educator professionals in these two districts and were in need of information on which to base decisions both practical and academic.

The measures of reliability on the instrument should
give an indication as to the appropriateness of further use
of the test with other groups of educators in other school
settings.

The instruments were administered in the early fall
of 1976 and were analyzed through the facilities of Auburn
University computer data processing using the SPSS computer
routines (Nie et al., 1975). It was proposed: (1) to do a
complete factor analysis on the instrument, (2) to determine
a reliability measure of internal consistency on the instrument, and (3) to make comparisons among mean scores for
all three groups on each of the four sub-scales as well as
the scale as a whole. The null hypothesis stated that there
would be found no differences among the three groups on the
Role Expectations of the Media Specialists on each of the
sub-scales or for the scale as a whole.

Measures of internal consistency on each sub-scale
and total scale were computed through the coefficient Alpha
which is equivalent to the Kuder Richardson formula 20.
The results of these computations indicated coefficients of
.82, .73, .91, and .86 for each of the four sub-scales respectively. A coefficient of .96 was computed for the scales
as a whole.

When the total scores of the instrument were submitted to a factor analysis, the results revealed a total of
five factors. A closer look at the Eigen values (Table 1),
however, indicated that the first of the five factors accounted
for 80 per cent of the common variance among all the items.

It was then decided to treat the scales as a unidimensional variable rather than examining the results of the four sub-scales separately. In the view of the investigators, this did

Table 1
Percent of Variance Attributable to Each of Five Factors*

	Factor	Eigen Value	Percent of Variance	Cumulative Percentage
1.		15.72672	80.1	80.1
2.		1.55803	7.9	88.0
3.		1.15837	5.9	93.9
4.		0.62047	3.2	97.1
5.		0.57474	2.9	100.0

*based on a factor analysis utilizing the principle components methods

not necessarily negate the possibility for usefulness of the four sub-tasks. It did indicate that these particular clusters of items did not constitute distinct traits as was suggested in the literature.

When the cumulative scores of the three groups, administrator, classroom teacher, and media specialist, were submitted to a simple analysis of variance test (Table 2) it revealed that the administrators and media specialists, together, differed from classroom teachers in their role expectations for the library/media specialist.

A closer inspection of difference on the sub-scales indicated the greatest differences between the two former groups and classroom teachers were on sub-scales three and four.

Summary

A graduate evolution has taken place in the last decade whereby the school library has expanded greatly in scope and function. In reality most libraries are now instructional media centers. This "new" profession of the library has tended to create more confusion and questions than it has solved, since few administrators, classroom teachers or even

Table 2
Analysis of Variance Test on Five Sub-scales and Scale as a Whole N = 231

Sub-scale	Source of Variance	D.F.	Sum of Squares	Mean Squares	F Ratio
1	Between Groups	2	11.5000	5.7500	1.104
	Within Groups	229	1192.3125	5.2066	
	Total	231	1203.8125		
2	Between Groups	2	42.2500	21.1250	*
	Within Groups	229	1359.9375	5.9386	3.557
	Total	231	1402.1875		
3	Between Groups	2	765.7500	382.8750	***
	Within Groups	229	5182.1875	22.6296	16.919
	Total	231	5947.9375		
4	Between Groups	2	30.7500	15.2500	***
	Within Groups	229	2435.3750	10.6348	1.434
	Total	231	2465.8750		
Total Scale	Between Groups	2	1781.0000	890.5000	***
	Within Groups	229	17610.0000	76.8996	11.580
	Total	231	19391.0000		

*P<.05

media specialists know what the precise identity or role of the media specialist should be. There has been much confusion of terminology applied to the role, since job descriptions tend to differ from system to system and state to state.

Since 1960 with a plethora of widespread standards there has been an urgency to "produce" school media specialists through higher education programs. The major problem that confronts the school system is how to make the most effective utilization of these graduates of school media programs. Research evidence indicates need for greater clarification of the changed role of this educational specialist. More precision in definition and interpretation of the role could lead to more effective training programs and better utilization of the services that they may potentially provide. If this confusion continues, neither teachers or students or school systems will benefit from the expanded service role that the school media specialists could uniquely contribute.

The attitudes and perceptions of classroom teachers and administrators are generally neutral or even negative regarding the abilities and responsibilities of school media specialists. Many elementary teachers readily admit that they cannot use the media center effectively.

There are several concepts of the school media specialist. There are those who think the position is primarily for the circulation of books; others view the media center as a place to take their classes so they can take a break. Other elementary teachers believe it is the job of the librarian to teach all library skills, and there appears to be little coordination between the librarian and elementary classroom teacher on teaching students these skills. Some teachers feel that there should be a scheduled weekly library period, without any need for coordination by a professional.

The results of this survey indicate that even though the perceptions of administrators and media specialists in the schools sampled do not differ, these two groups do view the function of the library/media professional differently from classroom teachers.

Among the items in sub-scales three which reflected the greatest differences are: the role that the media specialist plays in regard to faculty; the role in regard to curriculum and instruction planning; the role in regard to guidance for teachers and students in the selection and use of resources.   This is not inconsistent with other writers as reflected in the literature previously cited.

What can be concluded is that further work needs to be done at several levels.   First, professional training programs and media educators should reflect the changing patterns of schooling and school programs which demand changing functions of media personnel.   Second, considerable attention needs to be given to further interpretation of the potential role of media professionals in the public education. This may be done through in-service work in schools as well as in undergraduate training programs of pre-service teachers.   Finally, the discrepancies noted could be partially remedied as library/media specialists take seriously the task of developing policy manuals and handbooks for their school programs which will clearly illustrate the new thrust of the tasks and services that may be performed by the "new" media professional in schools.

References

American Library Association and Association for Educational Communication and Technology.   Media Programs: District and School.   Chicago: 1975.

Ball, Howard G.   "School Media Specialists' Perceptions of Media-Education Programs."   Southeastern Librarian, Vol. XXVI, Number 4, 1976.

Southern Association of Colleges and Schools.   Guide to Evaluation and Accreditation of Schools.   Atlanta: 1976.

Halpin, Gerald, acknowledged for assistance in data analysis of study.

SHIRLEY L. AARON is an Assistant Professor in the School of Library Science, Florida State University in Tallahassee, Florida.

ELENORA C. ALEXANDER is now retired from her position as Director of Library Services/Coordinator of Instructional Materials, Houston Public Schools.

MARTHA S. ANGEVINE is Coordinator of Instructional Materials and Services for the Lexington, Massachusetts Public Schools.

LaMOND F. BEATTY is an Assistant Professor, Educational Systems and Learning Resources, University of Utah, Salt Lake City, Utah.

SHIRLEY M. BLAIR is a Teacher-Librarian at Davie Jones Elementary School, Pitt Meadows, British Columbia.

D. JOLEEN BOCK is a Professor in the Department of Educational Media: Librarianship and Instructional Technology, Appalachian State University, Boone, North Carolina.

MARION A. BOND is a Media Specialist, Junior High School East, Arlington, Massachusetts.

ELSIE L. BRUMBACK is Director, Division of Educational Media, Department of Public Instruction, State of North Carolina, Raleigh.

FRANCES CARR is Director, Developmental Reading Lab, Centralia Jr. High, Centralia, Illinois.

CHARLES F. CHRISTENSEN is Principal, Junior High School East, Arlington, Massachusetts.

TED C. COBUN is Professor, Director of Instructional Communication Division, Media Services Department, East Tennessee State University, Johnson City, Tennessee.

MARGARET DEES is Principal of Yankee Ridge School, Urbana, Illinois.

ROBERT J. DIERMAN is Principal at Columbus Senior High School, Columbus, Nebraska.

R. KIM DRIGGERS is Assistant Superintendent for Curriculum and Instruction, Centralia City Schools, Centralia, Illinois.

HERMAN ELSTEIN is Head of Reference Services, Ocean County Library, Toms River, New Jersey.

BETTY FAST, now deceased, was Director of Media Services for the Groton, Connecticut Public Schools.

ALEXANDER FRAZIER was Professor of Education, Ohio State University. He retired in 1978 and now resides in Fountain Hills, Arizona.

MORRIS FREEDMAN is Director, Center for Library, Media and Telecommunications, Division of Educational Planning and Support, Board of Education of the City of New York, Brooklyn.

KAREN HARRIS is Associate Professor of Education, University of New Orleans in New Orleans, Louisiana.

FREDERIC R. HARTZ was Assistant Professor of Library Science, Trenton State College, New Jersey.

ALMA RUTH (FERGUSON) HESS is Librarian at St. Martin's Protestant Episcopal School, New Orleans, Louisiana.

WILLIAM E. HUG is Chairman, Department of Educational Media and Librarianship, University of Georgia, College of Education, Athens, Georgia.

HARLAN R. JOHNSON is Assistant Professor of Education and Library Science, Northern Arizona University, Flagstaff, Arizona.

PHYLLIS R. KUEHN is Media Specialist at Webber Junior High School, Saginaw, Michigan.

MARY LATHROPE is Librarian at Hawthorne School, Glen Ellyn, Illinois.

MILDRED LAUGHLIN has been a Department Editor for Learning Today since 1972 and is on the faculty at the University of Oklahoma, Norman.

RICHARD J. McKAY is Superintendent of Schools in Holbrook, Massachusetts.

MARY MARGRABE is retired but was a high school librarian (1964-1969), an elementary school librarian (1969-1976) and a high school teacher (1963-1964).

JUDITH K. MEYERS is Coordinator of Media Services for Lakewood Ohio Public Schools.

ROSALIND MILLER is Associate Professor of Library Media at Georgia State University in Atlanta.

DAVID M. MOORE is Associate Professor, College of Education, Division of Curriculum and Instruction, Virginia Polytechnic Institute and State University, Blacksburg.

MARGARET A. PEMBERTON is Library Media Specialist, Wilson Elementary School, Ft. Benning School System, Columbus, Georgia.

NANCY B. PILLON is a Professor in the Department of Library Science at Indiana State University, Terre Haute.

EARL P. SMITH is Associate Professor of Education, Department of Educational Media, Auburn University, Auburn, Alabama.

JANET SULLIVAN is Coordinator of Clinical Lab-College of Education at Bowling Green State University, Bowling Green, Ohio.

MARJORIE SULLIVAN is Assistant Professor in the Department of Librarianship, Kansas State Teachers College, Emporia.

PEGGY SULLIVAN is Dean of Students, Graduate Library School, University of Chicago and President of the American Library Association.

KEVIN J. SWICK is Associate Professor of Early Childhood Education, University of South Carolina, Columbia.

CAROLYN I. WHITENACK is retired but was Professor of Education and Chairman of the Media Sciences Curriculum at Purdue University, Lafayette, Indiana.

JOHANNA S. WOOD is Assistant Director, Department of Library Science, Public Schools of the District of Columbia, Washington, D. C.

RITA ZIEGLER is Media Specialist at Eugene A. Tighe School, Margate City, New Jersey.

BIBLIOGRAPHY

Aaron, Shirley L. "Personalizing Instruction for the Middle School Learner--The Instructional Role of the School Media Specialist, " Final Report School Library Media Section. Florida State Department of Education, August 27, 1975.

Aaron, Shirley L. "The Role of the School Media Program in the Curriculum, " Southeastern Librarian, Vol. 27, Winter 1977, pp. 221-26.

Aaron, Shirley L. "Teaming for Learning, " School Media Quarterly, 4:215-218, Spring 1976.

Alexander, Elenora C. "New Curriculum Trends and School Libraries, " Illinois Libraries, Vol. 47, April 1965, pp. 291-99.

Alexander, William M. , et al. The Emergent Middle School. New York: Holt, Rinehart and Winston, 1968.

American Association of School Librarians. Knapp School Library Project. Realization; The Final Report of the Knapp School Libraries Project. Peggy Sullivan, ed. Chicago: American Library Association, 1968.

American Association of School Librarians. School Library Standards Committee. Standards for School Library Programs. Chicago: American Library Association, 1960.

American Association of School Librarians, American Library Association, and Association for Educational Communications and Technology. Media Programs: District and School. Chicago: American Library Association/AECT, 1975.

American Association of School Librarians, American Library Association, and Dept. of Audio-Visual Instruction, National Education Association. Standards for School Media Programs. Chicago: American Library Association, 1969.

American Library Association. Committee on Post-War Planning. School Libraries for Today and Tomorrow, Functions and Standards (Planning for Libraries, No. 5). Chicago: American Library Association, 1945.

Angevine, Martha S.; Marion A. Bond; Charles F. Christensen; and Richard J. McKay. "People--The Ingredient Which Forges the Dynamic Relationship Between Media Center and School," International Journal of Instructional Media, Vol. 3, 1975-76, pp. 237-42.

Association for Supervision and Curriculum Development. Commission on Current Curriculum Developments. New Curriculum Developments; A Report. Glenys G. Unruh, ed. Washington, D. C.: Association for Supervision and Curriculum Development, 1965.

Ball, Howard G. "School Media Specialists' Perceptions of Media-Education Programs," Southeastern Librarian, Vol. XXVI, No. 4, 1976.

Barber, Raymond W. "The Open Media Center," Tallahassee, Florida: Department of Educational Administration, Florida State University, 1972.

Barber, Raymond W. "The Open School Media Services," Drexel Library Quarterly, 9:1-7, July 1973.

Barth, Edward Walter. "The Relationship Between Selected Teaching Structures and the Activities of Media Centres in Public Senior High Schools in the State of Maryland," George Washington University, Abstract of Doctoral Thesis, 1971.

Beachner, A. M. "Librarian: Consultant in Curriculum," in American Library Association, School Activities and the Library. Metuchen, N. J.: Scarecrow Press, 1964, pp. 102-106.

Beatty, LaMond F. "Do Media Specialists See Themselves As Others See Them?" Audiovisual Instruction, Vol. 21, Nov. 1976, pp. 44-45.

Birmingham, John. Our Time Is Now: Notes from the High School Underground. New York: Praeger Publications, 1970.

Blair, Shirley. "Teachers and the School Resource Center," Canadian Library Journal, Vol. 35, April 1978, pp. 93-100.

Bock, D. Joleen. "Role of the Library Media Specialist in Curriculum Development," Ohio Media Spectrum, Vol. 29, Oct. 1977, pp. 57-59.

Broderick, Dorothy M. "Plus ça Change: Classic Patterns in Public School/School Relations," School Library Journal, 14:31-33, May 1967.

Brown, J. W., and K. Norberg. Administering Educational Media. New York: McGraw-Hill, 1965.

Brown, James W.; Kenneth D. Norberg; and Sara K. Srygley. Administering Educational Media. New York: McGraw-Hill, 1972.

Brumback, Elsie L. "The Open-Classroom Concept and Its Effect on the School Library (Media) Program," Virginia Librarian, Vols. 18-19, Fall-Winter 1971/Spring 1972, pp. 3-4.

Bruner, J. E. "After John Dewey, What?" Saturday Review, June 17, 1961.

Bruner, J. E. The Process of Education. Cambridge, Mass.: Harvard University Press, 1960.

Bush, Robert N., and Dwight W. Allen. A New Design for High School Education: Assuming a Flexible Schedule. New York: McGraw-Hill, 1964.

Christine, Emma R. "Saturation Stations: A Plan for Media Center Classroom Collaboration for Better Learning," School Media Quarterly, 3:16-20, Fall 1974.

Clare, Sister Anne. "A School Becomes an Open, Individualized Learning Center: Let Us Strive On!" Catholic Library World, April 1977, 49:380-383.

Cobun, Ted C. "Media Specialist: Specialist in Media," International Journal of Instructional Media, Vol. 3, 1975-76, pp. 223-27.

Coleman, James S. "The Children Have Outgrown the Schools," Psychology Today, February 1972, pp. 72-75.

Committee for Economic Development. Innovation in Education: New Direction for the American School. New York: The Committee, 1968.

Condit, Martha Olson. "If Only the Teacher Had Stayed with the Class," Elementary English, 52:666, May 1975.

Cousins, Norman. "Are You Making Yourself Clear?" Saturday Review, Feb. 22, 1969, pp. 31-32.

Crawford, Lura E. "The Changing Nature of School Library Collections," Library Trends, 17:383-400, April 1969.

Dale, Edgar. Audiovisual Methods in Teaching. 3rd ed. New York: Holt, Rinehart and Winston, 1969.

Davies, Ruth Ann. The School Library Media Center, A Force for Educational Excellence. 2nd ed. New York: Bowker, 1974.

DeHart, Florence E. "Education of the School Library Media Specialist: Position Paper." Emporia: Kansas State Teachers

College, Graduate Library School, 1970. 34 pages. (Eric-ED 045 111)

Dierman, Robert J. "The Media Center and Continuous Progress," NASSP Bulletin, VoL 59: Sept. 1975, pp. 47-50.

Eisenberg, George O., and Virginia B. Saddler. "Dear Principal: Dear Librarian: A Dialogue on the Heart of the Matter," Wilson Library Bulletin, 48:55, 1973.

El-Hagrasy, Saad Mohammed. "The Teacher's Role in Library Service, An Investigation and Its Devices," Rutgers University, Abstract of Doctoral Thesis, 1961.

El-Hi Textbooks in Print 1973: Subject Index, Author Index, Title Index, Series Index. New York: Bowker, 1975, annual.

Erickson, C. H. Administering Media Programs. New York: Macmillan, 1968.

Fadell, Frances. "Factors Influencing Teacher Use of the High School Library," Chicago, Illinois, University of Chicago, M. Ed. Thesis, 1971.

Fast, Betty. "The Media Specialist as an Agent for Change," Wilson Library Bulletin, Vol. 49, May 1975, pp. 636-37+.

Finn, James D., et al. Studies in the Growth of Instructional Technology, I: Audio-Visual Instrumentation for Instruction in the Public Schools, 1930-1960: A Basis for Take-Off. National Education Association of the United States. Technological Development Project. Occasional Paper, No. 6. Washington, D. C., 1962.

Frazier, Alexander. "Curriculum Changes and the Librarian," Wilson Library Bulletin, VoL 39, January 1965, pp. 389-91.

Freedman, Morris. "Integrated School Resource Programs: A Conceptual Framework and Description," Audiovisual Instruction, 20:5-9, Sept. 1975.

Freel, Judy. "Is There a Media Specialist in the House?" Learning Today, 8:54-59, Fall 1975.

Gaines, Edythe J. "Accountability: Getting Out of the Tangled Web," Nation's Schools, Oct. 1971, pp. 55-58.

Geargiady, Nicholas P.; Louis G. Romano; and Walter A. Wittich. "Increased Learning Through the Multi-Media Approach," Audiovisual Instruction, 12:251, March 1967.

Gillespie, John T., and Diana L. Spirt. Creating a School Media Program. New York: Bowker, 1973.

Ginn, Reginald Alfred. "Individualizing Instruction Through the Elementary School Library Media Center," University of Alabama, Doctoral Thesis, 1974.

Godfrey, Eleanor P. The State of Audiovisual Technology: 1961-1966. National Education Association of the United States. Department of Audiovisual Instruction. Monograph No. 3. Washington, D. C., 1967.

Goodlad, John L, and Robert H. Anderson. The Nongraded Elementary School. Rev. ed. New York: Harcourt, Brace & World, 1963.

Goodman, Paul. "The Present Movement in Education," New York Review of Books, Vol. 12, April 1969, pp. 14-21, 24.

Grazier, Margaret H. "Effects of Change on Education for School Librarians," Library Trends, April 1969, p. 418.

Grazier, Margaret Hayes. "A Role for Media Specialists in the Curriculum Development Process," School Media Quarterly, 4: 199-204, Spring 1976.

Hanson, Connie. "Establishing an Identity," Illinois Libraries (part of "What Am I"), 60:570-579 (575-576+), Sept. 1978.

Hardman, Robert Richard. "Philosophy of Role and Identification of Critical Tasks Performed by Educational Media Specialists in Elementary and Secondary Schools of Iowa." Indiana University, Doctoral Thesis, 1971.

Hartz, Frederic R., and Herman Elstein. "Media Support System for the Secondary School," Journal of Secondary Education, Vol. 45, Jan. 1970, pp. 31-39.

Hawkins, David. "I-Thou-It," Mathematics Teacher, Spring 1969.

Hellene, Dorothy Lorraine Ingalls. "The Relationships of the Behaviors of Principals in the State of Washington to the Development of School Library/Media Programs," Doctoral Thesis, 1973.

Henry, Marion, and Curtis Mustiful. "Leadership Responsibilities of the Building-Level Media Specialist," Audiovisual Instruction, 16:76, June 1971.

Hess, Alma Ruth (Ferguson), and Karen Harris. "Agenda for Action: Teacher-Librarian Planning," Louisiana Library Association Bulletin, Vol. 36, Summer 1973, pp. 81-84.

Hug, William E. "Curriculum Renewal: Are We Prepared?" School Libraries, Vol. 21, No. 1, Fall 1971, pp. 43-46.

Hug, William E. Instructional Design and the Media Program. Chicago: American Library Association, 1975.

Hug, William E. "The Media Specialist: En Route and Terminal Competencies, " Improving College and University Teaching, 24: 59-60, Winter 1976.

Hutchins, Robert M. "The School Must Stay, " The Center Magazine, Vol. 6, Jan. - Feb. 1973, pp. 12-23.

Illinois Audiovisual Association. IAVA 1972 Leadership Conference Final Report. Illinois Audiovisual Association, 1972.

Ishikawa, Kivoharu. "Teacher Attitudes Toward School Library: An Investigation of Library Service Levels Related to Teacher Characteristics, " George Peabody College for Teachers, Doctoral Thesis, 1972.

Jay, Hilda Lease. "Increasing the Use of Secondary School Libraries as a Teaching Tool, " New York University, Doctoral Thesis, 1970.

Jetter, Margaret Ann. "The Roles of the School Library Media Specialist in the Future: A Delphi Study, " Michigan State University, Doctoral Thesis, 1972.

Johnson, Harlan R. "Teacher Utilization of Instructional Media Centers in Secondary Schools, " The Clearing House, Vol. 51, Nov. 1977, pp. 117-120.

Joyce, Bruce R. "Model for an Alternative Approach to Curriculum Development, " School Media Quarterly, 4:219-223, Spring 1976.

Kallet, Tony. "Some Thoughts on Children Materials, " Mathematics Teaching, Autumn, 1967, pp. 38-39.

Kemp, J. E. Instructional Design: A Plan for Unit and Course Development. Belmont, Calif. : Fearon Pub. , 1971.

King, A. R. , and J. A. Brownell. The Curriculum and the Disciplines of Knowledge. New York: Wiley, 1966.

King, Kenneth Lee. "An Evaluation of Teacher Utilization of Selected Educational Media in Relation to the Level of Sophistication of the Educational Media Program in Selected Oklahoma Public Schools, " University of Oklahoma. Doctoral Thesis, 1969.

King, Richard Lee. "A Study of Selected Factors Related to Variability in the Use of Certain Types of Instructional Media Among Teachers, " University of Missouri, Doctoral Thesis, 1967.

Kingsbury, Mary E. "Future of School Media Centers, " School Media Quarterly, Fall 1975.

Kirst, Michael W., and Decker F. Walker. "An Analysis of Curriculum Policy Making," Review of Educational Research, December 3, 1971, p. 492.

Knight, Douglas, and E. Shepley Norse, eds. Libraries at Large: Tradition Innovation and the National Interest. New York: Bowker, 1969.

Kuehn, Phyllis R. "The Principal and the Media Center," NASSP Bulletin, Sept. 1975, pp. 51-60.

Landerholm, Merle E. "A Study of Selected Elementary, Secondary, and School District Professional Staff Development Patterns," Ed. D. Project. Teachers College, Columbia University, 1960.

Lathrope, Mary, and Margaret Dees. "How Elementary School Teachers and Librarians Cooperate in Instruction," Illinois Libraries, Vol. 48, April 1966, pp. 285-291.

Laughlin, Mildred. "Action Activities," Learning Today, Vol. 7, Winter 1974, pp. 69-72.

Lee, Chi Ho. "The Library Skills of Prospective Teachers of the University of Georgia," University of Georgia, Doctoral Thesis, 1971.

Leopold, Carolyn Clugston. School Libraries Worth Their Keep: A Philosophy Plus Tricks. Metuchen, New Jersey: Scarecrow Press, 1972.

Levitan, Karen. "The School Library as an Instructional Information System," School Media Quarterly, 3:194-203, Spring 1975.

Loertscher, David Vickers. "Media Centre Services to Teachers in Indiana Senior High Schools, 1972-1973," Indiana University, Doctoral Thesis, 1973.

Loertscher, David V., and Phyllis Land. "An Empirical Study of Media Services in Indiana Elementary Schools," School Media Quarterly, Vol. 4, No. 1, Feb. 1975, pp. 8-18.

Lowrey, Anna Mary. "Components of Curriculum Innovation," Journal of Education for Librarianship, Vol. 12, No. 4, Spring 1972, pp. 247-253.

Machlup, Fritz. The Production and Distribution of Knowledge in the United States. Princeton, New Jersey: Princeton University Press, 1962.

McKay, R. J., and A. Ansara. "The Cluster Organization Pattern as a Model for Continuing Education for Professional Staff in Public Education," International Journal of Career and Continuing Education, I, Jan. 1976.

Madaus, James Richard. "Curriculum Involvement, Teaching Structures, and Personality Factors of Librarians in School Media Programs," University of Texas, Doctoral Thesis, 1974.

Mager, Rogert E. Developing Attitudes Toward Learning. Palo Alto: Fearon Pub. Co., 1968.

Mahoney, Sally. "Individualizing in the Library," Elementary English, Vol. 52, No. 3, March 1975, pp. 346-350.

Marantz, Sylvia. "Turned On, Not Punched Out: People in a Human Resources File," School Libraries, Winter 1969, pp. 49-53.

Margrabe, Mary. "The Library Media Specialist and Total Curriculum Involvement," Catholic Library World, Vol. 49, Feb. 1978, pp. 283-287.

Martin, Gordon E. "The Industrial Arts Teacher and the Media Specialist," Audiovisual Instruction, 21:36-38, April 1976.

Metropolitan School District of Perry Township. Meridian Middle School. Indianapolis: The Township, 1970.

Meyers, Judith K. "Media Services in the Open School: An Overview," Drexel Library Quarterly, 9:9-26, July 1973.

Miller, Rosalind. "Curriculum Delusions," School Library Journal, Vol. 99, Nov. 15, 1974, pp. 3028-3029.

Moore, D. M., and R. M. Brucker. "Technology and Teachers: Combatants or Collaborators?" Illinois Schools Journal, 52:80-84, 1972.

Moore, David M. "The Case of the Media Specialist: The Overlooked Educational Change Agent?" International Journal of Instructional Media, Vol. 3, 1975-76, pp. 109-115.

Mullen, Bennat Curtis. "A Survey of Problems, Practices, and Conditions Affecting the Use of the Library in Instruction in North Central Association Schools in Missouri," University of Missouri, Doctoral Thesis, 1966.

National Association of Secondary School Principals. Commission on the Experimental Study of the Utilization of the Staff in the Secondary School. Focus on Change: Guide to Better Schools. Prepared by J. Lloyd Trump and Dorsey Boynhann. Chicago: Rand McNally, 1961.

National Education Association of the United States. Research Division. School Library Personnel Task Analysis Survey. Chicago: American Association of School Librarians, 1969.

National Study of Secondary School Evaluation. Evaluative Criteria for the Evaluation of Secondary Schools. 4th ed. Washington, D. C., 1969.

Nieburger, Gayle D. "The Library and the English Program," English Journal 64:83-84, Feb. 1975.

Pemberton, Margaret A., and Earl P. Smith. "A Comparison of Role Perceptions of the School Media Specialist Among Administrators, Classroom Teachers and Library Media Specialists," Southeastern Librarian, Vol. 28, Summer 1978, pp. 92-95.

Phenix, P. H. "The Architectonics of Knowledge," in Education and the Structure of Knowledge. Chicago: Rand McNally, 1964.

Pillon, Nancy B. "Media Specialists Work with Teachers," Drexel Library Quarterly, Vol. 9, July 1973, pp. 59-69.

Prostano, Emanuel T., and Joyce S. Prostano. The School Library Media Center. Littleton, Colo.: Libraries Unlimited, 1971.

Prostano, Emanuel T., and Joyce S. Prostano. Public School Library Statistics, 1962-63. (OE-15020-63.) Washington, D. C.: U. S. Gov. Printing Office, 1964.

Roe, Ernest. "What Kind of Librarian?" School Library Journal, April 15, 1969, p. 1718.

Rogers, Carl R. On Becoming a Person: A Therapist's View of Psychotherapy. Boston: Houghton Mifflin, 1961.

Rutland, Thomas. "A Study of the Basic Physical Facilities and Educational Roles of Secondary School Libraries," University of Tennessee, Doctoral Thesis, 1971.

Sanders, Norris M., and Marlin L. Janck. "A Critical Appraisal of Twenty-Six National Social Studies Projects," Social Education, April 1970.

Saylor, J. Galen, and William M. Alexander. Planning Curriculum for Schools. New York: Holt, 1974.

Schmid, William T. "The Teacher and the Media Specialist," Media and Methods, 13:22-24, October 1976.

Schultzetenberge, Anthony C. "Interests and Background Variables Characterizing Secondary Librarians Who Work with Teachers in Curriculum Development and Improvement of Instruction," University of North Dakota, Doctoral Thesis, 1970.

Sharper Tools for Better Learning. Reston, Va.: National Assoc. of Secondary School Principals, 1973.

Sherman, Mendel, and Gene Faris. Quantitative Standards for Audio-visual Personnel, Equipment, and Materials in Elementary, Secondary, and Higher Education. Washington, D. C.: Dept. of Audiovisual Instruction, National Education Association of the United States, 1966.

Snygg, Donald, and Arthur W. Combs. Individual Behavior, A New Frame of Reference for Psychology. New York: Harper, 1949.

Southern Association of Colleges and Schools. Guide to Evaluation and Accreditation of Schools. Atlanta, 1976.

Stauffer, Russell G. "A Reading Teacher's Dream Come True, " Wilson Library Bulletin, 45:287, 1970.

Steinaker, Norman. "Ten Years Hence: The Curriculum Development and Usage Center, " Educational Leadership, Vol. 33, No. 6, March 1976, pp. 447-449.

Stephens, Charles S.; Marie P. Canfield; and Jeffrey J. Gardner. "Library, Pathfinders: A New Possibility for Cooperative Reference Service, " College and Research Libraries, Jan. 1973, pp. 40-46.

Sullivan, Janet. "Instructional Development in Media Programs, " School Library Journal, Vol. 25, April 1979, p. 24.

Sullivan, Marjorie. "The Media Specialist and the Disciplined Curriculum, " Journal of Education for Librarianship, Vol. 10, Spring 1970, pp. 286-295.

Sullivan, Peggy. "Librarian, Teacher, Administrator, Relationships, " Catholic Library World, Vol. 46, Feb. 1975, pp. 282-285.

Swarthout, Charlene R. "An Approach to an In-Service Program to Develop the Concept of the School Library as Part of the Instructional System. " Wayne State University, Doctoral Thesis, 1968.

Swick, Kevin J.; Frances Carr; and R. Kim Driggers. "The Librarian and Instructional Programs, " Reading Improvement, Vol. 12, Spring 1975, pp. 32-33.

Tanzman, Jack, and Kenneth J. Dunn. Using Instructional Media Effectively. Englewood Cliffs, N. J.: Parker Pub. Co., 1971.

Taylor, Kenneth L. "Creative Inquiry and Instructional Media, " School Media Quarterly, Vol. 1, No. 1, Fall 1972.

Taylor, Kenneth I. "Media in the Context of Instruction, " School Media Quarterly, 4:224-228, Spring 1976.

Tielke, Elton Fritz. "A Study of the Relationship of Selected Environmental Factors to the Development of Elementary School Libraries," University of Texas, Doctoral Thesis, 1968.

Toffler, Alvin. Future Shock. New York: Random House, 1970.

U. S. Bureau of Education. Public Libraries in the United States of America; Their History, Condition, and Management. Washington, D. C.: U. S. Gov. Printing Office, 1976.

U. S. Dept. of Commerce. Statistical Abstract of the United States, 1972. Washington, D. C., 1972.

U. S. Office of Education. Descriptive Case Studies of Nine Elementary School Media Centers in Three Inner Cities. Title IL (OE-10060.) Washington, D. C.: U. S. Gov. Printing Office, 1969; and _____. Emphasis on Excellence in School Media Programs. Title IL (OE-20123.) Washington, D. C.: U. S. Gov. Printing Office, 1969.

Van Orden, Phyllis Jeanne. "Use of Media and the Media Centre, As Reflected in Professional Journals for Elementary School Teachers," Wayne State University, Doctoral Thesis, 1970.

Welch, Fred. "Relationships Between Curriculum Variables, Attitudes, Teacher Characteristics and the Utilization of Instructional Media," University of Southern Calif., Doctoral Thesis, 1974.

Whitehead, A. N. The Aims of Education and Other Essays. New York: Macmillan, 1929.

Whitenack, Carolyn L. "School Libraries and Librarianship," in Miles M. Jackson, Jr., ed. Comparative and International Librarianship. Westwood, Conn.: Greenwood Pub., 1970, pp. 68-69.

Whitenack, Carolyn L. "The School Media Program: Emerging Multi-Media Services," Library Trends, Vol. 19, No. 4, April 1971, pp. 410-418.

Whyde, John S. "Comparison of the Subject Headings Assigned by Eight Major University Film Libraries with Those Assigned by the Library of Congress and an Analysis of the Deviation of the Former from the Latter," Kent State University, Master's Thesis, 1973.

Wiedrick, Laurence G. "Student Use of School Libraries in Edmonton Open Area Elementary Schools," University of Oregon, Doctoral Thesis, 1973.

Wight, Lillian, and A. Grassman. "Maximum Utilization of School Library Resources." Alberta: Edmonton Public Schools, 1977, 13 pages. (Eric-ED 154 781)

Wittich, W. A., and C. F. Schuller. Instructional Technology: Its Nature and Use. 5th ed. New York: Harper & Row, 1973.

Wood, J. S. "IDI: A Vehicle for Curriculum Change in D. C.," School Media Quarterly, Fall 1975, 4:43-44.

Wood, Johanna S. "Media Programs in Open Space Schools," School Media Quarterly, 4:197-228+, Spring 1976.

Wood, Johanna S. "The Role of the Library Media Specialist in the Instructional Program," School Media Services Office, Maryland State Dept. of Education, February, 1977.

Ziegler, Rita. "Miniguide Media Center Services for Teachers," NJEA Review, Vol. 50, Feb. 1977, pp. 84-85.

SUBJECT INDEX